AVID

READER

PRESS

The
Second
Life of
Tiger
Woods

MICHAEL
BAMBERGER

Avid Reader Press

NEW YORK · LONDON · TORONTO
SYDNEY · NEW DELHI

AVID READER PRESS
An Imprint of Simon & Schuster, Inc.
1230 Avenue of the Americas
New York, NY 10020

First Avid Reader Press hardcover edition March 2020

AVID READER PRESS and colophon are trademarks
of Simon & Schuster, Inc.

For information about special discounts for bulk purchases,
please contact Simon & Schuster Special Sales at 1-866-506-1949
or business@simonandschuster.com.

The Simon & Schuster Speakers Bureau can bring authors to your
live event. For more information or to book an event, contact the
Simon & Schuster Speakers Bureau at 1-866-248-3049
or visit our website at www.simonspeakers.com.

Interior design by Paul Dippolito

Manufactured in the United States of America

1   3   5   7   9   10   8   6   4   2

Library of Congress Cataloging-in-Publication Data has been applied for.

ISBN 978-1-9821-2282-9
ISBN 978-1-9821-2285-0 (ebook)

This book is dedicated

with gratitude

to

MD251MC.[†]

[†] A modest prize awaits any reader who can decode these
seven characters. Offer expires with the author.
Email: mbamberger0224@aol.com.

"Shivas, here it is!" I cried and picked it up. "It's here in the hole!"

"I'll be damned," he said, his eyes more cross-eyed than ever. "'Tis the first time I e'er shot a hole-in-one on the thirteenth." He looked at the shillelagh, and kissed its mean-looking burl. "Ye saved my life, ol' spoon," he said with enormous relief. "Thank ye kindly."

—MICHAEL MURPHY,
GOLF IN THE KINGDOM

The
Second
Life of
Tiger
Woods

Tiger's funny.

A while back, after Nike stopped making golf clubs, he was shopping for a new deal, trying every brand you've heard of and some you maybe have not. Tiger was on the phone with Davis Love. It was Christmastime, and the Love house looked like the United terminal at O'Hare, with so many people coming and going.

"How're things at your house?" Davis asked.

Tiger's first win on the PGA Tour had been over Davis in a play-off. Twenty years later, Davis was the captain of the U.S. Ryder Cup team and Tiger was one of his assistants. Golf does long well.

"My house," Tiger said, "looks like a PGA Tour Superstore."

When Tiger was in his prime but having a bad tournament, he'd sometimes tell Steve Williams, "Stevie, looks like I'll be opening TW's Car Wash pretty soon, and you'll be polishing cars." A droll line, but a reassuring thought. Even if Tiger played his way out of golf, his caddie would still have a job.

In the interest of candor, you should know that Tiger can work blue and often does. That makes him like millions of other American men with exposure to playground basketball or army veterans or both. After hearing that a male acquaintance had spent a productive hour with not one but two late-night pros in legal Nevada, Tiger's retort was immediate: "Which one had a dick?"

Blech.

But he has many moves. With a script in hand, he can do it all. He can be funny, serious, warm, contemplative, mischievous. You can imagine professional actors who wish they had Tiger's range. He doesn't do Method. He once told Bryson DeChambeau, when they were shooting an ad together, "You're overthinking it, bro." Tiger was playing a bored student to Bryson's mad professor, and he was nailing every take. He's a natural. Tiger has been playing for cameras all his life. In middle age, amid the wallop it packs, he has shown a depth he didn't have as a teenager or as a young man in his twenties and thirties. Self-deprecation has become part of his repertoire.

Here's an extreme example but a telling one, from the May night when he was charged with suspicion of driving under the influence, a camera rolling all the while. Tiger was in a holding cell at the Palm Beach county jail at four in the morning. He was about to take a Breathalyzer test. A police officer was posing a series of boilerplate questions. Tiger was barefoot and hatless. He was wearing baggy workout shorts and a long-sleeved Nike running shirt. His cuffed hands were behind his back and he was unsteady on his narrow feet. He was forty-one and not ready for his close-up. Still, he soldiered on, as pros do.

Your home address, Mr. Woods.

Your date of birth.

Your height, your weight.

Your eye color.

Your hair color.

"Mostly brown," Tiger said to the last. "And fading."

The officer chortled. Male-pattern baldness doesn't care how many golf trophies you have in your den.

Not quite two years later, Tiger won the Masters. What he did over the course of those twenty-three months is a monument to the human capacity to rise. Somehow, and not alone, Woods got from that depressing holding cell on Gun Club Road in West Palm Beach to the eighteenth green of the Augusta National Golf Club, the winner's green jacket being draped over his shoulders.

• • •

At the top of the order at Augusta National is the great triumvirate of American golf: Arnold, with four Masters wins; Tiger, with five; Big Jack, with six. Presiding over this unlikely threesome, now and forever, is Robert Tyre Jones Jr., founding father of the club, patron saint of American golf, host of the original Masters. Or, as Bobby himself called it in its early Great Depression years, the Invitational, when it was a decidedly southern golfin' jamboree for Jones's friends, amateur and professional.

By the 1950s, the Masters had cemented its place in American sports. It was a rite of spring, along with baseball box scores in morning newspapers and earthworms on weekend fishing hooks. Dwight D. Eisenhower, golf-nut president, was making regular trips to his Old South club, and Herbert Warren Wind, Yalie writer of sport, had given a gentle name—Amen Corner—to a back-nine nook where weird and memorable golf seems to unfold each year. By 1958, the year Arnold Palmer won his first Masters, Augusta National was already steeped in magic and mystery, and a win there was a ticket to the club's good life, in which working-class men (the players) and accomplished businessmen (the members) could drink on equal footing.

During the Tiger years and the long stock-market rise that accompanied them, anything bearing the Masters name became a status symbol. The club brought in executives from Disney and Ritz-Carlton to work in marketing and sales. The Masters became synonymous with tradition and southern courtliness to a national and global audience that couldn't get enough. The club opened new territories via amateur golf events in Asia and Latin America. Grow-the-game had supplanted fraternity as the club's MO. If you looked closely, you could see the manic pursuit of perfection bubbling below the surface, but the club was getting what it wanted. An Augusta National membership—actual (Warren Buffett, Condi Rice, Jack Nicklaus) or honorary (all the other former winners)—had immeasurable cachet. If you were in, you had something money could not buy.

All the while, the club wisely kept its eye on the prize. Each April, it continued to put on a terrific show. Some years were better than others, but that's bound to happen when you're staging a live outdoor sporting event. The Masters is unscripted drama at its best. As traditional life everywhere has languished, the club has doubled down on ritual. For one blessed week, you can take a break from the heartbreak of the real world and enter Augusta's twilight zone. The Drive, Chip & Putt contest. The release of the Champions Dinner menu. The chairman's annual State of the Masters press conference. The Par-3 Tournament. The annual jokes about getting thrown out for having a cell phone on the course. The ceremonial first shots. The opening round. The second round, the third. Masters Sunday. The Butler Cabin interview. The Green Jacket Ceremony. Yes, all that ritual can be cloying. (Bob Jones carries the title *president in perpetuity*.) But it's comforting, too.

Golf thrives on ritual. The game has a dress code, a language, a code of conduct. It has its own bible (*The Rules of Golf*) and Talmud (*Decisions on the Rules of Golf*). Golf tries to impose order and predictability where it can. You need it, because physical chaos (*How do you play a mud ball?*) and psychic confusion (*Where does your game go when it goes?*) are always lurking around the corner.

Tiger is a master of preparation. He dislikes surprises but accepts that they're coming. No matter how bad his situation is, his thoughts are settled by the time he plays his shot. It's an unusual mind that can do that again and again, forget the past and get lost in the present. It's an excellent athletic skill, and it's particularly useful on the back nine on Masters Sundays, with all that water waving at the contenders. Rae's Creek can kill dreams. You have to respect the back-nine water hazards without becoming frozen with fear. You could say the same of the greens, the bunkers, the hovering ghosts of Masters past. Man, it's fun.

The former champions have their own locker room, on the second floor of the time-warp clubhouse, up a set of corkscrew steps and adjacent to a dining room called The Library. All through the tournament there's a uniformed gent with a trim white beard and a cherubic face at the locker-room door. He has little to do. Who would even think about trying to enter without the necessary credential, a Masters title? Nobody.

Each former champion gets his own green jacket. By custom, the past champions leave their jackets at the club but the new winner, by special dispensation, gets to take his home for his year as the reigning champ. Each winner shares a locker. A half-locker, actually, but tall enough to accommodate a jacket. Tiger's locker mate is Jackie Burke, the 1956 winner. Long after they're both gone, they'll still share their gym-class locker, just as Bob Jones will still be the president in perpetuity, your cell phone will stay in your car's glove box, and the leaderboards will be changed by hand.

Augusta's an interesting place.

• • •

The first time I saw Tiger at Augusta in person was during the 1996 Masters. Tiger played the Thursday and Friday rounds with Ben Crenshaw, the defending champion. Crenshaw shot 77-74 in the Thursday and Friday rounds and missed the cut, but he stayed through the weekend. Come Sunday night, by tradition, he would help the new winner into his green jacket—Nick Faldo, as it played out. Ben was happy to do it. He and the club share a paternal grandfather, or so it seems. Tiger shot 75-75 and missed the cut, too, and by Friday afternoon he looked like he couldn't wait to split. He was due back at Stanford, where he was a sophomore.

The first time I saw Tiger Woods anywhere in person was at the 1995 U.S. Amateur, played in Newport, Rhode Island. I was a reporter on *The Philadelphia Inquirer*. Tiger was facing Philadelphia's best amateur, Buddy Marucci, in the final. In the insular world of suburban private-club amateur golf in Philadelphia, Marucci was famous. All through spring and summer, his name was often in the paper. I drove from Philadelphia to Newport early that morning, on the last Sunday in August.

By the summer of 1995, everybody who followed golf closely knew the outline of the Tiger Woods story. His father was black and his mother was Thai, and Tiger grew up playing public courses in Southern California. He had won the 1994 U.S. Amateur just as he was starting his freshman year at Stanford. He had a big smile and an intense fist pump, and he didn't look like any of his opponents.

I was thirty-five, and golf was an elemental part of my life. I was bitten by the bug in an eighth-grade PE class, hitting plastic balls off plastic mats at retractable backboards. I knew there was a chasm between what golf really was and how nongolfers often thought about it. Ted Knight—Judge Smails in *Caddyshack*, blowhard member of Bushwood Country Club—had played his role too well. In the mid-1990s, when Tiger was emerging, Smails was still the face of American golf.

This analogy is more recent and borrowed from a friend: I wished that golf, like soccer, could stand publicly in its beauty. *Fútbol*, "the beautiful game," was played wherever there were kids and a ball and anything resembling a field. Golf is at heart a primitive, overland stick-and-ball game. Like millions of other pilgrims, I had played the stripped-down, fast-paced, open-to-all aboriginal game, as practiced by actual Scots. American golf is still weighed down by its attachment to 1950s suburban prosperity. The country club! Courses in gated communities with man-made water geysers. A white-haired man cruising along an excessively manicured fairway in a rumbling golf cart. White belt, white sunscreen, white stomach beneath his logoed shirt. I thought Tiger could bring the game to people who did not have a passport to it, as my eighth-grade gym teacher (Mr. Greenlee) had done for me. I was projecting far too much on him. It wasn't fair. Tiger was nineteen. He had his mind on other things.

For *The Philadelphia Inquirer* the final of the 1995 U.S. Amateur at the Newport Country Club was a good local story. I was going to write up Buddy Marucci no matter what he did. But I had come to see Tiger.

. . .

Tiger's first Masters win was all about him and the man who made him. It came in 1997, when Tiger was twenty-one, and he won by twelve. You can imagine a younger winner but not a bigger winning margin, at any age. There's too much parity. Too much good training, instruction, and equipment. Tiger holed out and, in victory, fell into the arms of his father, Earl Woods.

Earl was a sociology major at Kansas State in the 1950s. He was an army officer in Vietnam in the 1960s. He was a self-taught golfer in the 1970s. He was a golfing theorist, a prodigious drinker, a world-class curser, a pantsuit-chaser, a midnight philosopher with a smoker's baritone and a bad heart. He is also the starting point for the unique life and times at play here.

Earl had three children from what he sometimes called "my practice family." (He could be funny.) In his second go-round, Earl married a woman, Kultida Punsawad, whom he met in Bangkok, and they had one child, Eldrick Tont Woods, future chairman of ETW Corporation and one of the great prodigies ever.

The caddies at Augusta National and other clubs got to know Earl because he liked to hang. He'd poke around, Tiger often beside him. They'd make the rounds at Pinehurst, at the National Golf Links on Long Island, at a public course called Forest Hills in Augusta, at other places. The photographic proof of those visits, curling and held up by a thumbtack or tape, can be found hanging here and there. Tiger looks so young in the snaps.

Here's a casually assembled lineup of prodigies who fulfilled their early promise: Mozart, Alexander Hamilton, Einstein, Picasso,

Michael Jackson, Babe Ruth, Julie Andrews, Bobby Fischer—and Tiger.

Yes, it's a little odd to see Woods with Picasso and Mozart, but there are powerful similarities. All three have brought a lot of joy to a lot of people. All three lived with the costs of their extreme gifts. All three started out crazily young. You've probably seen the clip of Tiger, as a two-year-old, hitting balls on the *Mike Douglas Show*, dwarfed by his father, by Mike Douglas, by Bob Hope and Jimmy Stewart. Earl Woods wore a tight red shirt and a heavy gold medallion around his neck. It was 1978. The camera loved Tiger. It was all beginning. Michael Jackson, particularly, would get this. Tiger was a reality-TV star before the term existed. It was the start of a life that has been recorded with and without his consent. It has allowed him to prosper and caused him to suffer, too.

Tiger's fourth Masters win came in 2005, followed by a fourteen-year wait for number five. No gap between wins there has ever been longer. In victory, Tiger hugged his son, Charlie, ten, and his daughter, Sam, then closing in on twelve. It was a Sunday in April and they were taking a break from their crowded lives at the Benjamin School, a private school in South Florida often populated by a half dozen or more students named Nicklaus. There have been times that golf's two greatest players, Jack Nicklaus and Tiger Woods, have attended the same middle-school soccer games, Tiger on hand to see his daughter, and Jack to see one of his granddaughters. Sam Woods and Nicole Nicklaus on the same roster. What are the chances of that?

When Jack won his sixth Masters in 1986, Tiger, then ten, was watching the tournament on TV for the first time. He was with his father in his parents' tidy, modest development house in Southern California, a classic Mike Brady design right down to the ski-jump roof line, but with only one child in it, not the *Brady Bunch* six. Jack and Tiger could not know it, of course, but that was when their circle game began. In 2019, Nicklaus watched Tiger win his fifth Masters from a boat with a TV while bonefishing in the Bahamas. It was Tiger's fifteenth major professional title. Only Nicklaus, with eighteen, has more. Jack has always been Tiger's main opponent.

"Tiger, your victory today is going to inspire not only children but adults all over the world," said an Augusta National member, Craig Heatley, wrapping up the winner's press conference. He was its host and moderator.

Heatley was wearing his green Augusta National members coat, with its coaster-sized patch depicting a green America with a giant flagstick planted in Augusta. Before long, Heatley's coat would be placed on a wooden hanger for safekeeping at the club. Tiger, seated beside Heatley, was wearing his own club blazer, but you know how that works: As the reigning champion, he could wear his home.

"Magnificent achievement," Heatley said, looking at the new winner.

Tiger, uncharacteristically, had his upper teeth resting on his lower lip. He was waiting.

"You're a very, very worthy champion, and we're proud that you're wearing that jacket for the fifth time today."

Tiger didn't bother to take a beat. He looked out at the nearly two hundred reporters, photographers, camera operators, and visitors in attendance and ended the press conference with the most charming thing I have ever heard him say: "Yeah—I'm excited about show-and-tell at school."

Tiger giggled, stood up, rolled his heavy desk chair back into place, and headed out, his green jacket covering most of his red shirt. Christmas in April.

That final line was some nod: to himself, to his kids, to their school, to his green jacket, to (stealing now) *this thing called life.*

Oh happy day.

NIGHT.

On Memorial Day 2017, Matt Palladino, in his second year as a road-patrol officer for the Jupiter Police Department, in South Florida, started his nearly twelve-hour shift at 6:45 p.m. He was in his mid-twenties, tall and slender. He was driving a 2014 Dodge Charger patrol vehicle, a white car with blue and gold decorative stripes. (A curling wave, a ray of sunshine.) At a little past two in the morning, about a mile and a half from police headquarters, Palladino saw a Mercedes on the west side of a flat six-lane north-south commercial road called Military Trail, named for a path cleared by U.S. Army soldiers in a nineteenth-century war against the Seminole Tribe. To the west was a housing development called Canterbury Place. To the east was a golf course called Admirals Cove. At two in the morning, on this stretch of Military Trail, you're more likely to see a coyote than a parked car, but it was the latter that prompted Officer Palladino to stop. The stopped car's brake lights were on, with the right turn signal flashing, and the left front and rear tires in Military Trail's slow lane.

Palladino turned on his vehicle's flashing red-and-blue rooftop lights and its dashcam. He called a command center to make certain the black Mercedes—a four-door 2015 sedan with an immense engine—wasn't stolen or connected to another investigation. It wasn't.

Palladino got out his flashlight, approached the car from the passenger side, and saw a lone person in it. There was a man sitting behind the steering wheel as the engine ran, a phone on his lap, his eyes closed. The driver, attempting to respond to the officer, could barely open his eyes. He struggled to locate his driver's license, insurance card, and registration. Eventually he handed the officer his Florida license, and that was when Officer Palladino knew with certainty that the man in the car was a black male born December 30, 1975, named Eldrick T. Woods.

Can you imagine running into Tiger Woods in some random setting? He's one of the most famous people in the world, and, try as you might, it would be hard not to stare and gawk. Most people only know him from TV, and there he is, in the flesh. The heart races.

Officer Palladino's response was nothing like that. He was dealing with an impaired driver, a stopped car in a dangerous place, the requirements of Florida law. He had a job to do.

Palladino asked Woods where he was coming from.

"Jupiter," Tiger said.

He asked Woods where he was going.

"Jupiter," Tiger said.

The officer repeated his second question.

"Home," Woods said.

Where, Palladino asked, is home?

"Jupiter," Woods said.

Woods's car was pointed south on Military Trail. His home is on Jupiter Island, eight miles north.

Backup was on its way. That's standard Jupiter Police Department procedure for any DUI investigation. Doesn't matter who the suspect is.

• • •

Jupiter Island is a narrow barrier beach and an incorporated town with a population in the high three digits. It's in southern Martin County, which is South Florida but almost the edge of rural small-town Florida. The town of Jupiter, crowded in places and largely suburban, is in the northernmost part of Palm Beach County, about a half hour north by car from the airport in West Palm Beach. The airport to Jupiter is just a straight shot up I-95, followed by a right turn on Indiantown Road, toward the ocean. Jupiter Island and the town of Jupiter are separated by the Indian River and the Loxahatchee River, both bountiful today, even with all the developments. It's easy to imagine Native Americans as fishermen and trappers on the banks of those rivers, centuries before the first Jiffy Lube went up. Today Indiantown Road, the main east-west route into and out of Jupiter, is choking with strip malls and the various signposts of modern American suburban life. A PetSmart, a Home Depot, a Publix. A Taco Bell.

Across a bridge, Jupiter Island is a spectacular oasis from all that, at least for the tiny number of people who live there, including Tiger Woods and his two children, when they're with him. (Shared custody after divorce.) Driving through Jupiter Island—driving past Blowing Rocks, a desolate and beautiful public beach—a powerful force comes off it, related not to its natural beauty but to its population, or its lack of population. There is no 7-Eleven to buy an emergency late-night pint of Ben & Jerry's. There are no kids playing H-O-R-S-E on the street. There are few sidewalks. It feels lonely.

. . .

Tiger has spent half his life in Florida and half of his Florida life in South Florida. Golf brings all manner of people to South Florida, for a variety of reasons. When you look at Martin County and Palm Beach County from a plane, or via Google Earth, the number of courses you see is astounding. Collectively, the many public courses, resort courses, development courses, country-club courses, and private-club courses are major contributors to the social, athletic, and economic life of both counties. To keep the dozens of clubs and courses up and running takes an immense amount of disposable income. It also takes the cooperation of the government, which regulates how the clubs and courses are taxed and assessed. Raise the taxes and the assessments, and green fees and annual dues will rise until some courses close. It's a balancing act.

Then there are the thousands of low-wage course workers and

clubhouse employees dedicated to keeping the greens green and the iced teas icy. You sometimes see these men and women in carpools, arriving in the early morning, driving in from distant places, years after being born in places more distant yet. Without these workers, the whole industry would shrivel up and die. Of course, you could say the same thing of the golfers on those playfields. No golfers would mean no golf courses, no driving ranges, no pro shops, no grillroom bars with terrace seating, umbrellas angled just so in the midday sun.

Jupiter has become a mecca for PGA Tour players, aspiring players, teaching pros, club pros, equipment salespeople, player agents, professional caddies, and professional amateurs. So has Palm Beach Gardens, Jupiter's more affordable neighbor to the south. The PGA of America has been based for years in Palm Beach Gardens. The Gardens Mall is on PGA Boulevard, where there's an Apple store frequented by Tiger's people, and a Yard House brewpub, where Joe LaCava, Tiger's caddie, has enjoyed some pops over the years. The Snuggery, a mile south on PGA Boulevard, is a caddie bar and has been for years, just as the Keys Bar, on Market Street in St. Andrews, is a caddie bar and has been for years. There's a Moe's on PGA where Tiger's young friend Justin Thomas will stop for a burrito. PGA Boulevard is the Main Street of the modern PGA Tour, and the Gardens Mall is its downtown. Rory McIlroy and his father met Jack Nicklaus for the first time in its vast parking lot. Tiger's been in that lot more times than he could count.

Nicklaus lives between the mall and the ocean in a development called Lost Tree, fifteen miles south of Tiger's compound on Jupiter Island. Nicklaus would go right by Tiger's corporate offices in Jupiter and his bar-and-restaurant if he were ever invited to make the drive from his house to Tiger's. That doesn't happen. There's a psychic closeness between the two golf giants, but that's really it. They're not in each other's daily lives. They've spent little time together, although

Donald Trump, as president, did get Nicklaus and Woods together by asking them to join him for a round at one of his courses, Trump National Jupiter. Rory McIlroy was invited, too, but passed, so Steve Nicklaus, the second of Jack and Barbara's five children, filled out the foursome. Tiger shot a 64 and Trump tweeted out the score. Tiger's play that day got Nicklaus's attention, too. Nicklaus started predicting then that Tiger's fifteenth major title was bound to come soon. That was ten weeks before the 2019 Masters.

Jupiter Island is dominated by an eleven-thousand-acre nature preserve with meager public parking and by a long row of estates, most with gated driveways and ficus-tree hedges, tall and dense. Tiger lives in one of those estates and Greg Norman lives in another, about a mile up the beach and up Beach Road. Norman moved to Jupiter Island from Orlando in 1991. Woods moved to Jupiter Island from Orlando in 2011. They pass each other regularly along narrow Beach Road, Norman typically in a Range Rover, Tiger most often in a Mercedes sedan, though each has other options.

Norman enjoys telling about the time he was driving behind Tiger on Jupiter Island with his wife, Kirsten, in the passenger seat. Tiger got to the drawbridge leading off the island just as it was going up. Norman positioned his car beside Tiger's. "I got ahead of his security detail," Norman said, describing it playfully. "We're side by side. Had to be the longest eight minutes of Tiger's life. I'm talking to Kirsten, so I'm looking his way. She rolls down the window. I said, 'Hi, Tiger!' Nothing. Tiger storms off. Kirsten says, 'What was *that* all about?'"

• • •

Many of the courses in and around Jupiter have big, bold golf names attached to them. Greg Norman was the founder of Medalist Golf Club. Jack Nicklaus redesigned, for a fee of one dollar, the municipal course in the village of North Palm Beach, where he lives. He also designed the course at Lost Tree, the gated development in North Palm Beach where he and Barbara raised their kids. Nicklaus redesigned the Champions Course at PGA National, where the Honda Classic, a fund-raiser for the Nicklaus Children's Health Care Foundation, is played each year. (The synergy is so thick you could cut it with a 1-iron, if you could find one.) McArthur Golf Club, three miles up the road from Jupiter on U.S. 1, was designed by Nick Price, working with Tom Fazio. There are courses designed by various other notables. Rees Jones, Dick Wilson, Joe Lee, Pete Dye. George Fazio, Jim Fazio, Tom Fazio, his nephew Tommy Fazio. Trump likes to use architects named Fazio.

Tiger doesn't have his name on a South Florida course yet—he first discussed his interest in course design with Trump years ago— but he did design a practice area on three and a half manicured acres, on turf he's always trying to get drier and faster to duplicate tournament conditions. This rectangle of golf in Tiger's backyard has four greens, seven bunkers, and enough space to invent a variety of par-3 holes. On his website it looks spectacular.

Tiger, when he's home, does most of his practicing and playing at Medalist, which Greg Norman designed with Pete Dye in the mid-1990s. Seeing Woods work on the practice tee alone there, dirt-soiled clubs leaning on his Tour bag, is a stunning sight. People watch him, but at a distance. Tiger requires space. The longtime pro there, Buddy Antonopoulos, once told the writer Craig Dolch, "You'd watch Tiger hit thirty drives and they'd go through the same cloud." Tiger knows what Hogan knew: the secret's in the dirt.

Medalist has a distinct high-octane energy, and it's loaded with successful people. It's one of the reasons a dozen or more notable Tour players play there and actually enjoy the members, even if they're 93 shooters.

Nobody confuses Medalist with Seminole Golf Club, a late-1920s Golden Age classic on the Atlantic designed by Donald Ross.

Seminole oozes the confidence that comes with age and inheritance. There are no Tour players who belong there, although Raymond Floyd and Rory McIlroy's father are members. Tiger played Seminole as a guest once on a day when he was in no mood to charm anybody. The tenor of his round was captured as the group played the last hole. Seminole's eighteenth is a beachfront dogleg par-4 with an elevated back tee that's practically on a dune and so near the heaving ocean that you can't wait to finish your round and get in the surf. Woods was told to aim for two wrecking-ball cranes in the distance and on the beach. Tiger, in the retelling, said, "I know about those cranes—I'm paying for them." Contractors working for his former wife, Elin Nordegren, were knocking down a waterlogged 1932 oceanfront mansion. She was starting over.

As he was leaving the club, with its pink clubhouse and pebbled driveway, Woods told a club employee that Seminole was a "nice little course." It's his habit to use diminutives, to call even the most meaningful moments of his life "pretty special," to refer to a stretch when he has won multiple consecutive events as "a nice little run." He's been overcompensating for his father's verbal grandiosity all his adult life. But "nice little course" was a dig. Every dues-paying golfer knows the sentiment that Herb Wind, in the language of his time and place, captured for posterity: "You may sooner insult a man's wife than his golf club." Tiger, playing the course for the first time, had shot something in the mid-60s without batting an eye or working up a sweat. His afternoon plan was to drive to Medalist and get in some practice.

• • •

Memorial Day weekend is not sleepy in greater Jupiter, and it's not solemn. Thousands of college students are home, cooling their jets while getting reacquainted, and many of their parents are off, too. On the beaches and along Jupiter's rivers and inlets, there are docks, backyards, hotels, bars, and nightclubs teeming with people seeking a reprieve from their gotta-check-my-phone lives. Workday norms are blessedly snuffed out by the holiday that jump-starts summer, by warm South Florida days spent in the surf, in the wind, in the sun. By nightfall, inhibitions take a further beating, owing to the steady flow of Funky Buddha (a South Florida beer), Tito's (a yellow-corn vodka), and Corazón (a small-batch vodka). Plus weed, coke, Ecstasy, various other club drugs. No different than anyplace else.

The three days of Memorial Day weekend in 2017 were hot in Jupiter, ninety or warmer each day. Time slowed. On Sunday, Jason Cardinal, an *America's Got Talent* alum, played a sultry afternoon gig at the Square Grouper, on Jupiter Inlet. All over town—on the golf courses, in the surf, at the bars—the pace was languid. It was too hot to rush around.

Most of the prominent PGA Tour players who live in and around Jupiter—Brooks Koepka, Rory McIlroy, Dustin Johnson, Justin Thomas, Rickie Fowler, Keegan Bradley, Lucas Glover, Ernie Els, others—were off. They weren't at the tournament concluding that Sunday at Colonial Country Club in Fort Worth. It was a good weekend to be home. Spring break, in March or April, is a time for tourists to shake-shake-shake. It's amateur hour. Memorial Day weekend in Jupiter is a far different thing. It trends more local, for one thing. It's more mature.

Tiger wasn't at the 2017 Colonial, and he wouldn't be in the next event—Jack's tournament, the Memorial, played outside Columbus—despite his five wins there. Woods was recovering from his fourth back surgery five weeks earlier. Golf for him was on the back burner with the gas off. Tiger's annual two-day charity fund-raiser, Tiger Jam, had been a week earlier at the MGM Grand in Las Vegas, but Woods wasn't there, either. Still, he had things to keep him occupied: the different tournaments he oversees; his yacht; the many schools with his name on them. He was doing his post-surgery rehab. His kids were on summer break. Plus, he had side businesses up and running, most notably his golf-course design company and his restaurant. Ever since he turned pro, Tiger's life has been busy, expensive, and pressured. He doesn't have much down time.

The Woods Jupiter was doing well, both the restaurant and its bar. Yelp reviewers were consistently praising it without confusing it with the local Outback Steakhouse. A modest dinner for two at the Woods Jupiter—a full rack of "Woods ribs," in this menu sampling, with a twice-baked potato and Brussels sprouts, along with a bottle of wine and a single order of s'mores with two forks—would run about two hundred dollars with tax and tip. Of course, factored into the price is the prospect of seeing Tiger Woods. It can happen, but he's not exactly what Mickey Mantle was at Mickey Mantle's restaurant, in its red-meat prime. Even when Tiger's in the house, he could be eating in a private room and you would never know it.

A more likely Jupiter nightspot to see a professional golfer, well known or not, is the Square Grouper, a down-home tiki bar on Jupiter Inlet. You might see Ernie Els there, or Dustin Johnson. You could see a golfing minor-leaguer, somebody good enough to dream (in the phrase of a long-ago Utica Blue Sox GM). The pale left hand, covered all day by a golf glove, is just one tell. If you're good at name-that-pro, you might recognize the journeyman Steve Marino, who once looked like he might be the game's next Mark Calcavecchia. You might see Will MacKenzie, a touring pro more interested in snowboarding and kayaking. Tiger always liked Willy Mac. His play was erratic, but as a free spirit he was irresistible. Once, at Torrey Pines in San Diego, after MacKenzie had been off the PGA Tour for several years, Tiger saw him, hugged him, and said, "You have no idea how happy I am to see you here." Tiger's internal life shows up in unexpected places.

In his South Florida years, Tiger would sometimes frequent the better chilled-glass hangouts with their expensive martinis, but over time he grew tired of drawing crowds and making money for others. That has been cited as one of the reasons he wanted to open the Woods Jupiter, located in an outdoor mall called Harbourside Place. The restaurant was still in its planning stages when Tiger got to know Erica Herman, a former nightclub owner in Orlando who was involved in its design and the hiring of its staff. The *u* in Harbourside is surely a clanging alarm for pretentiousness, but Tiger's restaurant is not, if you can get past the special menus for cognacs and cigars. The name, the Woods Jupiter, doesn't roll off your tongue, but the rights to your own name are complicated when you're Tiger Woods and your name is worth millions. That's what the man who developed the mall once told me.

The Woods and the Square Grouper are only a mile apart as the gull flies, across two inlets and a park named for Burt Reynolds, but one establishment might as well be planted on East Egg and the other on West, they're so different. You park your own truck at the Grouper, and the bands there play right through midnight. At the Woods, the valet guy will handle any European key you drop in his palm, along with a crisp green gift, and the house band is Joe Buck doing play-by-play on a flat-screen above your head. What both places have are well-stocked bars, sure-handed bartenders, and thirsty guests.

When you do all the math and take out all the recycling bins, you can only conclude, for good and for ill, that drinking is one of our great American hobbies, in Jupiter and most everywhere else, and Memorial Day weekend is a particularly prime time to indulge in it. The Jupiter police have a delicate job. There's serve and protect and something even more elemental than that: the responsibility to keep people safe. The local cops have to know the closing times at the Woods, at the Grouper, at Ralph's and Joe's and Uncle Mick's and the others. Jupiter has 55,000 residents and 310 miles of paved roads, three of them carrying the name Military Trail. Drivers speed, they stop in odd places, they drive when they shouldn't, they fight with their passengers, they get into accidents. The fifty Jupiter police officers on road patrol have their hands full. And now, early on the morning of Memorial Day, there was Tiger Woods on the side of one of their roads, in no shape to be driving—not even close.

"Have you been drinking tonight?"

The question was put to Woods by another Jupiter police officer on the scene that night.

"No," he said.

"No? Are you sure about that? Because there's some odor coming from you," Christopher Fandrey said.

Normally, nobody says anything to Tiger Woods even remotely that direct or challenging. That's because in almost every relationship, except maybe the ones with his mother and former wife, Tiger is the dominant personality. He holds the cards and has the power. But then he did not.

• • •

Greg Norman was the best player in the world when Tiger Woods turned pro, and no player had more power or charisma. Norman first met Tiger in the early 1990s, when Tiger was fourteen or fifteen. Hughes Norton of IMG, which represented Norman and had designs on Tiger, had arranged for them to play together at Old Marsh Golf Club, a development course in Palm Beach Gardens. They played nine holes, just the two of them, walking. Tiger was inquisitive and better than any junior golfer Norman had ever seen, and he told IMG how impressed he was. He remembers Tiger asking, "Why do you play so aggressively?" By 1993, Tiger had begun working with Butch Harmon, Norman's teacher, but Norman and Tiger never saw each other. In 1995, when Woods played in his first Masters, Norman played a Tuesday practice round with him. Norman remembers Tiger asking a litany of specific questions about how to play the course, and Norman answered them as best he could while still preparing for the tournament himself. But Earl felt Norman hadn't shown Tiger enough respect. That was one of Earl's moves. He liked to stir the pot. He liked the idea of *us against the world.*

Norman wasn't alone. There was something awkward about Tiger's relationships, early in his pro career, with Tom Watson and Nick Faldo, among others. Curtis Strange made some critical remarks about Tiger no-showing at a college awards dinner, and Earl never forgot that. Even Arnold Palmer said that Tiger was being talked about with too much awe. Faldo and Norman and a hundred other guys were trying to beat Tiger. They saw no reason to coddle him.

Various golf reporters, present company included, were doing enough coddling for everybody. Golf Channel began broadcasting in 1995, the year before Tiger turned pro. Golf websites were becoming popular for the first time. There was suddenly so much space to fill, and along came a player to fill it. Tiger was the game's first great Cablinasian player (his term for being white, black, Indian, and Asian) and the first golfer since Bobby Jones to win USGA titles in *six* consecutive years as an amateur. Interest in him was almost insatiable even before he collected his first Tour check. Tiger and especially Earl had the power, and they were taking names. If you dared to say that Tiger would have been wise to return to Stanford for his last two years instead of turning pro, your name went on a list. Sandy Tatum, the former USGA president and a legendary Stanford golfer in the early 1940s, found that out. The power of the traditional golf establishment has been in decline ever since.

Tatum was close to another Stanford golfer, Tom Watson, who turned pro after getting his degree in psychology. Watson and Woods have always been a curious pair, linked by far more than their initials. They have major areas of overlap—Stanford, U.S. Open wins at Pebble Beach, a knack for links golf—but they have never been close.

Watson was the captain of the U.S. Ryder Cup team in 2014, a year in which Tiger was feuding with his back. In the months leading up to the Ryder Cup, there was an ongoing debate (among people who clearly had too much time on their hands) about whether Tiger would play on Watson's team. They weren't talking. Mark Steinberg, Tiger's agent, said to one of Watson's confidantes, "Have your guy call my guy." It was the old thing, the caller loses. Tiger, aided and abetted by Steinberg, had a knack for turning the most mundane request into a show of power. You see it in every walk of life. For some people, it's a way to feel alive.

Things changed after Thanksgiving 2009, the starting date of the Tiger Woods sex scandal, which turned various lives upside down. It also empowered a disparate group of people. The editors at the *New York Post*. Matt Lauer. Tiger's wife, Elin Nordegren. Tom Watson. Newspaper columnists. It was absolute hysteria there for a while, at the end of 2009 and the beginning of 2010. The Stiletto Parade was in full swing, with a long series of Tiger's alleged lady friends offering their rendezvous histories. You would have thought Tiger was a United States senator, the way his infidelity was being covered. But he wasn't an elected official, a clergyman, a university president. He was just an exceptional athlete making millions on the side by selling a false version of himself in the name of Buick and American Express. The *National Enquirer* was treating him as if he were Gary Hart seeking the presidency. As the *Miami Herald* spied on Gary Hart, the *Enquirer* spied on Woods.

This wasn't MeToo before the movement existed. Yes, there were mighty gaps between Tiger and the women, in wealth and fame and power. But none of the women even implied that the relationships were anything other than consensual. Still, people were going crazy.

Arnold Palmer did what he wanted, and nobody wrote about it. Thirty years later, Michael Jordan did what he wanted, and there was no public shaming of him. But the rules were changing, and maybe

Woods, had he been more aware, could have seen the pattern. Or maybe arrogance got the better of him. In any event, he was exposed. No star had ever fallen so far and so fast. His rise had been steady. It took decades. His fall took three days.

All those hiked-skirt, in-the-parking-lot revelations cost Woods his marriage, his image, a chunk of his money. And that was when the long road to his fifth Masters victory began, in the aftermath of Thanksgiving 2009 when he ran over a fire hydrant in his front yard in a development near Orlando called Isleworth, and all hell broke loose. This is painful: We were surely culpable in his fall. We bought the tabloids. We clicked on TMZ. We judged. The ripples of Woods's affairs went far.

His fall had to be a staggering blow to his psyche, no matter how it came about. Whatever mind-games training Tiger got as a junior golfer from Jay Brunza, a navy psychologist, it could not have prepared him for the daily assault he was getting at the hands of TMZ.

Can you imagine the impact it would have on you—you, me, Tiger, anyone—if your sexual life were exposed for the world to see? For your friends, your colleagues, your parents, your spouse, and your children to read about? Imagine just *one* itty-bitty leaked text about a private fantasy, online and available for anybody to read. Can you imagine the stress that would bring? The anger and the confusion? It would be impossible for your mental health not to take a hit.

And sooner or later your mental health is going to show up in your physical health. This is not New Age crazy talk. It's René Descartes, Norman Cousins, Dr. Bob Jones IV, clinical psychologist and grandson of Bobby. "In many instances, if not most, there's a biological connection to stress," Jones told me. "If you're prone to spinal issues, and then you endure great stress, your spinal issues will likely get worse. It's to be expected."

Yes, Tiger Woods hit a million golf balls, and that's the starting point of his back problems. But Jamie Jungers, one of the women in the parade, talking about Tiger on the *Today* show surely didn't help. Neither did the twenty straight days when Tiger appeared on the cover of the *New York Post*. The headline on the fourth day wasn't artful, but it did its job: 2 MORE SEXY GALS COME OUT OF THE WOODSWORK WITH THEIR STEAMY TALES.

The tabloid covers, the *Saturday Night Live* skits, the Conan and Letterman stand-up bits, the Radar Online updates. Who could possibly withstand all that intact? Where a human being once stood for millions to see and admire, there was now a cardboard cutout, like Keanu Reeves as John Wick, greeting you at your AMC 20. Say whatever you want about that cutout, step on it if it falls over, it doesn't matter—it's not Keanu Reeves or even John Wick. It's just a piece of cardboard.

· · ·

The second officer at Woods's car on that Memorial Day night was a Jupiter police sergeant named Don Hennessy. When Palladino called for backup, Hennessy was the first to respond. The sergeant observed that Woods, on a warm night and with the car's engine off, kept the windows of his car up when the officers weren't talking to him. Palladino told Hennessy that he believed Woods was impaired, and it was Hennessy who called in Christopher Fandrey, a road-patrol officer, to conduct a series of field sobriety tests. It had now been six minutes from the time Palladino pulled behind the Mercedes.

Before Fandrey arrived, another Jupiter officer, Nick Imperiale, was on the scene, although only briefly. When Palladino was in his patrol car, Imperiale's job was to monitor Woods. When Woods began to reach into his pockets, Imperiale asked him to stop. He did, and then he fell asleep.

Later that night, Imperiale returned to take an inventory of Woods's car and to fill out the paperwork for its towing. The officer noted that Woods was driving a black 2015 Mercedes-Benz AMG

S65 registered to the ETW Corporation. The officer wrote that the driver's-side front and rear tires were flat and that their rims were damaged. He mentioned that the front bumper was damaged and the back bumper had scrape marks on it. He looked for car parts on and around Military Trail but found none.

The car was towed away by North County Towing, a Jupiter company that had been in business for forty-five years. Over the years, North County towers have towed their share of golf carts out of swamps, but now they were towing away a $200,000 Mercedes-Benz belonging to Tiger Woods. It was going to an impound lot. Imperiale removed a range finder and two pairs of sunglasses and took them to police headquarters for safekeeping. For a professional golfer, a range finder is an essential tool of the trade. A golfer without one is practicing naked.

·   ·   ·

The last officer to arrive that night had the biggest role. Christopher Fandrey was twenty-four, tall and baby-faced, living in an apartment in Jupiter, making about fifty thousand dollars a year as a Jupiter police officer after seventeen months with the department. He was also the grandson of a police detective on Long Island, a college graduate with a degree in criminal justice, and a veteran of the U.S. Marines, in which he had enlisted at eighteen. It was Fandrey who told Woods that he was emitting an odor.

Yes, in polite society that observation would be beyond the pale, but from an investigating police officer, and said the right way, it was all in a shift's work. Body language and actual language, along with some other things, subtle and otherwise, can make or break these encounters. We've all seen the evening news. Fandrey was appropriate in every way, and that made all the difference. As Fandrey noted, Woods was trying to cooperate. On some level, Woods must have understood that Fandrey didn't want to further humiliate him or make a show of power over him. Fandrey's first job was to assess the situation, a mess of Woods's making.

It was Fandrey who let out a quick laugh when Tiger, at the Palm Beach county jail, described his hair as "brown—and fading." In that moment, there was a serious imbalance of power between the two men. Woods was alone in a holding cell, standing barefoot on a stained linoleum floor, cuffs around his wrists, his brain function impaired. Fandrey was in his heavy blue police uniform, carrying a gun. Despite all that, Fandrey was going to treat his prisoner with humanity. In doing so, he revealed his own.

Fandrey's poise through all his taped and now public interactions with Woods, both roadside and at the jail, showed his professionalism. But all the while, there was never any doubt about the seriousness of Fandrey's purpose or Woods's recklessness. Woods could easily have killed somebody, including himself, that night. "He could have *died*," Tiger's friend Notah Begay said later. In the twelve pages of police reports that came out of that night, there was a rectangular box on one page marked VICTIM. It was a question. In filing the report, an officer entered a single word: SOCIETY.

When he arrived at the scene, Fandrey parked his patrol car in front of Woods's Mercedes. He turned on his spotlight and left on his headlights to shine a path for the sobriety tests he would conduct on a dark stretch of road on a dark night. Woods struggled to get out of the driver's seat and took off his running shoes after being unable to tie the left one. You almost can't believe it. At a tournament, and in about five seconds, Woods can stand on a tee and talk with a playing partner while tying a shoelace without looking at it.

Woods first told Fandrey that he was in Los Angeles, on his way to Orange County. He was wobbly, his speech was slurred, his eyelids were droopy, his hair was messy, his face was bloated, and he looked like he hadn't shaved in a week. Palladino and Fandrey half-caught Woods at one point to prevent him from falling. Woods couldn't follow Fandrey's pencil light with his eyes. He couldn't walk a heel-to-toe line. He struggled to bring his finger to his nose. He couldn't answer Fandrey's basic mental-function questions. He was gone.

Fandrey asked Woods to recite the English alphabet and not in a singsong manner, then asked him to repeat the assignment, to show that he understood it.

"Not to sing the National Anthem backwards," Woods said. His confusion could not have been more obvious.

When he finally did recite the alphabet, Woods finished it off with a triumphant "and z," sounding like a proud preschooler. Most of the other tests could not be completed.

There are thousands of hours of tape of Tiger on YouTube. He's playing golf, giving interviews, appearing at functions. He's with presidents, other players, business leaders, reporters, Tiger Woods Learning Center students. All those hours where he is nothing but appropriate and in control. And then there was this night. Nothing in his taped canon can prepare you for the Memorial Day recordings. They're hard to watch, though many have. They're primitive and real. Tiger Woods, without his usual power. Tiger has always been impressive, from age two on. But on that night, he was vulnerable. What a sad scene. He was lucky nobody died that night. And still your heart went out to him. Tiger was practically screaming, he was in such pain.

·   ·   ·

In early November 2009, two women, employees at a downtown New York nightclub that catered to men with heavy credit cards and thin-soled loafers, called the main number for Time Inc. in midtown Manhattan. The switchboard operator steered them to the golf editor at *Sports Illustrated*, a Time Inc. magazine.

That editor, Jim Herre, spoke to one of the women and could hear the other in the background. Though they were giggling, their purpose was serious. The woman said she had a friend named Rachel Uchitel who was having an affair with Tiger Woods. The two women, one on the phone and other near it, were looking for a buyer for their story. They wanted twenty-five thousand dollars.

Herre told the woman that *Sports Illustrated* didn't buy information from sources. But he didn't want to lose her, either. He was surprised by what he was hearing. Tiger's reputation was so Buick, so AT&T, so clean. He took the woman's number (she didn't offer her last name) and said he would speak to his boss. After that, he said, they could speak again. The woman said she was talking to other publications as well. She mentioned the *National Enquirer*. Herre asked, "Why are you ratting out your friend like this?" There was no meaningful response.

Herre spoke to his boss, the managing editor of *Sports Illustrated*, who showed little interest in the story. He left the matter to Herre, who called me. (I was an *SI* writer). Herre gave me the woman's number and told me to call her and find out what I could.

"What would we do with it if we got it?" I asked. *It* was the goods, the scoop. I remember thinking, if Tiger Woods was having an affair, that wasn't news for *Sports Illustrated*.

"I don't know," Herre said. "But I'd like to know." I got that. Reporters often gather information they will never use directly, but it informs whatever else you write.

I called the woman. Her cell phone had a Las Vegas area code. She did not call back. From what I was able to gather, she had made a deal with the *Enquirer*. She didn't sell her Tiger-Rachel story, as I understand it, but got paid for telling the *Enquirer* when Rachel Uchitel would be leaving her Manhattan apartment and flying to Melbourne, Australia, for a rendezvous with Woods, who was there playing in a tournament.

The *Enquirer* got a photo of Uchitel leaving her building. Then the *Enquirer* had a stringer in the elevator of the Crown Towers Hotel as

Uchitel was going to Tiger's penthouse suite, and the stringer confronted her. The *Enquirer* had its story, what turned out to be the first of many. That's how the unraveling of Woods's private life began. It seems unlikely that the Founding Fathers had in mind stories that came out of that kind of sordid newsgathering when they ratified the First Amendment.

The *National Enquirer* was creeping in on him, and *still* Tiger won the 2009 Australian Masters at Kingston Heath. That was on November 16. On November 25, the print edition of the *Enquirer*, featuring the Woods-Uchitel tryst, was published. November 26 was Thanksgiving. On November 27, at 2:25 a.m., Tiger left his house in a hurry, crashed his Cadillac Escalade, and was unconscious for six minutes. Police and emergency workers were called in.

Now there was a new kind of Tigermania, completely unlike the first version, which began with Tiger's win at the 1997 Masters. Everybody got swept up in it. Or most everybody. Jack Nicklaus didn't. He said that Tiger's private life was Tiger's business, not his. But you didn't hear that take much.

You didn't hear it from Billy Payne, the chairman of Augusta National. His eleven-year run as chairman will be remembered for what he did to bring golf in general and the Masters in particular to more people across the world. But in the highlight reel of his tenure you would have to include his State of the Masters address on the Wednesday of the 2010 Masters, when he apparently confused the dais in his club's press building for the pulpit at his church. That afternoon he offered a two-minute sermon about Tiger's return to competitive golf in the wake of his sex scandal. A snippet: "It is not simply the degree of his conduct that is so egregious here, it is the fact that he disappointed all of us, and more importantly, our kids and our grandkids. Our hero did not live up to the expectations of the role model we saw for our children."

I speak only for myself: Tiger Woods didn't disappoint me; he wasn't my hero; and I never had any kind of thought about what kind of role model he needed to be for our son and daughter, both in high school at the time. Tiger Woods was an excellent and exciting golfer from an uncommon background, and I was mesmerized by his ability to do a difficult thing at such a high level, again and again. Also, I liked the way he walked. That was more than enough to sustain my interest in him.

The chairman, like many others, was empowered by Tiger's fall. Here's how Payne concluded his remarks: "We at Augusta hope and pray that our great champion will begin his new life here tomorrow in a positive, hopeful, and constructive manner, but this time, with a significant difference from the past. This year, it will not be just for him, but for all of us, who believe in second chances."

Can you imagine praying for Tiger to do *anything*? But I have to be careful not to be too judgy here, as we all have our breaking points. Once, while caddying in a long-ago Masters, I talked my player into going for the green with his second shot on the par-5 fifteenth hole, despite the yawning pond that guards that green like a moat. With the ball sailing limply through the air, I could imagine the coming splash, and I never prayed so hard in all my life: *God, please—make it fly!* Seems kind of nutty now.

There were and are many reasonable people who thought Payne's remarks were not only appropriate but necessary. The chairman of Augusta National is a leader in the game, and golf's most significant figure was returning to competition, and to Billy Payne's club, after a public sex scandal the likes of which modern life had seldom if ever seen. How could the chairman not say something? It's one view.

I asked Bob Jones, the psychologist, how his grandfather would have handled Tiger's post-scandal return to the Masters. Here's Dr. Bob: "He would have said, 'Hello, Tie-*guh*.' In private." Jones did his grandfather's patrician Atlanta accent, an old-guard brogue now nearly dead.

33

Tiger despised (I've been told) Payne's remarks but has never said a public thing about them except this: "I was disappointed in myself, too." As it happens, Tiger never won a Masters with Billy Payne as chairman. Nearly ten years later, Payne said, "I would say, and I would hope and believe Tiger would confirm, that we are dear friends."

The Monday, Tuesday, and Wednesday before the 2010 Masters were downright strange. Tiger played practice rounds with Fred Couples, Mark O'Meara, Steve Stricker, and some of his other regulars. It *looked* like business as usual. He still had some of his earned status. On Tuesday morning, he had his regular tee time, first off at eight a.m., with Phil Mickelson right behind him. For that round and others, Tiger wore shirts that were on the loose side, and some of his pants were downright baggy. Nike considers every piece of clothing worn by Tiger, and that was not the week to sell Tigerwear on the basis of his sex appeal.

At times, Tiger looked sheepish and unsure of himself, and the people around him were walking on eggshells. Mark Steinberg, following Tiger closely, looked pale and tired, in the fifth month of his crash course in crisis management. Tiger's caddie, Steve Williams, was robust by nature, but his vitality, even the customary bounce in his walk, seemed forced in those practice rounds. Phil Knight of Nike was on the scene during the tournament, much more prominent than usual, walking with Tiger's mother, talking to reporters with a county sheriff nearby. Woods, in a press conference, said his wife, daughter, and son would not be coming to Augusta, and mentioned how his family had been hounded by paparazzi. Nobody close to Tiger had come out of this scandal unfazed, most of all Elin. Her former life was over. *Poof.*

But when the bell went off on Thursday, Tiger's play was excellent, despite his five-month layoff. He was playing for keeps, and he was his old self. The way the practice rounds had gone, you didn't know what he was going to be like. That's how good at golf he was then.

Practice-round days used to be slow, and some of the writers would sneak out to play nearby courses. A nice memory. Following the example set by the Super Bowl, golf figured out that the days leading up its biggest events were prime selling days. On Masters Wednesday, the day when Billy Payne made his hope-and-pray remarks to a roomful of reporters, Nike aired its memorable "Dead Earl" ad. The thirty-second spot featured only one visual, Tiger's impassive face in black and white, filling the screen, the shot getting tighter and tighter over the half minute. It has the feel of a homemade movie but with two camera flashes going off near the end, an apparent nod to his public life. He blinks seven times as he listens to his father, in voice-over, from the great beyond: "Tiger? I am more prone to be inquisitive, to promote discussion. I want to find out what your thinking was. I want to find out what your feelings are, and did you learn anything."

It was brilliant, mixing private life and public life, comingling father and son, teacher and student. It was also hilarious. Stephen Colbert had a field day with it.

Earl's dialogue was lifted from a documentary that had aired about eight years earlier. The first word—*Tiger?*—was spliced in. In the documentary, Earl was not addressing Tiger but comparing himself to Tiger's mother. But Nike's people weren't making a documentary. All's fair in love and advertising. They wanted to push our buttons, knowing that button-pushing is good for business, at least at Nike. Brand awareness is Nike's god.

Nike and Phil Knight have shaped Tiger's life in some ways that can be measured, and many that cannot. It was Phil Knight who made Tiger rich before he struck a single shot as a professional golfer. Nike gave Tiger the freedom to say to his father, as he was concluding his amateur career, "I'm never flying coach again." He knew that his first Nike deal, reportedly for $40 million, was coming. Nike sold Tiger every way a free man can be sold, but Tiger signed willingly.

He must have wanted the clothes, the clubs, the fame, the money, the attention. The proof is that he never walked away. He was set for life—for money, anyway.

. . .

Tiger's professional greatness has always been rooted in his otherworldly ability to be in control. Of his situation, his swing, his body. His thinking. His employees and his fans. (If a child in a crowd touched him, Tiger's glare would send the kid into a hole.) He was in control of his sponsors, golf executives, reporters, broadcasters. Other players, at least at times. Woods could make players try desperate things, because they knew it would take a miracle to beat him. They knew and Woods knew that Woods was better. He was better in every category there is, so their nervousness was well founded. If Woods had the fifty-four-hole lead, and he often did, he didn't have to do anything special to win. But the chasers did.

At the 2007 U.S. Open at Oakmont, Aaron Baddeley had the fifty-four-hole lead. Tiger was in second, two shots behind him. Tiger stepped on the first tee on Sunday in a red T-shirt so tight you could almost see his pounding heart. The leader flinched. You could actually see it. Baddeley looked like a prizefighter getting ready to take a hit, and he shot 80. Woods didn't win that day, but Baddeley had no chance. In their twosome, Woods had a TKO before they made the turn.

By tradition, the fight and conflict in stroke-play tournament golf is practically invisible. That's one of the reasons golf is a niche sport. The whole enterprise is too subtle. But it wasn't a niche sport when Tiger was leading majors. He drew millions of people to TV screens who, under normal conditions, would have been out washing the car or doing some other productive weekend activity. They wanted to watch Tiger Woods because he was the heavyweight champion of the world. Because he was consistently, reliably, and relentlessly great.

Because he buried the competition. He was Mike Tyson in the 1980s, General Motors in the 1950s, the U.S. Army in the 1940s, the New York Yankees in the 1920s. Rooting against him was a waste of time. Woods left his opponents gasping for air, and by Sunday night you could see their blood all over those beautiful country-club greens. Before the cleaning crews could get out there, Tiger would talk into a TV microphone held by a smiling broadcaster. He might be exhausted, but you wouldn't see even a scratch on him.

He'd give up little pieces in those interviews, but you had to mine the material. To try to understand him, you needed to watch closely. And that was difficult, because you could feel how uncomfortable he was, knowing that three thousand people were staring as he walked from the putting green to the first tee. His eyes told you when his allergies were bothering him, when he was cold, when he had suffered a particularly bad bout of insomnia. Would you look at any other golfer so closely? You wouldn't even have the interest.

There was always something more purposeful about him. You could see it in his walk, through parking lots and clubhouses, across driving ranges, down fairways. He didn't wing anything, except when circumstances required him to invent something on the spot, and he could do that, too. He could play a shot left-handed, he could grip the club on the metal, he could blade a shot by design. But he always had a plan, for his pre-round warm-up sessions and his post-round interviews and for all that he said and did in between. He was unwavering in his devotion to his predawn workouts and his red-and-black Sunday costumes. He could dictate intra-round conversation with his playing partners on body language alone. The stage was his.

The ultimate goal for Tiger, as it is for any golfer, was to be in control of his golf ball, to the degree he could. (Golf balls have an annoying tendency to do their own thing.) But when you can really golf your ball, to use a dying phrase, when you are truly in control of it, a feeling of ecstasy washes through you. Every golfer at every level has experienced that, even if it's fleeting. At Tiger's level, it leads to all manner of prizes: silver-plated trophies, direct-deposit checks, carnal pleasures, preferred tee times. But the starting point is to be in control of your ball. Golf tests control in every possible way.

But people need to be out of control, too. It's in our nature. Witness: the dance floor at an August wedding, ties loose, shoes off, ice buckets spent.

· · ·

On those police tapes, Tiger seems relieved. That's not an observation many would make, but that's Billy Harmon's take. Billy, a prominent teaching pro and Butch Harmon's youngest brother, has been around Tiger. He's also a recovering alcoholic and drug addict who is open about his own sobriety and who knows firsthand the relief that comes from being caught. In the sine curve of life, being discovered can be a fast way to define the bottom of the trough. It was for Billy. On the day of his reckoning, a small group of club members came into his apartment on the second floor of the columned clubhouse at the Newport Country Club, in Rhode Island, and told him what they could see and he could not. The jig was up. He felt the lying and the booze and the coke start to wash out of him.

You've never heard Tiger be more polite than he was that night. After Fandrey and Palladino handcuffed him and placed him in the back seat of Fandrey's patrol car, Woods asked, "Could you loosen the right one just a little bit?" They did, and Woods said, "Thank you so much."

· · ·

After Thanksgiving in 2009, all hell broke loose, and Tiger disappeared. His location became a national guessing game. Then, three weeks into the New Year, a *National Enquirer* photographer snapped a grainy long-lens picture of him. He was carrying a tall Styrofoam cup and was wearing gym clothes. He was almost concealed, with the hood of a hoodie on his head. But there was no mask on his face and you could tell who it was. The photo ran across the world, another nail in the coffin of privacy. Tiger was in Hattiesburg, Mississippi, as an in-house patient at a facility for sex, alcohol, and drug addiction called Pine Grove.

We all know how these centers work, at least when the recovery story makes it onto *Celebrity Rehab with Dr. Drew*. Patient bottoms out, *admits to having no power over specified addiction(s)*, enters facility as a ticking time bomb, endures weeks of cold sweats and tough group therapy, comes out clean and sober and saying these words right on cue: "Now the real work begins." Mental illness as mass-market entertainment will lead to distortions, but these facilities have been demystified over time. If Bill W. and Dr. Bob were starting Alcoholics Anonymous today, maybe they would drop the second word. Billy Harmon would be fine with that. He doesn't think there's anything to be ashamed about. For that, Betty Ford should take a posthumous bow. She paved Tiger's path to Hattiesburg. But privacy, for Tiger, has always been an issue. *Privacy* is the name of his yacht.

Pine Grove and places like it are selling hope, but you have to think they're saving lives, too, even if the proffered stories sound too easy. It's not like these facilities can perform plastic surgery on a patient's mental health. The follow-up is the rest of the person's life. In *Clean and Sober*, Michael Keaton's character is a cocaine addict and an embezzler. He enters rehab because he's trying to stay out of prison. That isn't the ideal reason to go to rehab, but it's a good one, and by the end of the movie you feel like he has a chance. Tiger went to rehab looking to save his marriage. That's a good reason, too, even if it's not what the classically trained twelve-steppers would ideally want to hear. When it comes to saving souls, gatekeepers can't be too fussy.

Tiger had to be way outside his comfort zone. Pine Grove asks its patients to be open and trusting, and Tiger is not. He was accustomed to luxurious hotels and homes, but at Pine Grove he lived in Spartan quarters. Tiger's humor can run homophobic, and at Pine Grove he was living in close proximity to two gay men. It's unlikely that Pine Grove's communal dining and food offerings in the winter of 2010 brought to mind the gourmet options in the team room at the 2009 Presidents Cup in San Francisco, with Fred Couples and Michael Jordan and Phil Mickelson popping in and out. But Tiger had a powerful incentive to be there: to try to address his serial adultery, along with his drinking and his drug use, in the name of keeping his family of four under one roof.

Tiger has been a drinker all his adult life. Earl Woods once described, in an interview with Matt Rudy for *Golf Digest*, his first drink with Tiger, when his son was home for Thanksgiving during his freshman year at Stanford. Earl: "We walked over to the park and we sat down and Tiger said, 'I just want to share this first drink with you. This is the first drink we've ever had, the two of us.' And we sat there and talked and talked and talked. One of the most beautiful moments of my life." For millions of people (this is not a news flash), drinking promotes intimacy. Growing up, Tiger had seen Earl and his military buddies enjoy post-round drinks at the Navy Golf Course near their house. Golf has always been swimming in drink. It takes effort to avoid it, and most golfers wouldn't want to.

By his tight-lid standards, Woods has been open about his drinking. At that 2009 Presidents Cup, you could see Woods sipping out of Michael Jordan's Scotch glass, although that might have been more of an exercise in male bonding than anything else. Over the years, after some of his wins, Tiger has made cheeky references to his celebratory drinking plans, particularly if the flight home was long. He sometimes mentioned *libations* or *adult beverages*. He liked rum and Coke. He liked Corona and ginger ale. Nothing in his public life would tell you whether he was or was not an alcoholic, a word that resists definition anyhow. But it was not a secret that Tiger liked to drink.

His issues with insomnia have been well-known for most of his professional career, mainly because he has mentioned them in press conferences and interviews. So if he went to Pine Grove dependent on or addicted to sleep meds, that would not have been a surprise.

Across the developed world, alcohol and drug issues are about as common as the cold. Untold numbers of people have them, and just saying no is one way—but not the only way—to address them.

Which brings us to Door No. 3: Tiger and *sex addiction*. Another phrase that's resistant to a doctor-certified consensus definition. Some wonder if it even is an addiction, as addiction implies a change in brain function and a disease that can be treated. But that's not a debate for the people at Pine Grove, where sex addiction is a house specialty.

On the Pine Grove website, there's an eleven-question yes-or-no quiz that includes this layup: "Do you ever feel anxious or irritable if you are unable to engage in sexual behaviors?" If you answer yes to any of the eleven, you're encouraged to call Pine Grove's toll-free number. They must have a lot of operators standing by.

This is fertile ground for comedians, as most people would like to have more sex. Tiger's stay at Pine Grove helped inspire a *South Park* episode called "Sexual Healing." In it, a cartoon Tiger and a cartoon Bill Clinton, among other cartoon creations, are in rehab for sex addiction. A cartoon therapist asks, "In order to make sure we are no longer destroying our lives with any of these behaviors, we must avoid—anyone? Avoid getting—anyone?" And a cartoon Michael Douglas says, "Caught."

The actual conversation at Pine Grove is the opposite. Lives are on the line, and patients are looking to make changes. Therapists and patients are on a group dig, and what they excavate can be alarming and insightful. For starters: The core problem for the sex addict is not an insatiable desire to have sex. The heart of the matter is the soullessness that comes from lacking the empathy gene. There's a missing chip. Try finding it.

Sex addicts can race through sex partners like French fries out of a bag because they don't care about the person they're having sex with. They're not thinking about their spouse or partner, if they have one. They want what they want. They feel entitled, superior, untouchable. If they're not full-blown narcissists, they're heading there. Lack of empathy is the starting point of the talk therapy. There ought to be a word with real oomph to describe this emotional bankruptcy. *Apathy* isn't it. *Coldhearted* comes close. This might be closer yet: *me-me-me-me-me.* Tiger on the course had that in spades. He was coldhearted. He had *me-me-me* in his bones. Whatever character defects he might have had, they were useful on Sunday afternoons.

His six-week stay passed. What he got out of it is impossible to say. Tiger left Hattiesburg and resumed his public life. He gave two TV interviews for which his people dictated unusual terms: Each interview could be only five minutes, and Tiger had to be standing. He returned to his home at Isleworth, now an empty one. His wife and kids had moved out. He returned to the range there. He returned to competitive golf and public life at the Masters. Billy Payne was there to greet him.

We all looked at Tiger differently, Billy Payne and everybody else. We knew too much. Whether he had changed, or had even started to change, we couldn't know. The next seven years would be telling. That is, the time between the day he checked out of Pine Grove and the night a Jupiter police officer took him to the Palm Beach county jail.

• • •

Tom Watson is a forthright man, unusually so. He has always enjoyed a reputation for being candid (to the point of arrogance), for knowing golf's rules and playing by them, for owning his mistakes. He has all the answers. He's "Carnac II," in an old Tour nickname. (Nicklaus was the original.) Lord knows Watson can be preachy.

When Woods was at the treatment facility in Hattiesburg, Watson was in Dubai for a golf tournament. This was about a half-year after his second-place finish in the 2009 British Open—at age fifty-nine. His stock was way up. Watson was asked about Tiger at a press conference. Here (lightly edited) is what Watson said: "He has to take ownership of what he's done. He must get his personal life in order. I think that's what he's trying to do. I don't know.

"And when he comes back, he has to show some humility to the public. If I were him, I'd come back and I would come out and do an interview with somebody and say, 'You know what, I screwed up. I admit it. And I'm going to try to change. I am trying to change. I want my wife and family back. I have to earn her trust back.'

"It's going to be interesting, to see how he handles his return to public life. And I wish him the best. He messed up. He knows he messed up. The world knows he messed up."

Watson was then asked about Woods's on-course demeanor. "I feel that he has not carried the same stature as the other great players that have come along, like Jack or Arnold, Byron Nelson, Hogan. The language, the club-throwing on the golf course. I think he needs to clean up his act there and show the respect for the game that the people before him have shown."

There was more in those comments than the ordinary American sports fan could possibly process on a weekday in February while still getting over the Super Bowl. Watson was addressing a broad issue that worried a generation of old-guard golfers: Over the course of a century of American golf, the game's sacred mantle had been handed down seamlessly. Jones to Sarazen, Sarazen to Nelson, Nelson to Snead, Snead to Hogan, Hogan to Palmer, Palmer to Nicklaus, Nicklaus to Watson, Watson to Norman. What they were actually handing down was a reverence for golf's oldest and richest events, for the players who came before them, for an unspoken code that made the game, and those who played it, so . . . *special*. Yes, there was a smug self-importance in this whole discussion, and in this cloistered world populated only by white men. But there was something real there, too, something manly, appealing, timeless, clubby in a good way. Those golfers earned their way onto that list, with their golf and with their demeanor.

Then came the attempted handoff from Norman to Woods. That part had not gone well. There were complaints from on high, though nearly always whispered, about Tiger's cursing, his spitting, his whole *second sucks* routine, his empty victory speeches. But after the Stiletto Parade, the floodgates opened. Tiger didn't have a constituency. It was obvious that the game's elder statesmen admired Woods the golfer. That didn't mean they liked the man. Watson was asked about Woods, and he didn't hold back.

Only one part of Watson's remarks was widely circulated: *He needs to clean up his act.* Watson was talking about Woods's comportment on the course, but nobody took it that way. Several years later, when Watson and Woods sat next to each other at a dinner for former U.S. Open winners, they barely got past the weather and the length of the Merion rough.

Nick Faldo and Johnny Miller had similar experiences with Tiger. Faldo, from his perch in dozens of broadcast towers, deigned to critique Woods's swing changes and his strategy, and those comments were not well received. Johnny Miller, the legendary NBC golf analyst, was far more critical, and Woods once said of him, "Johnny knows everything, doesn't he?"

And then, in this group of Hall of Famers who have had frosty relationships with Woods, there was Greg Norman. There are interesting parallels. For several years, Butch Harmon taught both Norman and Tiger, but then Norman was pushed out. ("Tiger told Butch point-blank: It's either me or Greg," Norman told me. "I told Butch, 'You've got a great chance with this kid. You go with him.'") Norman had been managed by IMG, and Tiger followed suit. Tiger hired Norman's former caddie, Steve Williams. Norman moved from

Orlando to Jupiter Island mid-career, and Tiger moved from Orlando to Jupiter Island mid-career. Norman's estate manager became Tiger's estate manager. Norman's home club, Medalist, became Tiger's home club. Norman was the best player in the world, and then Tiger was. That happened, if you want to go by something called the Official World Golf Ranking, for the first time in June 1997. Tiger was one and Norman was two.

So first Tiger dethroned the man. Later he wouldn't give Norman a neighborly wave at a drawbridge. Oh, why can't these superstar golfers just get along?

· · ·

When the parade was over, and after Tiger returned to professional golf with a fourth-place finish in the 2010 Masters, he endured what was then the longest dry spell of his career. He didn't win in 2010 or 2011. He and Elin divorced. Sponsors dropped him. Steve Williams—Tiger's Stevie, his faithful sidekick and enforcer—left him.

In golf's cloistered world, the Steve-Tiger breakup was big news. The story, as it was written, was that Williams had been fired, and that was what Williams said, too. But you could also say he was asking to be fired. When Williams agreed to caddie for another star player, even on a one-week basis—Adam Scott at the 2011 U.S. Open, in which Tiger did not play—he was essentially quitting. The unwritten understanding was that caddying for Tiger Woods was a full-time job that required the caddie's complete and undivided attention. Woods had no use for a caddie who was willing to fraternize with the enemy. Tiger had been the best man at Williams's wedding in New Zealand, but that was five years earlier. That was in another lifetime. When Tiger mentioned Williams at all, he was no longer Stevie, but Steve. Tiger brought in a new caddie, Joe LaCava. In the years when Joe worked for Fred Couples, he would sometimes pick up a different player when Fred wasn't playing. Joe would not be doing that with Tiger.

Tiger's first win with Joe, and his first win since the scandal, was at Arnold Palmer's tournament at Bay Hill in March 2012. Tiger called the victory "pure joy." It wasn't readily apparent. Damon Hack, writing about the win for *Sports Illustrated*, captured the tenor of the day perfectly when he described Tiger on that Sunday night, getting into his black Mercedes with two dry turkey sandwiches and two cans of Diet Coke. Dinner for his two-hour drive home.

He won two more times that year and five times the next. When Woods reclaimed his ranking as the number-one player two weeks before the 2013 Masters, Nike unleashed an ad with the message "*Winning takes care of everything*" superimposed in white on Tiger, reading a putt. The quotation marks make obvious who owns the idea. It's hard to imagine a single sentence that degrades the meaning of sport more efficiently. It's also hard to imagine a single sentence that reveals more about a corporate culture, unless you want to count Gordon Gekko, of Gekko & Co., when he said, "Greed is good." But that was in a movie.

Tiger Woods couldn't possibly have believed that winning takes care of everything. He *couldn't* be that shallow, could he? But there he was, crouching on a green, with those words, in quotes, bisecting him at mid-body.

He wasn't carrying himself like a man who believed that winning takes care of everything. There was no lightness in his step, as there had been. One victory in particular, at the 2013 Players Championship, was telling. Sergio García, not one of Tiger's friends, had a share of the lead through three rounds and was in the last group on Sunday. But with balls in the water on the last two holes, he had squandered whatever chance he had to win. Tiger won, but not the way he was accustomed to winning. He won while watching the tournament on TV in the scorer's room. For about two seconds he looked at the screen and showed absolutely nothing, no emotion of any sort. He then stood up, saw LaCava behind him, and, with a camera operator hovering nearby, gave his caddie a little touch-football shove. He smiled and said, "How 'bout *that?*" It looked like a performance.

•　•　•

In 2013 Tiger played in only sixteen events on the PGA Tour. In three of them—the Masters in April, the Players Championship in May, and the BMW Championship in September—he was involved in rules disputes over issues that (borrowing Watson's list here) Nicklaus, Palmer, Nelson, and Hogan surely would have handled differently. You could add to that list Bobby Jones, Tom Watson, and thousands of others, famous and obscure and in between.

Tiger's first rules issue of the year was in his first event of the year, at a tournament in Abu Dhabi in January. It was relatively minor. He thought he was entitled to embedded ball relief in an area covered with leafy vegetation but sandy underneath. Woods called his playing partner, Martin Kaymer, to look at the lie. Kaymer agreed with Tiger, that he was entitled to relief. Turned out they were incorrect. Despite the vegetation, Woods was playing out of a bunker, a hazard. You can't take embedded ball relief out of a hazard. Tiger was given a two-shot penalty and missed the cut. It was avoidable and it was odd, but odd things happen in golf all the time. The playing fields are big and varied, and the rule book is dense.

Then came one of the most famous incidents in the history of golf-rules jurisprudence. It occurred three months after Abu Dhabi, in the second round of the Masters, when Woods played a full wedge shot on the par-5 fifteenth hole that hit the flagstick and ricocheted into the pond in front of the green. That part was nothing more than bad luck. Flagsticks are skinny things. The wedge shot was his third on the hole, and his fourth was the penalty shot, a consequence of hitting his ball in the water. Golf can be cruel, but the rules are the same for everybody.

For his fifth shot, Woods tried to do again what he'd done on his third, but from at least a yard farther back. There are three options for taking relief (a phrase from the rule book) in that situation, but what Woods did is not covered under any of them. Under the option he chose, he was required to drop the ball *as near as possible* to where it was played from originally. His unfilled divot hole told him exactly where his ball had been—so an inch or two or three behind that, after dropping a ball from shoulder height. That's what the rule required.

One TV viewer, David Eger, a former USGA and PGA Tour executive and a former rules official, was watching at home. Eger saw what to him was, in the vernacular, a bad drop, an obvious one. From what he could see on TV, Eger estimated that Woods played his second wedge at least three feet behind where he was required to be. This might sound absurdly persnickety, but without precise rules adhered to with High Orthodox devotion, the game would turn into chaos. Three feet or more is not as near as possible.

Eger called a rules official he knew who was working the tournament, and word got to Fred Ridley, the chairman of the tournament's rules committee. Eger knew as well as anybody how these situations unfold. If Woods signed his scorecard, thereby swearing to its accuracy, and somebody later questioned his drop on fifteen, he would be disqualified from the tournament for signing an incorrect scorecard. The clock was ticking. Because of Eger's call, Ridley watched the tape from fifteen, and did so before Woods finished his round.

Ridley's job was to help keep the tournament fair for all the players. Had he reviewed the drop with Woods, after the round and before Woods signed his card, Tiger almost surely would have received a two-shot penalty for playing from the wrong position.

But Ridley, a former U.S. Amateur winner himself (and Billy Payne's successor as club chairman) didn't do that. He watched the tape and decided that Woods was close enough to the original spot. He let the matter go. To do otherwise, he wrote in a text to another rules official that afternoon, would be "splitting hairs."

When Ridley wrote that, he did not know that Woods would soon go on live TV and tell Tom Rinaldi of ESPN in a post-round interview that he went "two yards" behind where his ball originally was. His statement to Rinaldi was proof, by testimony, that he had inadvertently broken a rule. He wasn't cheating. But it was also proof—again, by Tiger's own testimony—that he had broken a rule. Eger, watching on TV, thought it had been at least three feet. Tiger, not realizing he had done the drop incorrectly, was saying *six* feet. That's not even close to *as near as possible*.

A golfer is responsible for any rule he or she breaks, no matter how it is broken. Signing an incorrect scorecard for a score lower than what you actually shot had long resulted in automatic disqualification. It was how golf preserved the sanctity of a golfer's score. That act, signing your name for your score and owning it, is at the absolute core of the game.

A mess.

The tournament's rules committee added two shots to Woods's Friday score the following morning. The committee was bending over backward to be fair to Tiger, because it had not acted on Eger's call. Despite signing for a score lower than he had actually shot, Tiger was not disqualified from the tournament. That does not happen.

Tiger could have owned the moment, the problem, the solution. He could have stood up like a grown man and said, "This is my responsibility, and I'm going to make it right." All he had to do was withdraw. Nick Faldo, a three-time Masters winner and the lead golf analyst for CBS, urged Woods on Golf Channel that Saturday morning to do just that. "He really should sit down and think about this and the mark this will leave on his career, his legacy, everything," Faldo said. His words have never stopped ringing true.

Later, at a news conference, Ridley said quietly, "There's not a day that goes by that there are not some things I wish I would have done differently." You could feel his discomfort and his regret.

The club was too gracious, or too something, to say what Faldo was saying: the problem began with Woods, and Woods was the one person who could really fix the problem. Ridley owned his action. Imagine if Woods had done the same. It would have become a shining example of golf's value system.

Woods's decision to continue to play made for a distraction that lasted through the weekend and far beyond. Had he won that Masters, you could have put an asterisk on the lapel of his green jacket forever, like Hester Prynne's *A* in *The Scarlet Letter*. His whole march to eighteen would have looked different. In the end, he finished fourth, four shots behind Adam Scott, who won his green coat with Steve Williams caddying for him.

That Saturday, Woods put himself ahead of the tournament, the hosts of the tournament, the game's tradition of sportsmanship, the other players in the field. Woods had nobody in his camp, or in his life, who could convince him that going home would have been the best thing to do in the long run, for everybody and everything. But it wasn't in him to do that.

· · ·

One month later, on the Sunday of the Players Championship, Tiger was in the penultimate group, playing with Casey Wittenberg, former wunderkind golfer. In the 2004 Masters, as a nineteen-year-old amateur, Wittenberg was paired for the first two rounds with Tiger. On the first hole, on the first day, Tiger hit a poor tee shot, but on the second hole he hit a good one, and Wittenberg saw his opening. He tried to start a conversation while they walked along the broad, downward-sloping second fairway. Tiger's responses were barely north of curt, but it didn't seem to faze the kid. By Sunday night he was getting the tournament's medal as the low amateur in Butler Cabin. The winner, Phil Mickelson, was beside him. They both had shot back-nine 31s in the finale to get there. Casey Wittenberg was nothing but promise. Three years later, he was playing in (and winning) the Flora-Bama Lounge Classic. Pro golf is hard. You get what you can where you can.

Sunday at the 2013 Players, Woods and Wittenberg were on the tee of the 461-yard par-4 fourteenth hole, near each other physically, otherwise separated by a chasm. Tiger was trying to win the tournament while also trying to further cement his status as the best player in the world. Wittenberg was trying to cash the best check of his career while also trying to find regular employment on the PGA Tour. Woods had the honor. He went to the left side of the tee box and aimed right, away from a pond that runs down the left side of the hole's fairway. But he made a poor swing with a 3-wood, coming down steep, his body way in front of the ball.

And then it was Wittenberg's turn. He had to block out the short par putt he had just missed on thirteen. He had to block out the cameras, the fans, the Tiger-on-Sunday swirl, the pond in which Woods's ball had just landed with a splash. The fairway was narrow, and the wind was right to left and quartering in. Tee shots don't get much more difficult, but Wittenberg hit a good one, long and down the right side of the fairway, far from the pond. What a relief.

Now, nine years after the Masters when Wittenberg and Tiger played together, Tiger needed something from Wittenberg. Tiger, the most powerful person in golf, needed Wittenberg to tell him where he "crossed." To play his third shot, after adding a penalty shot for his tee shot into the water, Woods needed help to figure out where to drop. To do so, he needed to know where his ball had last crossed the imaginary vertical window that separated land and pond.

Wittenberg came off the tee and he and Tiger had a brief conversation. A golfer's playing partner is also his opponent, and these conversations can be tricky. This one was not. Wittenberg told Tiger what Tiger had hoped to hear.

A minute or so earlier, Mark Rolfing, an NBC Sports on-course reporter and the least hyperbolic of men, had offered a description of

Tiger's tee shot while it was in the air. It doubled as haiku: "This is not good. Fat. High. Ballooning. Left. And I believe wet." Then came the splash, ten or more feet from the pond's bank. "Oh my gosh," Rolfing said.

Woods said nothing, but his body language was screaming. With the ball still rising, he spun to his left and looked away in disgust. For a half second, you thought he might bite his shaft. (It's been done before.) His response was telling. When a ball is hooking over land and heading toward water, you don't spin left like that. You watch your ball like a hawk eyeing supper. You beg for your ball to stay dry. But this ball was left from the get-go. When Woods spun left and suffered in silence, you knew he knew his ball had no chance. Hitter knows.

Some people, though not Tiger, would say the next part defied logic. Tiger dropped his ball 206 yards ahead of the tee, which left him a 250-yard shot to the front of the green. He dropped in a place—and from thin brownish rough that he could get a 3-wood through—where he had an outside chance of reaching the front of the green, or at least getting close to it. From there, he could definitely make bogey and possibly a miracle par. The outcome of the tournament was on the line.

For Tiger's tee shot to have crossed at the point where he dropped, it would have had to start by flying toward one o'clock on an imaginary dial and over the fourteenth hole's pale green fairway. Then, after sailing along for about two hundred yards, it would have had to bank a late, sweeping left-hand turn before dropping deep into the pond. That would be a bizarre, if not impossible, flight pattern for a shot that's fat, high, ballooning, and left.

Woods had consulted with Wittenberg—Wittenberg said later that the drop was "perfect"—so on a technical level, Tiger was in the clear. Tiger, in his mind, could call it a good drop. But it's the usual thing: When something is too good to be true, it is.

Tiger could have gone to other sources. He could have asked La-Cava what he saw, as Tiger himself hadn't been watching it. He could have asked Rolfing what he had seen, standing near the tee, or a marshal, way up the fairway. The rules allow that, and you could say they encourage it. The rules want the player to get it right in every instance. Tiger could have consulted with a Tour official and asked what the NBC broadcast had shown. Two months earlier, at Doral, Tiger had hit a ball that got stuck in a palm tree. On that occasion, he used whatever information source was available, including fans with binoculars and close-ups from an NBC camera, to try to identify his ball and save himself a shot. It worked.

At the Players, on the fourteenth on Sunday, NBC's footage from a blimp showed Tiger's tee shot over water as soon as it crossed the front part of the tee. A white ball over dark water, clear as could be. That was consistent with what Rolfing had said, that the shot was left. On the basis of that *Snoopy Two* blimp footage, it appeared that Woods had dropped well over 100 yards ahead of where he needed to drop, and probably more like 130.

Tiger could have done everything in his power to make sure he wasn't pushing that drop. He was the first person down the fairway, understandably anxious and eager. But that would have been the best time to slow things down and take the full measure of the situation. That would have been an excellent time to put sportsmanship ahead of expedience.

You can imagine Nicklaus there. Once, while playing from a pot bunker at a British Open, he felt something hit him. A voice-of-God rules official, Joe Dey, told Nicklaus he had been hit by a rock that had ricocheted off the bunker's wall. Nicklaus accepted Dey's judgment and has regretted it ever since. He couldn't say with certainty that it wasn't the ball that hit him. Had the ball hit him, he would have incurred a penalty. Which means he doesn't know if he signed a correct scorecard on that Saturday at Royal Lytham in July 1974, when he finished third in an Open won by Gary Player. Nobody's perfect and the rules are complicated, but the player's card is the player's responsibility. You can't respect it too much. It's the starting point for everything in tournament golf.

"That Tiger drop was really, really borderline," Johnny Miller said on live TV from the NBC broadcast booth. It didn't matter that Woods made a 6 on the hole. "I can't live with myself without saying that," Miller said.

An hour or so later, Tiger won while watching the telecast in the scorer's room. And then there were those two seconds, before seeing Joe, when he showed absolutely nothing.

• • •

On the walls in the heavy-wood men's locker room at the Oak Hill Country Club, near Rochester, New York, you can see giant score-cards from past championships. Each box has a color-coded number in it: green for bogey, black for par, red for birdie. It's the combination of our faith in those numbers and the stories behind how they got there that explains our love affair with tournament golf. Lee Trevino winning the U.S. Open at Oak Hill in 1968 with a 4 out of the gnarly left rough on the final hole. Can't you just see his red socks?

Cary Middlecoff won the 1956 U.S. Open at Oak Hill. He shot 281. Two hundred and eighty-one swings, big, small, and in between. Ben Hogan and Julius Boros each took one more over the four rounds, and that made all the difference. The scores from Dr. Middlecoff (he had been an army dentist during World War II) are hanging for posterity, and theirs are not. Each number in each box is both a cog in the machine of tournament golf and a tribute to a system at work. If we didn't believe the boxes, we wouldn't be watching. If the players didn't believe each other, they'd be at each other's throats all day and into the night.

Golf really is a game of honor. It's grand to say, but it's true. The system depends on players writing down their scores accurately, without adult supervision, and with strict adherence to the rules. You sign your scorecard as you sign your tax return, under penalty of perjury.

But there's more than the player's honor that keeps the scorecards on the up-and-up. In golf, Big Brother is always watching or assumed to be. Playing partners, caddies, spectators, officials, marshals, sundry others—camera operators looking through their lenses—can help a player make sure the scorecard is accurate. And the player should welcome that, because he or she *wants* to turn in the most accurate scorecard possible. After all, the player isn't trying to get away with anything, right? Which brings you back to golf's honor code.

It's pointless to compare golf's officiating to any other sport's, although many people, including Tiger, have done that often over the years. When Tiger was asked before the 2013 Players how he felt about TV viewers calling in with potential rules violations, he said, "I don't call in when Kobe travels, which does happen." It was an amusing answer, but basketball is not golf. Trying to get away with something is in basketball's DNA. If you can step on the guy's foot in the paint, you do. In his transcendent career, the late Kobe Bryant never raised his hand and said, "I traveled." Part of his job was to fool the refs. Not his teammates, not his opponents, not the fans, just the refs. It was the job of the refs to catch him. Cops and robbers. Golf works under a far different principle.

But golf has been struggling in this upstream swim by adhering to a code that is alien to modern life. Tiger's view on TV call-ins was the prevalent one, and his influence on any golf issue is massive. By late 2017 the governing bodies had raised the white flag of surrender: No more call-ins. Big Brother could still watch from a hillside blanket behind the seventeenth tee, but not from a BarcaLounger at home. The odd thing was, it was actually David Eger's call from home that kept Woods *in* the 2013 Masters.

Golf's two governing bodies, the USGA and the R&A, published a new rule book in 2019, and on its first page is a summary of the game's three "central principles," accumulated over centuries of play:

- Play the course as you find it and play the ball as it lies;
- Play by the rules and in the spirit of the game;
- You are responsible for applying your own penalties if you breach a rule.

Four months after the Players Championship, Tiger had his last rules dispute of 2013. It was a doozy. It came at the BMW Championship, played at Conway Farms Golf Club in Lake Forest, outside Chicago. In the playing of one shot, and in its aftermath, Tiger made a mess of each of those three central principles.

- He didn't play his ball as it lay. (It moved, incrementally but visibly, while he touched a stick that was touching his ball.)
- He didn't play by the rules or in the spirit of the game. (When you cause your ball to move, it's a shot.)
- He didn't apply his own penalty. (A PGA Tour rules official, Slugger White, had to do it for him.)

By the end of that September day, there had been, over the course of eight months, four occasions in which a golf official felt compelled to make a public statement explaining a rules issue involving Tiger Woods. Yes, Tiger gets far more attention than any other golfer ever has. But four explain-this-to-me rules events in eight months? That's never happened before.

Of the four, the dispute at the BMW tournament is the simplest to explain—and the hardest to fathom.

In the second round, on the short par-4 first hole, Woods hit a poor second shot that finished over the green and in a wooded area. There were no spectators nearby. Joe LaCava stood about ten feet from Tiger's ball, and the next nearest person was a PGA Tour camera operator standing behind Tiger, off to his left. Tiger's ball was leaning on a decaying twig about the size of a large Tootsie Roll.

The rules allow a golfer to remove *loose impediments*, but the ball cannot move while he or she is doing so. Tiger pushed down on the twig with his right thumb and forefinger as he started to remove it. He stopped because the ball changed positions ever so slightly. It had been sitting on a perch of soft forest dirt and it rolled off. It was practically nothing. It moved maybe one quarter of an inch. But it moved.

That's being stated as a fact here because that's the conclusion Slugger White reached. Slugger had no dog in this fight. He took over the adjudication of the dispute because it was obvious to him what had happened, and Woods, for whatever reason, could not see it. After the round, Woods and White repeatedly watched a videotape clip of the attempted twig removal. It's apparent on the video that the ball's logo rotates and sinks just slightly. Gravity doing its thing.

But Woods, in the scorer's room and all wound up, argued that the ball "oscillated." That's an old rule-book word. It describes a ball that goes from being stationary to wobbly before returning to its original position. There's no penalty in those cases, rare though they are, usually in exposed, windblown conditions. Slugger wasn't buying what Tiger was selling. It wasn't logical, and it wasn't what the tape showed.

Also, Tiger hadn't said anything about his ball oscillating to his playing partners, Henrik Stenson and Adam Scott. (Steve Williams was around as well, as Scott's caddie.) Players aren't required to explain unusual circumstances to their playing partners, but they often do, in the interest of honesty—or at least the desire to appear honest.

Slugger White, a former Tour player and a respected veteran rules official, reached his conclusion by looking at magnified footage shot from at least twenty yards away by a Tour camera operator. He shot between Tiger's feet, heel to toe. But Tiger, in real time, had a far better view of it. Bent over, his eyes were maybe three feet over his ball, and he was looking right at it.

You might be wondering: Who cares about a five-dimple rotation? Well, as Woods has often said, "A rule is a rule," and a ball has either moved or it hasn't. Whenever a golf ball moves, there has to be an accounting of that movement. Also, it's inherently unfair if some players are going to call such a trivial movement on themselves while others do not. The rules have to be applied uniformly or the whole system falls apart. In tournament golf, there can be only fundamentalism.

There are only two reasons why golfers stop moving loose impediments. The first is that they fear the ball will move if they keep at it. The second is because the ball moved. When the ball moves, no matter how little, you incur a shot. The rules then require you to move the ball back to its original position, no matter how impractical that might be.

There was a 6 on Tiger's scorecard in the box for that first hole. It should have been an 8. By the time he walked off that first green, that's what he had made, and that's what he should have told his playing partners. He had caused his ball to move, and that's a shot. Then he didn't move it back, and that's another.

In dealing with Slugger, Tiger never budged. He said, "I just don't see it, Slugs." Tiger didn't seem to understand that, by the hierarchical nature of tournament golf, Slugger had the power in that situation, that he was the judge and the jury. Slugger had to take over Tiger's card for him and give him an 8 on the first instead of a 6. Slugger wasn't being harsh. He was doing what the rule book, and his job, required him to do. He was looking out for the game, the tournament, and the rights of the other sixty-nine players in it.

Tiger could have withdrawn from the tournament in protest. He didn't. But for years afterward, he showed his annoyance in other ways. Slugger White is married to Joe LaCava's cousin Shelley Green White. Her introduction to the PGA Tour came as a caddie, working for her brother, Ken Green, starting in the mid-1980s. Joe succeeded her as Ken's caddie. Joe and Slugger have a good relationship. Slugger has a good relationship with nearly everybody on Tour. But ever since that BMW event, Tiger has been giving Slugger the silent treatment. It wouldn't be like Slugger to talk about it, but others have observed it. For Slugger, it was a cost of doing his job without fear or favor. The rules are an ethics test.

The next day, during the NBC broadcast, Johnny Miller offered a brief analysis of the latest Tiger Woods rules debacle: "This one will raise a few more eyebrows among the players, that's all I'm gonna say." It was always hard for Johnny to bite his tongue, but he did.

There was no public evidence that eyebrows were raised. When the 2013 golf season was over, the lodge brothers voted Tiger as their Player of the Year for his five victories. That got him the Jack Nicklaus Trophy for the first time since 2009. The players have never been shy to admit that when Tiger wins, everybody wins. He's been good for business from the day he turned pro.

In the late winter of 2010, on the heels of the scandal, Mark Steinberg, Tiger's agent, predicted that Tiger the golfer would come back swinging. He said that the post-scandal Tiger would look a lot like the pre-scandal Tiger. It took a while, but by 2013 Steinberg looked like a swami. By then everybody had fallen into line: Tiger was back, and Nike could claim that winning takes care of everything.

Well, maybe not *every* last person. This was (and is) a minority view: What Tiger showed in 2013, in addition to his singular skill and drive, was his desperation to "reclaim his identity," to use a borrowed phrase. Tiger wasn't carrying himself like a man who was in some kind of recovery program. He didn't seem to be a man trying to lead a reconfigured life. Not at all. When he had those three issues—at Augusta, at the Players Championship, at the BMW Championship—he was putting his soul in an open MRI for anybody to see. What you could see was his extreme self-absorption.

At Augusta, he had the chance to take responsibility for a mistake he had made, and he couldn't do it. He put his own needs ahead of the tournament's. At the Players Championship, he took what I would call a fantasy drop, and in so doing he put his own ambition ahead of the rights of his fellow competitors. At the BMW Championship, he had a 6 in a box when it should have been an 8. Reliable numbers in boxes: They *are* the game. They're the blocks at the start and the tape at the finish and everything in between. The difference between 6 and 8 is a world. *By whatever means necessary* is not golf. It's the opposite of golf.

Yes, Tiger Woods won five times in 2013, with a swing that could knock the breath out of you just by watching it. Golfers swing to their personalities, and his swing was furious. The five wins represented great playing by a great player. That's clear. But so what? Arnold Palmer understood this better than any other golfer I have ever known: Golf, really and truly, is not about winning. It's about being in the game, no matter the level at which you play. Arnold *relished* being in the game—he was the opposite of *me-me-me*—and that's why people were so drawn to him. Yes, you want to win. But for millions of us, the ultimate joy of the game is being in the community of golfers. That's why golf shares so much with this thing called life.

Good luck finding anybody interested in selling *that*.

• • •

For over fifteen years, Tiger kept to himself, despite appearances to the contrary. He really wasn't "on tour," in the traditional sense of the phrase—a group of golf gypsies, going from city to city, playing golf for prize money. Tiger dropped in, won or didn't, and split. He put his life in compartments. You could round up three hundred prominent players, players' wives, agents, caddies, manufacturer reps, TV broadcasters, reporters, trainers, dieticians, and PGA Tour officials, and not find two people who could say they had anything like an intimate relationship with him, or really knew him at all. "You guys know me," Tiger will sometimes say at press conferences. Guys scratch their heads. Gals, too.

Tiger, over many years, has described Steve Stricker—his buddy *Stricks*, his now-and-again putting coach—as one of his best friends on Tour. But that didn't mean they went out for dinner together. There have been times when players have wanted to set up practice rounds with Woods but were stymied in the end because they didn't have his phone number and saw no easy path to it. The circle around Tiger is tight. On something *really* sensitive, like whether he used performance-enhancing drugs, there would be very few people who would know.

In general, the glasnost movement you see in other sports has not reached the PGA Tour. The Tour doesn't reveal player fines for using profanity on live TV, it doesn't reveal the details of Player of the Year voting, it doesn't reveal drug-test results unless there's a suspension. In the face of a failed drug test for what the Tour calls *drugs of abuse* (recreational drugs, in the vernacular), the commissioner has broad powers to suspend or to warn or to negotiate terms for treatment. For years, there were players who were critical of how lax, and how irregular, the Tour's random drug testing was, for both drugs of abuse and performance-enhancing drugs. The only semi-prominent PGA Tour player to serve a suspension for using a performance-enhancing drug is Scott Stallings, and his ninety-day suspension came not from a failed drug test but from his own admitted and self-described accidental PED use. And that admission came after he had *passed* a drug test.

To the question of whether Tiger has used performance-enhancing drugs, you might consider:

- Woods has never been suspended;
- Woods says he hasn't.

Also, in all walks of jurisprudence, it's not simple to prove you did *not* do something. If Tiger says he didn't take PEDs, why not just take him at his word? Many do. Many don't care.

The counterargument has focused on various pieces of circumstantial evidence:

- His size.

Anyone could see how Tiger's body changed over his first decade as a pro. At twenty, he was Gumby. At thirty, he was a Pac-12 free safety, if you could find one with a twenty-nine-inch waist. There were times in his mid-thirties when he had the upper body of a thickly muscled middleweight boxer and the legs of a distance runner. His physique was nothing like his mother's or father's or any other professional golfer's.

- His frailty.

PED use can promote excessive weight lifting, workouts, and practice sessions that can contribute to the breakdown of body parts. Woods's career has been marked by repeated knee, back, ligament, and tendon issues, along with a litany of surgeries.

- His *just-win-baby* mentality.

You could see that nearly from his professional start, as when he had a dozen men move a one-ton boulder interfering with a fourth-round shot at the 1999 Phoenix Open. Tiger asked a rules official if the boulder was a "loose impediment." The rules official said that it was, provided the boulder was "readily movable." You could say the question alone violated golf's underlying spirit-of-the-game principle, even though the USGA backed the official's decision. How can a boulder that weighs at least a ton be considered loose?

• His ample opportunity.

For the first twelve years of Tiger's professional career, the PGA Tour didn't have a drug-testing program. And when testing began in 2008, the Tour's protocols were far from intense. Karen Crouse of the *New York Times*, a dogged reporter, polled fifty-four players in February 2013, including Woods, and asked each one if he had ever been tested for drugs away from a tournament site. A Tour official told Crouse that testing on the Monday, Tuesday, or Wednesday of a tournament week fulfilled the World Anti-Doping Agency requirement for out-of-competition testing. The WADA list is the basis of nearly every sport's list of banned drugs, including the PGA Tour's. The Tour didn't seem too interested in catching anyone. For years, the PGA Tour tested only urine, and masking drug use in a urine sample does not require a PhD in chemistry. The use of human growth hormone doesn't show up in a urine test at all, only blood, and the Tour didn't start even semi-widespread blood testing until 2017.

• Some of Tiger's willfully naive public statements about PEDs in golf.

For instance, when Tiger said in 2007 that he could see golfers testing positive for nothing more serious than "a hangover." A good line, but not a believable position from someone of his intelligence and sophistication, from someone who spent long days with trainers and logged many hours in gyms. After all, there were *bobsledders* in the news for failing drug tests in that period. Professional golfers were chasing speed—clubhead speed, in their case—just like other athletes. That need was accelerated wildly by the death of the old balata-ball finesse game and the rise of the graphite-and-titanium smash game. Gary Player, a fitness-nut golfer born in 1935, started saying as early as 2007 (not very early, really) that he was aware of at least one case of a golfer using performance-enhancing drugs and suspected there were more. But when it suited Tiger, he tried to present golf as stuck in its steak-and-Scotch past, where you could make it with any kind of physique.

At other times, he sang a different song. In 2006 he said the Tour should start testing as soon as possible: "Tomorrow would be fine with me. I think we should be proactive instead of reactive. I just think we should be ahead of it and keep our sport as pure as can be. This is a great sport, and it's always been clean."

• His on-course intensity and occasional outbursts.

That behavior, when exhibited by buffet-flipping baseball players and other athletes, used to be described as 'roid rage. Tiger seemed to be taking his cues from other sports, but his fits were mild, mostly profane language and club slamming. After the sex scandal, he started spitting on the course. He typically spat after a poor shot—disdain spitting—and eventually stopped. (Jim Bouton, right-handed pitcher and author of *Ball Four*, used to say that ballplayers spit to mark their territory, like dogs in a public park.) But the spitting did show an uptick in his intensity. As a young pro, Tiger was far more collected. As his successes mounted, he became more tightly wound, not less.

• His impressive sex drive, as implied by the list of lady friends that emerged after Thanksgiving 2009.

This point is included because anecdotal evidence (also called locker-room talk) suggests that PED use increases sex drive. Studies show that can be true, but there are many mitigating factors. If the subject interests you, you might want to read "Anabolic-Androgenic Steroids and Appetitive Sexual Behavior in Male Rats," published in a journal called *Hormones and Behavior*.

If the subject bores you, you have company. Years ago, I was writing about Donald Trump and the many golf courses that bear his name. He spoke knowledgeably as a golf, football, baseball, and boxing fan. The conversation turned to steroids in baseball. Manny Ramirez had just been suspended for violating baseball's PED policy. Trump asked my opinion of PED use in sports. I gave him some high-minded answer out of the NPR playbook. He said, "I do not care. I just want to see them hit the long ball." He couldn't be the only person with that view.

But here are four quick questions to consider, if the subject of golf and PEDs interests you:

- If medicine exists to promote healing and health, is it ethical to use medical science in the name of lowering golf scores?
- Does the use of PEDs by some golfers but not others upend golf's underlying concept of fairness?
- Are PEDs safe to use?
- Does their usage reveal a value system that's out of whack?

Across professional golf, wherever it's played, there have been few known cases of golfers being caught using banned performance-enhancing drugs. That tells you there are either few golfers using them, the testing is lackadaisical, or the golfers are skillful at passing the tests.

Fairly or not, the question of a golfer using PEDs clings to Tiger. His success, his size, and his secretive nature about anything medical all have a lot to do with that. If you ever walked inside the ropes at a PGA Tour event during the height of Tigermania, you were likely asked some version of this: Do you think Tiger uses PEDs? In 2010, near the peak of sex-scandal hysteria, *Sports Illustrated* conducted a poll of seventy-one Tour players that included that question. Even in that overheated environment, nearly 75 percent of the respondents said they thought he had *not*. Still, that leaves 25 percent who thought he had. Really, though, the chance that any player knew the actual answer is close to zero.

. . .

In 2019 I spent three interesting mornings in the company of a man named Tony Bosch, an expert on the use of performance-enhancing drugs. He got his expertise by selling these drugs, illegally, to a long list of clients. But his real skill, he said, was developing "formulations" for these drugs and "protocols" for their use without so much as a CVS internship. His most famous client was Alex Rodriguez, but that was before Bosch became a witness for Major League Baseball in the investigation that led to A-Rod's season-long suspension in 2014 for violating baseball's drug policy. Some years before that, Bosch had harbored a hope of landing Tiger as a client through, indirectly, A-Rod. A-Rod didn't like many people, Bosch told me, but one person he did like was Tiger.

Bosch said he had close to five thousand clients who came to him out of garden-variety vanity. They were seeking the fountain of youth, or they had weekend-warrior aspirations. He said he had another three hundred clients who were professional athletes. Bosch had a good business in baseball, football, and boxing. Golf looked like a wide-open and untapped market to him. This was in 2008 and 2009. Talking to Bosch was like entering a time warp. Names from old drug scandals were back in circulation: Biogenesis, Bosch's "wellness" center near Miami; Victor Conte, the founder of BALCO, the San Francisco–area steroid lab; Anthony Galea, the Canadian doctor who treated an impressive list of name-brand athletes, A-Rod and Tiger Woods among them.

Bosch thought Galea was good at his job but overrated. Maybe Bosch had sentence envy. When the dust had settled from various investigations into performance-enhancing drugs in sports, Bosch received a four-year federal sentence. Galea served one day.

Or maybe Bosch had degree envy. Galea is an actual medical doctor. Tony Bosch's mother and father were both doctors, and Bosch could sound like one, but he hadn't spent a day in medical school. That didn't slow him down. He was cited once by the Florida Department of Health for practicing medicine without a license. Guilty, he admits, as charged!

He doesn't try to be entertaining. He just is. Here's Bosch describing how A-Rod felt about Tiger: "Alex doesn't respect a lot of people. He would have a bunch of TVs on. And he'd go, 'That guy's a dick.' Or 'That guy's an asshole.' He hated everyone. Jeter. Oh my God—he *despised* Jeter. David Ortiz. Despises him to this day. But he didn't have that hate for Tiger. He understood that Tiger was the best, just like Alex was the best. But if Alex had decided to play golf, he would've been better than Tiger."

There was something cheerful about Bosch. He wasn't in a traditional twelve-step program, but he did speak about how, since getting out of prison, he had been making a daily effort to be kinder, more truthful, and more empathetic. Some of his stories came from his stints in different federal prisons—hanging out with Jeffrey Skilling, for instance, to trot out another name from yesteryear. Bosch said he and Skilling, the former CEO of Enron, were both making the rounds among different prisons by bus. Along the way, Bosch learned the phrase *diesel therapy*.

Bosch told me he was a recovering cocaine addict. Part of what made him such a compelling character was his candor about his past. He pointed me to an entertaining documentary about A-Rod's PED circle called *Screwball*, which depicts Bosch as a comically inept businessman and criminal.

What Bosch knows about Tiger is secondhand at best, so please keep that in mind. Bosch and Tiger never met, although Bosch said they were once at the same party in a swanky Palm Beach hotel. Bosch was there on a "recruiting trip, looking for new clients." He said that Galea was at the party, too.

There's going to be a lot of that in this section—*Bosch said, Bosch recalled*—and about things far more sensitive than Tiger at a party. Also, there's a list of people who would dispute many of Bosch's claims. This is going to get messy, so some of you may want to skip ahead and get back to Tiger and his golfing life (page 90). But if you're interested in knowing more about Tiger's caddies and swing instructors and business partners, you might want to know more about his former medical team, too. Enter Tony Bosch, who, in addition to his insights into Galea, describes his alleged interactions with a chiropractor and a massage therapist associated with both Galea and Woods. If you're interested in the intersection of Tiger's medical life and his golfing life, and you understand the caveats about the source, then you're in the right place.

· · ·

For a brief while, Anthony Galea's name was in the sporting news on a recurring basis. That was due to the legal problems Galea was having in Canada, where he lives and works, and in the United States, where he was charged with practicing medicine without a license. In Canada, he was charged with smuggling human growth hormone—a substance on the World Anti-Doping Agency banned list—from Canada into the United States. He was not convicted. Related to those charges, Canadian medical authorities revoked Galea's medical license for a nine-month period for "fundamental dishonesty." Galea faced a smuggling charge in the United States as well, became a cooperating witness to a broader investigation, and pleaded guilty to a lesser charge. Galea was interviewed by the FBI and asked about his treatment of Woods. "Galea didn't say anything," Rodriguez later told Bosch, according to Bosch. "He was a gentleman."

· · ·

Before we go on, let's hear from Galea, in an attempt to sow more doubt about Bosch. Galea, it should be noted, never faced a charge of any sort in connection to Woods.

His job, Galea told me in a phone interview, was not to improve performance but to "heal damaged tissue back to baseline." His treatment of Woods, he said, was strictly about accelerating recovery from injury and surgery. He said that he never used human growth hormone or any other PED with Woods.

Regarding Bosch, Galea said, "I never met him, never had a discussion with him, don't know him, never corresponded with him. I have no knowledge of him, have never interacted with him. I definitely know that I was never at a party with Tiger Woods, and I've never met Bosch at any party. I don't go to parties."

Galea's speech was deliberate and emphatic. His voice sounded almost like it was coming through a distortion machine, but the warbly quality was actually the residue of a long-ago bike accident in which his larynx was damaged.

"I'm going to Google Bosch to see what he looks like. How do you spell *Bosch*?" Galea asked.

"B-O-S-C-H."

Galea said he was looking at photos of Bosch. If you do the same, you'll see he looks like a character from *Get Shorty*, with his black sunglasses and oiled-back hair and three-day beard stubble.

He's Miami. "You want to do business here, you better come bearing gifts," Bosch likes to say.

Galea apparently spent a few seconds looking at Bosch photos on an office screen and said, "Nope. I've seen his picture before. I've seen him in the media. But I've never met this gentleman."

He likes the word *gentleman*. Galea said that when he made house calls to Tiger's home in the gated Isleworth development, he found the master of the house to be "a complete gentleman, the only guy to grab my bags. He was kind, generous, sincere, humble. A great guy. A great human being."

•   •   •

Tony Galea and Tony Bosch are footnotes, really, in the life and times of Alex Rodriguez, but their passing association with him will endure, particularly if A-Rod never gets to Cooperstown because of his PED use.

But before A-Rod, Bosch logged (he said) some long nights with another baseball legend, Manny Ramirez. Ramirez abruptly quit baseball in 2011 with a second PED suspension looming over him, this one for a hundred days. Like a lot of retirees with homes in South Florida, Ramirez has dabbled in golf. But when Bosch knew Ramirez, he was still the great and unpredictable slugger for the Boston Red Sox. Bosch said he loved hanging with Manny. He described Ramirez checking in to hotels and getting three rooms, one for his performance guy (Bosch), a second for himself, a third for his girlfriends. Bosch said he injected Trimix, an erectile dysfunction drug, directly into Ramirez's penis, for added efficacy. You could make up a story like that, but why would you want to?

Bosch shared that tidbit at one of our three long, taped breakfast interviews at the Miami Marriott Biscayne Bay. Bosch has lived near the hotel since his release from prison after pleading guilty to conspiracy to distribute testosterone. But he went in and came out as a true believer in performance-enhancing drugs, and he wishes they could be used openly and legally and with more oversight for their safe use. Regarding PEDs in golf, Bosch thinks they can and do help golfers in every aspect of the game, from driving distance to green reading and everything in between—provided the golfer is willing to do the work, both on the course and in the gym. He noted that performance-enhancing drugs help with any sort of recovery, from a workout, from an injury, from a surgery. How could that *not* help a golfer?

One last personal note about Bosch, though less personal than the Manny-being-Manny note above. Bosch has five children and is active in their lives. He repeatedly took calls from them when we were together and spoke about their accomplishments with pride. He said his prison stint got him off drugs, put him on an "empathy journey," and taught him gratitude. He absolutely showed ample appreciation for the miracle of the Miami Marriott Biscayne Bay breakfast buffet in all its colorful glory.

• • •

Bosch said he met Galea and Mark Lindsay, a noted Canadian sports-medicine chiropractor, through Alex Rodriguez and A-Rod's cousin Yuri Sucart. After Tiger's knee surgery in 2008, it was Lindsay who oversaw Tiger's rehab, working in conjunction with Galea. Lindsay and Galea shared patients and office space in Toronto for years. Bosch recounted how Sucart set up the evening when Bosch met Lindsay.

> **Yuri:** "Are you going to see the Chief tonight?"
> **Bosch:** "Yeah. What time?"
> **Yuri:** "Eleven."
> **Bosch:** "Eleven—again?"
> **Yuri:** "I want you to meet somebody."

Bosch: "Who?"

Yuri: "You'll see. It's about another athlete."

The Chief was Rodriguez. The somebody was Mark Lindsay. The athlete was Tiger Woods.

Tiger Woods, it hardly needs to be said, had nothing to do with setting up the night. But you could also say that the only reason the meeting happened was because Tiger was working with Alex Rodriguez's Canadian chiropractor, Mark Lindsay, and A-Rod's Canadian doctor, Tony Galea. Bosch believes that investigators knew to ask Rodriguez and Galea about Tiger because baseball investigators had seen *TW* written in Bosch's notebooks.

Bosch said he didn't write down all his activities, especially the more incriminating ones. Also, his writing was more legible some days than others. Baseball investigators, attempting to play hardball with Bosch, threatened to take the hundred-thousand-dollar cash payment he received from "Dr. Oposal" and report it to the IRS, certain that Bosch had not paid taxes on the sum. They had turned a sloppily written *proposal* into *Dr. Oposal*. "I told them, 'That's a hundred-thousand-dollar business *proposal*, you dumbasses,'" Bosch said.

According to Bosch, he and Lindsay were together at a long late-night treatment session in Rodriguez's office, in his mansion on Star Island, off Miami Beach, sometime after Tiger's win in the 2008 U.S. Open and the knee surgery he had had shortly afterward. Bosch could not offer a precise date, but he remembers that A-Rod and Lindsay were discussing Tiger's playoff win and how he walked with a limp.

There were four people in the room that night: A-Rod, A-Rod's cousin, Mark Lindsay, and Tony Bosch. (This is all by Bosch's account.) Lindsay was wearing, Bosch said, "sneakers with those little white socks, shorts, a little golf polo shirt. He was in shape. Trim, not muscular. Soft-spoken. Very nice guy. I remember thinking, *This guy is vanilla. He's not going to make a splash.* That's a great thing in our business."

Bosch would stand out anywhere. He has a loud voice, a loaf of thick hair, dark skin, and an unusually personable manner. You wouldn't call him trim. His parents were both born in Cuba and their medical practices were first in Queens and later in greater Miami, with its lively and large Cuban population. Bosch grew up in Queens, mad for baseball in a baseball-loving borough, and later moved to Miami.

Lindsay had brought his own folding chiropractic table that night and set it up by a black sectional sofa. When Bosch entered the office, Cousin Yuri nodded in Lindsay's direction and said, *"El Tigre."* That was when Bosch knew why he was there—to meet the chiropractor who worked on both A-Rod and Tiger. Cousin Yuri and Bosch were business partners, the owners of Biogenesis, a strip-mall "antiaging" clinic in Coral Cables, although much of their work was done elsewhere. This night had the potential to start their golf business in a meaningful way.

Lindsay went through his paces, working on different parts of A-Rod's body. When Lindsay was done, Bosch went to work, putting an oxygen mask on Rodriguez, hydrating him intravenously, injecting him with drugs. The two medical professionals, though only one with formal training, talked. "I felt that I was in an interview," Bosch said. "He was vetting me, if you will. They were big on growth hormone. They were, 'HGH and HGH and HGH.' And I'm thinking, *These guys solve everything with HGH. It doesn't work like that.*"

Bosch described how he inserted an intravenous drip into a vein in Rodriguez's left arm and, he said, "started pushing my drugs" into the baseball player's bloodstream. Banned drugs, purchased illegally. Bosch told Lindsay he had Rodriguez use testosterone in liquid form on his days off and in cream form on playing days.

This is how Bosch remembered the conversation, a decade or so after it occurred: "Mark says, 'Oh, you're hydrating here?' I say, 'No, I'm doing more than hydrating.'" There was growth hormone in the IV he was using, Bosch told me.

"Mark goes, 'I do a type of hydration.' I say, 'You or Galea?' He goes, 'We. We, we. We have our own protocol.' He goes off on Galea and how great his protocols are. I let him go. But at this time, remember, I'm an arrogant prick. I'm thinking to myself, *My protocols are better than yours.*"

If Lindsay was interviewing, Bosch was selling. In some manner, this was another recruiting trip for an athlete even more famous than the one sitting on a sofa in his man cave in a mansion on Star Island. Bosch was sharing information with Tiger Woods's chiropractor in the hope of getting some useful information back.

"Every time I would tell Mark one of my protocols, he'd go, 'Yeah, we do it exactly like that,'" Bosch said. "Or 'No, we use citocoline instead of just the choline by itself.'" Both are on the WADA banned list. "It was a lot of 'My dick's bigger than yours,'" Bosch said, despite Lindsay's modest and unassuming manner. Bosch said there was no question in his mind that Lindsay was discussing how he and Galea treated Woods.

"Mark asked, 'What do you do for fatigue?'" Bosch said. Not garden-variety fatigue but adrenal fatigue. "Straight-up growth hormone and peptides," Bosch answered, in his recounting. Both were and are on the WADA banned list. Bosch said he told Lindsay that he delivered the drugs into the bloodstream through an IV.

"Mark goes, 'Yeah, I like that. I do similar with my clients, especially with Tiger.'"

. . .

Tony Galea was an early proponent of a procedure that supposedly accelerated recovery from injury or surgery. The shorthand for it is PRP, for platelet-rich plasma. In a PRP therapy procedure (and this is a crude description) a doctor draws several ounces of a patient's blood and spins it in a centrifuge. The goal is to get the patient's platelets—the healing cells in the blood—into a revved-up state, on the theory that they will then do their job even faster. Does it work? Many doctors have said it does not. Galea's twist on the procedure, at least at times and according to law-enforcement officials who investigated him, was to infuse the drawn blood with growth hormone in an effort to further accelerate the healing process and to deepen the strength of the repair. Regular PRP therapy, with no additives, is legal under WADA guidelines. The infused method, with a banned substance, is illegal.

Would Tiger fly a doctor, one with a super-specialty, from Toronto to his home in Orlando for private and discreet medical appointments and not get the full-monty treatment? Bosch believes the answer is no.

I asked Bosch if Woods could claim he didn't know in detail how Galea was treating him. Bosch said, "He could claim anything. But could he claim it credibly? Nobody's going to believe him. He can say, 'Well, he gave me an IV, and I thought it was sodium static water for recovery.' He could say that. But everybody who knows Galea knows that he ain't going to do that."

•   •   •

The 2008 U.S. Open concluded on June 16. Bosch watched with interest, struck by Tiger's body. Tiger still had the same spindly legs, forearms, and narrow waist he did as a young pro, but now he had a pickle-barrel chest and tree-trunk upper arms. Not a combination you see in nature, but excellent for golf: a lower body built for speed and an upper body built for strength. "I would laugh every time I'd see him on TV," Bosch said. "I knew the protocol."

On June 24, Tiger had surgery on his left knee, repairing a torn ACL with a tendon from his right thigh. Mark Lindsay worked closely with Woods after that. The PGA Tour's drug-testing program, based on WADA guidelines, began on July 1. Tiger returned to the Tour on February 25, 2009, after an eight-month absence.

Tiger's 2009 golf year was great, frustrating, and hectic. He played a lot and at an intensely high level, but he didn't win a major, despite having a two-shot lead through three rounds at the PGA Championship. On that Saturday night, his fifteenth major title seemed preordained. It wasn't. Y. E. Yang won. By the time he hoisted the Wanamaker Trophy, he was being called the Tiger Killer.

Tiger's first win in 2009 came at Arnold Palmer's tournament, in March at Bay Hill, about a fifteen-minute drive from his house. He won Jack Nicklaus's tournament in June. He won his own tournament in July. He won two Tour events in two weeks in August, the first by three strokes, the second by four. He won in Chicago in September by eight. At the end of the month, he finished second at the Tour Championship in Atlanta. In October, in San Francisco, he played for the U.S. Presidents Cup team, captained by Fred Couples. The American team defeated the Internationals, captained by Greg Norman. In early November, Woods played in China and finished five shots behind the winner, Phil Mickelson. On November 15, Woods won the Australian Masters by two. All that golf plus a dozen corporate sponsors to keep happy, Gatorade and TAG Heuer and all the rest. He was going good, and he was gone a lot. Get it while you can. Janis Joplin famously screamed those words. Mark Steinberg and Tiger were living by them. It's a lot easier to board your plane when you know somebody else is paying for the jet fuel.

With the end of a long year in sight—on Friday, November 27, 2009, at about 2:25 in the morning—Tiger crashed his car outside his home. And after that, every aspect of Tiger's life became open for dissection, including the medical treatments he received in his home.

·   ·   ·

In 2009 and 2010, ESPN, the *New York Times*, and the *New York Daily News*, among other publications, covered Anthony Galea intensely, with reporters getting behind the curtains of different criminal investigations. The athletes on Galea's patient list, Rodriguez and Woods, were collateral damage. Later, different books were written about these investigations. Interest may not have been broad, but it was deep. The use of drugs in sports challenged our ideas about competition, and raised questions about the mental and physical health of the athletes using them.

In the first eight months of 2009, according to the book *Blood Sport*, Galea saw Woods fourteen times. At least some of the visits, if not all, were in Tiger's house in Isleworth, near Orlando. Galea's fee for Woods was $3,500 per visit, plus first-class round-trip Toronto-Orlando air travel and hotel charges. All told, Galea charged Woods $76,012. Mark Lindsay made forty-nine visits in a twelve-month period and charged $118,979. The two reporters who wrote the book, Tim Elfrink and Gus Garcia-Roberts, got the figures from a Florida Department of Health investigation. Florida loves Canadians as super-polite snowbirds with credit cards, but state investigators don't like Canadians, or anybody else, coming to Florida to practice medicine without a license.

"I was the only one doing it," Galea said, explaining why Woods would fly him in for PRP treatments. "I had the most expertise." Galea told me, as he has told others, that he did not use any banned substance while performing those procedures with Woods. Not EPO, not HGH, not any other growth hormone, not anything.

• • •

Bosch's descriptions were often loaded with detail. Regarding that night with Lindsay at the Rodriguez home, Bosch said, "I can see the whole thing." He remembered Rodriguez's spotless garage and a hallway wall with a LeRoy Neiman painting of Darryl Strawberry. He described the other three men in colorful and physical terms. He recalled that professional poker was on one of the TVs in the office and that Derek Jeter was being interviewed on another. He said that A-Rod was wearing an oxygen mask as he talked about how much he despised Jeter. Bosch said Rodriguez's nails were shiny and perfect from an at-home manicure he had received that day. He said that Yuri was telling jokes in Spanish and that Lindsay was talking about lymphatic drainage. Bosch seemed to be a human movie camera with built-in audio.

Does that mean Bosch's statements are true? No. Breakfast interviews at a Marriott do not have penalty-of-perjury hanging over them. Each time I saw Bosch I asked variants of the same questions. He emphasized different things at different times, but his answers were largely consistent.

There were discrepancies. Shaquille O'Neal was at the party at the Palm Beach hotel in one telling, and in another Bosch was less sure—it might have been LeBron James. The party might have been at the Brazilian Court Hotel in Palm Beach, but it could have been at another hotel. (The society reporter for the *Palm Beach Daily News* said such a party sounded vaguely familiar but she couldn't find a clipping for it, and neither the hotel's former publicist nor its former manager could recall it.) Bosch said Galea might have been at the party—or was it Mark Lindsay? Or Mark Lindsay might have been at another party. Bosch was a heavy drinker then, and a cocaine addict. The session in Rodriguez's man cave went till one a.m. in one telling and two in another. You get the point.

But for the most part his stories were consistent. He enjoyed telling them. Bosch was reliving, believe it or not, a fun chapter of his life. "I was having a *great* time," he said.

Bosch never claimed that he was offering verbatim recollections of what was said. He did say he was capturing the spirit and the nuance of the evening's conversations. That's important to consider as you read this next part.

"What do you use for stamina?" Lindsay asked Bosch that night, as Bosch recounted it. Rodriguez was on the sofa, texting on two cell phones.

Bosch told Lindsay about the different drugs he used for stamina, all on the WADA banned list. This was high-level late-night shop talk in a private setting where illegal activity was taking place. Nobody needed to say that the cones of silence were down.

Bosch asked Lindsay about PRP treatments. "Listen, I don't understand all that drama of taking out blood, doing this, the spinning," Bosch said. He told Lindsay he'd never considered any sort of PRP treatment. His go-to healing drugs were Neupogen and Epogen, growth hormones typically used in cancer treatments, which he injected directly into the stomach. Both are on the WADA banned list.

"Interesting," Lindsay said.

"What do you use?" Bosch asked.

"EPO," Lindsay said, as Bosch recalled it. EPO is a hormone produced by the kidney that can also be made synthetically. It has been used by athletes for decades to stimulate red blood cell production. It's on every banned list there is, and has been since the early 1990s.

"EPO?" Bosch said. "EPO is for amateurs." Lindsay laughed.

"You know what? I like you," Bosch said to Lindsay. "This one's free." He then shared details on his preferred use of Neupogen and Epogen.

"How do you get it?" Lindsay asked.

"You buy it on the black market," Bosch said. "I have nurses in hospitals. I have pharmaceutical-grade."

• • •

It sounded like some night. Everyone was on. Cousin Yuri, an unusually large man with a mustache, would interrupt to pump up Bosch's credentials with Lindsay. A-Rod, by way of a hand gesture and a big smile, indicated how one drug improved his sex life. Bosch could see Lindsay taking it all in.

Some days later, Yuri asked Bosch, "Can you do the same protocol that you did for Alex, can you do it with Tiger?" They often spoke in Spanish, but Bosch was relaying it to me in English.

"Who's asking? Mark?" Bosch said.

"No, Galea's asking," Yuri said.

"Galea's asking who?" Bosch said.

"Galea's asking Alex if you can do the same thing to Tiger," Yuri said.

"Sure, I can," Bosch said. "Let me know. Tell me when that's going to happen."

Subsequently, Bosch said he received a call from Galea. He said Galea asked Bosch if he could treat Woods.

"Yeah, absolutely," Bosch said. "Let's just arrange it."

Later, Cousin Yuri told Bosch that there had been a change in plans, that Bosch would not be seeing Tiger and Mark Lindsay would be going instead.

Soon after, in Bosch's telling, Yuri told Bosch that a man would be coming to the Biogenesis office to pick up and pay for vials of Neupogen from him. Bosch said the man's name was Tom, that he worked with both Galea and Lindsay, and that he had been seeing Tiger, under Galea's direction, as a massage therapist. I asked Bosch several times if he knew Tom's last name or had a way to get it, but I never learned it.

Cousin Yuri told Bosch that Tom wanted six or seven vials. Bosch told Yuri that he didn't have that many.

Tom came to the Biogenesis office, Bosch said. He thought that was the only time he ever saw Tom, but he said it wasn't the only time he ever talked to him. Tom paid Bosch in cash. "No trace," Bosch told me. Bosch said he charged Tom exactly what he had paid. In one telling the price was $913 per vial, and in another it was $970. In one telling he sold two vials, and in another it was three. He said he bought the vials of Neupogen from a nurse who had stolen them from a hospital. Each vial represented treatment for one week.

I asked Bosch why he thought the drugs were for Tiger.

"Because they told me they were for Tiger?" Bosch said in the exaggerated tone used in sitcom dialogue to indicate obviousness.

I asked Bosch if he was disappointed that he didn't get to treat Woods himself.

"Minor irritation," Bosch said.

I know I'm tripling down here, and excuse the shouting: Even if everything Bosch has described here happened as Bosch said it did, there's no evidence that any of that Neupogen ACTUALLY ENDED UP IN TIGER WOODS'S BLOODSTREAM.

. . .

Bosch believes that Mark Lindsay and Tom had more regular contact with Woods than Galea did. He also believes that Galea oversaw Woods's treatment in 2008 and 2009, at least the covert side of it. Bosch said, based on his phone conversations with Tom, that Tom had a good understanding of pharmacology and elite athletes.

Bosch said that Tom called him and asked, "That peptide that you're using, that fragment, the 176-191: You think it's good for Tiger?"

"It's absolutely good. What do you want to use it for, recovery?" Bosch asked.

"No, for performance," Tom said.

"Yes, so take it like this. Take the 176-191 and add the CJC-1295 to it. Tell him to take 1.2 IU a.m. and then 1.6 IU p.m., because it works better with fasting. He's not going to eat during the night. And let me know how it works out; give me a call in ten days."

The 176-191 refers to an HGH peptide fragment. The CJC-1295 is a synthetic growth hormone. Both are banned substances. *IU* refers to international units.

Ten days later, Bosch said, he heard back from Tom. "He loved it," Tom said.

I told Galea what Bosch had said about Tom's drug purchase and all the rest. "Mr. Bosch is making up stories," Galea said. "This is the first I've heard of this. The story is completely false. It's actually very impossible. Totally impossible."

I asked why.

"It would be impossible because there was no one in our office who would do that. They're crossing a line into something that's completely illegal. It would never be on my behalf. That would be one hundred percent a lie."

• • •

A semi-endorsement of Anthony Bosch: Eddie Dominguez, a former Boston Police Department detective and later a prominent baseball investigator, had an antagonistic cat-and-mouse relationship with Tony Bosch. "He's quite a character, and he's a great storyteller," Dominguez told me. Does he believe every last word out of Bosch's mouth? No. But when Dominguez and his fellow agents compared notes, they found that Bosch's street-level observations rang true. Bosch saw a lot. He saw trainers behaving like pharmacists and ballplayers with slush funds for cash purchases. He saw a rising baseball executive checking out skirts late-night at a midtown bar. Bosch had a good eye and a good ear. Most significantly, Dominguez said, Bosch's testimony about Alex Rodriguez, and what Bosch told baseball's investigators about drug use in baseball, checked out. In those areas, Dominguez found Bosch credible. He said Bosch knew which ballplayers were using PEDs and how and when they were using them. Eddie Dominguez could not have been clearer: When it came to his understanding of the underbelly of major league baseball, Tony Bosch was a self-made expert.

• • •

I made repeated efforts to reach four of the people Tony Bosch referred to regularly: Manny Ramirez, Alex Rodriguez, Yuri Sucart, and Mark Lindsay. I didn't get far. I also followed up with Bosch a handful of times and asked if he could figure out Tom's surname. He could not.

I spoke several times to Ramirez's agent and told him what Bosch had said about Manny's late-night, back-in-the-day activities, but I never heard from Ramirez, directly or indirectly.

I tried to reach Rodriguez, both by text and by email. (I can't be certain I had his current contact information, but nothing bounced back.) Rodriguez has a company called A-Rod Corporation, and I sent them an email requesting an interview with one of his colleagues. I did the same with Rodriguez's outside PR person. I went zero for four.

I spoke to Yuri's son, Yuri Sucart Jr., who played college baseball at Point Park University in Pittsburgh, from which he graduated in 2019. Four years earlier, his father had been sentenced to seven months in federal prison on a charge of conspiracy to distribute human growth hormone. Since then he has faced various health, legal, and financial issues. In a phone conversation, the son, who sells life insurance, mentioned in passing that his father had met Tiger and admired him. Later, by text, Yuri Jr. said his father didn't want to discuss Bosch now but might in the future. If so, the younger Sucart said, I would be welcome to come to his parents' house in Miami "for coffee." It was a reminder that there are innumerable people like Yuri Sucart who are in the news for brief and intense periods, and then they're not. But that doesn't mean their lives don't go on, because of course they do.

I tried to reach Mark Lindsay, Tiger's chiropractor, by phone and by text. Again, I can't be certain I had his current phone number. I wrote and called the Toronto lawyer who has represented him. No responses were forthcoming.

Lindsay did address his relationship with Tiger in the 2018

biography *Tiger Woods* by Jeff Benedict and Armen Keteyian. (This book has the same editor.) Lindsay is prominently featured in a chapter called "Miracle Workers." The authors write that in 2008 and 2009, "Tiger underwent hundreds of hours of treatment at the hands of Dr. Lindsay." The chapter ends with a long statement from Lindsay about Woods and PEDs, submitted to the authors through Lindsay's lawyer. This is the first paragraph of it:

> During this extended period of time, I was very close to Tiger. At no time during this intensive process did I ever witness Tiger Woods take, discuss, or ask for any banned or performance-enhancing substances, nor did he even indirectly hint about the subject matter of banned substances. Anyone suggesting or implying otherwise is misinformed and wrong. To the contrary, Tiger Woods was fully committed to a proper and highly disciplined rehabilitation process.

If you want to read the full statement (without committing to the whole book), you might find *Tiger Woods* in your local library and turn to page 305. You could also—and this is kind of upsetting—Google any sentence from the passage quoted above, and Lindsay's entire 390-word statement should pop right up.

I read the whole book. I found it to be rigorous, revealing—and semi-depressing. The last major event in it is the Memorial Day arrest. The last event of any kind is Tiger's twenty-third-place finish in his first event of 2018, at Torrey Pines.

·   ·   ·

The most comprehensive comment directly from Tiger on the subject of performance-enhancing drugs and Tony Galea came at his pre-tournament press conference at the 2010 Masters, when the sex scandal was still alive and kicking. The balance of power had shifted, and Tiger was more likely to answer personal questions than he ever had been. Below is a question posed to Tiger by Christine Brennan of *USA Today* and Tiger's (lightly edited) response.

Brennan: You've been known as a great proponent of drug testing on the PGA Tour. As you probably know, Dr. Anthony Galea was arrested with performance-enhancing drugs in his possession, and as you know, Dr. Galea said he's been to your home four times. Why did you feel it was necessary to have this particular doctor come to your home, and what did he specifically do for you?

Woods: Okay. Well, Christine, he did come to my house. He never gave me HGH or any PEDs. I've never taken that my entire life. I've never taken any illegal drug, ever, for that matter.

I had PRP, platelet-enriched plasma, treatments. Basically, what that is, they draw blood from your arm and spin it in a centrifuge. As you all know, in 2008 I blew out my ACL, and part of my reconstruction was with my LCL. It wasn't reacting properly. It was a little bit stuck. And so I had the PRP injection in my LCL.

And then in December I started to train, started running again, and I tore my Achilles in my right leg. I then had PRP injections throughout the year. I kept re-tearing it throughout the year and throughout the summer. I used tape most of the year to play, and so I also went to hyperbaric chambers after the injections. It does help you heal faster. I did everything I possibly could to heal faster so I could get back on the golf course, through the PRP injections.

In January 2020, I sent an email to Mark Steinberg in which I told him about my interviews with Bosch. I mentioned Rodriguez,

Galea, and Lindsay. I asked if Tiger would want to update his comments from 2010. Steinberg got back to me within an hour: "We will respectfully pass."

.   .   .

You might be wondering what Bosch's motivation is in saying what he's saying here. He despises Alex Rodriguez, and that's part of it. He genuinely believes that performance-enhancing drugs should be used openly and safely. And, off drugs and out of prison, he has a desire to tell the truth. The truth as he sees it.

.   .   .

Woods had his Thanksgiving crash, and his life collapsed. The reverberations reached Bosch. "I was freaking the fuck out," Bosch told me. He started huddling intensely with Cousin Yuri, paranoid that Tiger's problems would somehow become his. Bear in mind, he was using cocaine regularly in this period, and cocaine use can promote feelings of paranoia.

"Rumor-wise, one of the fears that Tiger had was that his wife was going to out him with all the PEDs," Bosch said. Bosch was worried that his sale of Neupogen to "Galea's guy" would be part of that reckoning. Bosch said A-Rod tried to call Tiger and could never get him, but A-Rod had another path to semi-reliable information: Mark Steinberg. (In 2001 Woods, Rodriguez, and Steinberg had attended the Orange Bowl together.) Eventually, Yuri told Bosch, "Tiger's going to give her whatever she wants to shut her up," and that was when Bosch started to calm down. His arrogance returned. He told Yuri, "They're going to blame Tiger's libido on the testosterone, they're going to blame the crash and the chaos on sleep meds. Can we at least get credit for some of the wins?" His *we* was Bosch and Yuri and their industry, so dedicated to improving athletic performance through hard work, talent—and drugs.

There is, by the way, no police evidence of drug usage by Woods related to his car accident that November night. No toxicology report was ever made public. In the annals of jurisprudence it had gone down as a single-car accident. Woods was cited for careless driving and fined $164.

Okay, one last thing from the Miami Marriott: Tony Bosch on the warrior-athlete. That is, the athlete—name your gender, name your sport—who lives beyond the boundaries of what any normal person could understand. Here comes a long preamble to what is, in effect, a closing statement from Tony Bosch to us, in our innocence, about a tiny, select fraternity of athletes he knows in ways we cannot. Athletes who, from toddlerhood on, are trained to do only thing: perform at the highest level possible.

Yes, there's a great deal of whatever-it-takes in all of this. A great deal of *just do it.* Most of us cannot relate. If anything, we're repulsed. We grew up on the idea of the level playing field and clean living. But elite performers are not of this earth. You can almost smell A-Rod's office from that night, four grown men, the door closed, midnight come and gone. Who would call that normal medical treatment, or a normal night at all? Bosch doesn't imagine that things were much different at Tiger's house, except no Cousin Yuri, and no Bosch.

There are A-Rods at the extreme end of every human endeavor. Is there much difference between his playing career and Judy Garland's? Not really, except hers ended at forty-seven, with her death by overdose. The health risks are staggering for any artist-performer-athlete using any sort of performance-enhancing drug. Tom Simpson, a great British cyclist, died during a mountain climb while competing in the 1967 Tour de France, his death connected to his race-day amphetamine usage. He was twenty-nine. We pause to remember F. Scott Fitzgerald (forty-four, alcohol); Janis Joplin (twenty-seven, heroin); Jean-Michel Basquiat (twenty-seven, heroin). If Judy Garland had to be doped up to perform, to wake up, to go to sleep, to stay skinny, she did what she needed to do and kept it to herself (forty-seven, barbiturates). A-Rod's MO for his drug use was about the same—get in the game, stay in the game, dominate the game—until he got caught and could lie no more.

It was painful, that peek at A-Rod through Bosch's lens: the great Rodriguez on a random night, one night among his thousands, in his sealed-off office, in his gated mansion, on his gated island. All that effort to get the man's body ready for battle, one courtier in charge of outside operations (Mark Lindsay), a second handling internal affairs (Anthony Bosch), Cousin Yuri in some kind of management role. But A-Rod was an artist. Dave Anderson, sports columnist for the *New York Times,* used to say that turning a double play was baseball's ballet. Rodriguez was a star dancer, one who turned hundreds of double plays. Tiger is an artist. Anybody who has seen the pitch shot he played for his second shot on sixteen in the fourth round of the 2005 Masters would say that. He banked it off a slope *just* so. In golf, the swing is a dancework, and the shot is an artwork. If you ever saw Tiger play live—or Arnold Palmer or Seve Ballesteros or Johnny Miller or Lee Trevino—you know how stirring golf can be. On a good course in difficult conditions with a trophy in the clubhouse with Gene Sarazen's name on it? For sure. You can't shoot 66 without a paintbrush.

But at the end of the day, golf is a number. You can't fake it. A ballplayer can hide it for a night or two. Judy Garland could, too, on her bad nights. The band could play louder, or a singing partner could be hastily organized. In golf, that player is exposed and alone. Even Tiger has had rounds where he couldn't break 80. But there were many more times when he shot 66.

You can take Tiger at his word, that he has never used performance-enhancing drugs. You can take him at his word and still conclude he has led an extreme life. Here he is, rising in the middle of the night for a morning tee time, needing hours to stretch and be stretched, to go to the gym and lift, to get heat or ice or both, to eat a first by-the-numbers meal that leaves nothing to chance. (And we call it breakfast. How quaint.) His road to all those first tees only became longer over the years. Hogan could have told him how that goes. The body and brain can only take so much. Hogan had his own PEDs—nicotine in the morning, alcohol at night. The pressure, the disappointment, the obsession with perfection—it's a heavy load. Consider Tiger, after Thanksgiving in 2009 and Memorial Day in 2017. Do you think those nights were one-offs among *his* thousands? Not likely.

Still, your heart goes out to him, no matter what choices he made, no matter what choices his father made for him. We can't know the tax rate on his greatness.

So here, finally, is Tony Bosch, in an informal summation (not a verbatim statement), talking about athletes he has known intimately, about X, about Y, about Z after the bonfire of desire has been lit, after National Letter of Intent Day has come and gone, after science has exploited every gift assigned at birth:

Now he's a finely tuned machine. Drugs to lower anxiety. To drop the pulse rate. To deepen breathing. To tighten ligaments. To recover. To increase stamina and speed. To be explosive. To sleep. He wants to perform. He wants to conquer. But what's he going to do the rest of the time? He's the best, and being the best is an aphrodisiac. Women want to be protected, and if you're the best, you can protect them better.

He's a machine. He has to perform. So sex becomes part of the hunt, part of the kill. He's performing. He's conquering. He's a fucking porn star! He's like those warriors in ancient Rome. They battle. They conquer. Then they eat, they drink, and they bang.

•   •   •

One last last thing on this whole subject. If you thought Woods used PEDs before you waded through this muck, you probably still do. If you came in thinking he didn't, nothing here likely changed your mind. And if you didn't care before about the whole question, you almost certainly don't care now. After a while, who can keep track of all this drug stuff anyhow? What Lance Armstrong or Barry Bonds or Marion Jones did in the back of a van or on a cushioned table, what drug tests they passed or failed, what happened to their trinkets or their records. We're much more likely to remember Armstrong on the Champs-Élysées, Barry Bonds hitting number 756, Marion Jones with five medals around her neck at the Sydney Olympics. Moments with emotional impact.

Galea practices medicine in Toronto today. Bosch is trying to start a business in Miami based on performance-enhancing *nutrition*. Bosch's four-year federal sentence was reduced to fourteen months, plus time in a halfway house and under house arrest. He said he wished it had happened earlier in his life. Prison got him off cocaine.

Tony Bosch is a casual golf fan. He's like a lot of people: When Tiger is playing well, he watches. But he's not a big fan. "The road to recovery for Tiger, the road to happiness, is winning." And that, Bosch said, is not sustainable. He wasn't playing psychotherapist. He was looking at Tiger's life though his own. This was in March 2019—a half year after Tiger's win at the Tour Championship at East Lake, when Tiger won for the first time in five years—and a month before his win at the Masters. Whenever Bosch saw Tiger on TV, playing golf or being interviewed about a round, this is what he saw in the man: "A better version of his former self."

• • •

Tiger didn't win in 2010 or 2011. He won three times in 2012. His fifth and last win in 2013 came in early August at the Firestone tournament in Akron, Ohio. He could not of course have known that his win there would mark the start of the longest winless period of his career by far. You don't have to play anything like perfect golf for four days to win tournaments, but if your body and head are both off, it's almost impossible. Golf is too hard.

In mid-August 2013 there were again hints that Tiger's body was betraying him. They came during a tournament at Liberty National in Jersey City, New Jersey, at a course built on a former landfill with a view of the Statue of Liberty. In the Wednesday pro-am, Tiger played the front nine, but from the tenth hole to the clubhouse, he didn't hit any full shots, he just walked the course and putted. He said he had awakened that morning with a stiff neck and back that he attributed to the "soft bed" at his hotel. That comment generated this headline: TIGER WOODS INJURED BY SOFT BED. Maybe the headline writer was punch-drunk. A year earlier, at another tournament near New York City, Tiger attributed lower-back pain to "soft beds at the hotel." At Liberty National in 2013, after playing a second shot from the fairway on a back-nine par-5, he fell to his knees, racked by back pain. Whatever was going on, it was more than a bad mattress. Not that you were going to get much on the subject from Tiger.

As Dr. Jones, Bobby's psychologist grandson, says, mental stress can show up in the damnedest places, including the back. In the moment, Tiger on his knees, the view is so narrow: *How bad is it? Will he play next week?* Then some years pass, the camera zooms out and rises, and you see the same event in a different way: *Tiger fell to his knees on a golf course.* You've never seen or heard of another golfer doing it. As cries for help go, it's practically biblical. (Charlton Heston at the end of *Planet of the Apes*, on a beach, on his knees, looking at a half-submerged Statue of Liberty, screaming in anguish.) The stress in Tiger's life, the pressure on him to perform, must have been unbearable.

Three public rules issues in five months: stressful. Going five years without winning a major: stressful. Being a single father: stressful.

Having sponsors (AT&T, Gatorade, others) drop you in the wake of an epic sex scandal: stressful.

In the wake of those departures, Tiger made some odd choices about what do with some of the most valuable marketing space in golf, the sides of his golf bag. First he signed with one company that tanked, Fuse Energy. Then he signed with another, MusclePharm, that paid to terminate its deal with him. All the while, he was signing an endless series of checks. All those bills. The jet and the yacht, estate maintenance, lawyers and doctors and accountants.

He was never a good sleeper. Sleeping away from home is a struggle for many people, and sleeping when your head is filled with problems and your body hurts of course makes matters only worse. At least for the Honda Classic, at PGA National in Palm Beach Gardens, Tiger could sleep at home. He doesn't play in that event often, but he did in March 2014. He opened with rounds of 71 and 69 and made the cut on the number. Then he shot an early-morning third-round 65, buoyed by tremendous putting. Nobody shot lower. Sunday arrived and he shot 40 going out, followed by pars on ten, eleven, twelve, and thirteen. After holing out there, he shook hands with his playing partner, Luke Guthrie, and quit the tournament with only five holes to play. That's beyond rare.

Tiger walked in holding hands with his daughter, Sam, dressed to match her father in his traditional red-and-black Sunday colors. Like Tiger, Guthrie had been wearing a red shirt, but only out of wardrobe desperation. "It was a pleasure playing with you," Woods told the young golfer. "I can't go anymore." He offered nothing more than that.

But a player is obligated to give a reason, to a playing partner or a tournament official, for withdrawing during a round. Slugger White said that Tiger had fulfilled his obligation. Yes, Slugger again. The Tour is a fishbowl, a crowded one. As Frank Sinatra once had a cold, Tiger Woods had, he said, a "bad back." His withdrawal left some of the lodge brothers shaking their heads: *Just finish the tournament, even if you have to bunt it around—there are people out there who have paid money to see you.* But nobody would ever say that to Tiger's face or to reporters with their notebooks out. Tiger was too big.

The rest of the year—for Woods and Mark Steinberg, for Tom Watson, the captain of the 2014 U.S. Ryder Cup team, for many others—was a long series of medical bulletins. Tiger didn't play in the Masters or the U.S. Open. He played poorly in the British Open, then withdrew after eight holes in the fourth round of the Firestone tournament. In his next outing, at the PGA Championship, he missed the cut and said, "I felt old a long time ago." Tom Watson had been saying all year that if Woods were healthy, he'd be picked for the team, if he didn't qualify for it on points. He didn't qualify for it on points. He wasn't picked for the team. The U.S. lost in Scotland. Watson took a beating, chiefly at the hands of Phil Mickelson. Woods was at home.

· · ·

If 2014 was muddled for Tiger, 2015 was downright weird. The first instance of weirdness came on a trip to Italy that Tiger made in mid-January, to watch his girlfriend at the time, the skier Lindsey Vonn, compete in the finals of a World Cup event, which she won. It was her sixty-third World Cup win, a record.

Upon his arrival at the event, Woods was wearing a cloth mask with an image of a skeleton head printed on it. The mask itself was from an Xbox game called *Tom Clancy's Ghost Recon* that simulates the experience of being a U.S. Army tactical shooter. Tactical shooters, in combat, will sometimes wear masks to keep dust and insects out of their mouths and nostrils, so the mask was a logical tie-in, like a plastic Flintmobile in a box of Fruity Pebbles. Tiger has a long history with Xbox, as both a paid endorser and an amateur enthusiast. He's way into it.

Tiger can be unpredictable in his public appearances. Goatees come and go with him. At the 2001 Orange Bowl, the one he attended with Mark Steinberg and Alex Rodriguez, his hair was bleached a yellowish blond. He'll step out sometimes wearing a tailored suit and other times in dad jeans. He showed up at that World Cup event in Italy wearing a *Ghost Recon* mask and a Nike ski jacket. No biggie.

When Tiger offered Lindsey a congratulatory kiss, his cloth black-and-white mask was covering his lips. Soon after, he was photographed with the mask below his lips and his mouth open. All his teeth were there except one. There was a gaping hole where you expected to see his front left tooth, a tooth that had long shown signs of discoloration, particularly in comparison to its neighbors, so bright, white, and perfect. It was odd. The British papers were calling it Toothgate. Tiger was mum. Mark Steinberg issued a statement saying that a media member with a shoulder-mounted camera knocked out Woods's tooth in a crowd near a stage.

Two weeks after the event, Tiger played in his first tournament of the new year, the old Phoenix Open. He looked great, as he often does. With his new prosthesis, he was again smiling for the cameras. At a pre-tournament press conference, he seemed more than ready for the inevitable Toothgate questions.

He told the assembled reporters that he had worn the mask so that he could come in unnoticed and surprise Vonn. He repeated what the statement said, that the tooth was knocked out when he was struck in the mouth by a video camera. The incident happened, Tiger said, during the awards ceremony—outside, on the mountain—when a kneeling photographer suddenly stood up and turned around, and the camera on his shoulder caught Woods squarely in the mouth. Tiger said his blood would have been all over the place had it not been for his *Ghost Recon* mask.

But of the many photos from the day, a day when the most famous couple in sports was together in public, not one shows any blood on the mask or anywhere on Tiger. There was no public effort to find the knocked-out tooth, nor any sign that Woods was in distress. No odd sounds from one of the most famous people in the world. He was never whisked away for medical attention. No race official came forward to corroborate his account, and one actually refuted it. No photographer came forward, either.

Could his story be true? It could be. But it didn't make sense.

In the hundreds of press conferences Tiger has given over the years, there have been few where he had to do that much selling. As performance art, what Tiger did that day at the Waste Management Phoenix Open was solid. It was held outside, with natural lighting on a cloudy day, so he had that going for him. Nike had him in a handsome blue crew-neck sweater that made him look mature and responsible. He made good use of hand gestures and eye contact, and he offered his megawatt smile more than once. He had a forced but friendly moment with a reporter. He mixed in some humor, noting that there were "not a lot of brown dudes at ski races." And then there was the pièce de résistance, his moment of righteous indignation. That came when a reporter asked Woods if the videographer knew what had happened. Woods dropped his voice and said, "He didn't care." His disgust was palpable. He owned the stage.

But at other times his words came out too quickly. A couple times, he dropped words, which he never does. His breathing at times was out of rhythm. Maybe it was the thin desert air. Maybe he was nervous.

Tiger is not typically asked anything too far outside his comfort zone at his press conferences, so it was surprising when a reporter said, "So many people are not believing your story."

"Dude, you guys," Tiger said. "It's just the way the media is. It is what it is."

Those five words had become one of his go-to phrases.

"It's not just the media," the reporter said.

"It is just what it is," Tiger said.

The next question was about the sixteenth hole at TPC Scottsdale, a par-3 ringed each year by famously raucous fans.

• • •

The week only got more peculiar. In the second round, Tiger shot an 82 on a course that no Tour player would ever call difficult.

If you're new to golf, some context might be helpful. Let's say your mother-in-law is an avid golfer, and she can break 100 most days. Then one day she shoots 126. That's Tiger shooting a Friday 82 at TPC Scottsdale, on a soft course, with little wind and easy pins, even if he played through a light rain for some of it.

Watching him play his poorest shots, in person or not, made your skin crawl with discomfort. As he mangled a series of simple chip shots, pitches, and bunker shots, he looked (except for his remarkable athlete's physique) like an ordinary Sunday beer-in-the-cart duffer en route to a newspaper 93. Facing one ten-yard chip, Tiger skulled the ball nearly fifty yards. At another point, he went looking for his ball amid prickly cactus bushes, looking lost and confused and a lot like us.

He bladed a bunker shot; he had the chip yips; he missed short putts; he drove his ball into a water hazard: 82.

A trio of Golf Channel analysts offered their insights into Tiger's play. His short game had been showing signs of problems for a while—it had become scoopy, like he didn't trust the club to do its job—but now these panelists were treating his short-game woes as a full-blown health crisis. Brandel Chamblee described Tiger in his prime as maybe the greatest artist the game had ever seen. But now, Chamblee said, he looked like something out of *Frankenstein*. Tiger's friend Notah Begay compared Woods to a catcher who could no longer make the child's toss back to the pitcher. Arron Oberholser, clinging to the natural beauty of Tiger's youthful game, offered the theory that the only teacher who could help Tiger was the one he started working with as a teenager, Butch Harmon. Brandel and Notah took a different view, one almost out of the recovery movement, arguing that Tiger ultimately had to help himself and find his own answers. "There's intellectual power in solitude," Brandel said. Some phrase.

A winter desert rain was falling behind them. It was unexpected and unscripted, both Tiger's score and the ten minutes of emotional weekday cable TV about his travails. But that's how invested that threesome was in Tiger's rise and in his domination—and how worried they were that this was Tiger's version of Jake LaMotta on Valentine's Day 1951 in Chicago, the day the Bull's boxing career died and everybody knew it except Jake LaMotta.

Seeing the flub reel from that 82, John Daly, one of the greatest natural golfers ever, came to mind. In his prime, Daly was a savant for every type of greenside shot that golf can present. But he wrestled with various addictions and demons, and his short-game magic evaporated for long stretches. His golf went dark.

The affinity between Daly and Tiger was real but limited. They genuinely liked each other, although Daly was never able to get Tiger to come out drinking with him. Tiger would have been fine with the drinking but not John's smoking (Tiger got enough of that with Earl). Tiger's name for Daly was JD, and Daly's name for Tiger was BJ, for Black Jesus, because Tiger's golf gifts, in Daly's half-jokey estimation, were divine. Well, Daly's were, too. They shared all that and some other things. They both won British Opens at St. Andrews.

In 2005, during an event at Harding Park in San Francisco, Daly and Woods were in a playoff for the title. Tiger won when Daly missed a three-foot putt on the second playoff hole. "You don't want to win tournaments like that," Tiger said. It was striking. Tiger's whole career had been about taking no prisoners, but that moment was an exception. That was the first act of empathy I had ever seen from Tiger for another player. It was as if he understood what it was like to be on the other side. Daly lost, and Tiger was in pain. It was beautiful.

In Tiger's hour of darkness, Daly thought he might have something to offer. "You get in a circle where it's just your agent and a couple of other people who don't have the experience of what it's like to deal with some of these issues," Daly told me. "I reached out to Tiger but never heard anything back."

Justin Thomas was playing in that 2015 Phoenix Open. He considered Tiger's score and said, "It's disheartening for me. I've never met him. He's been my favorite golfer my whole life. It's a bummer. I'm upset for him." He was twenty-one, starting out in a cutthroat business, but he had his heart on his sleeve. Tiger Woods had shot 82.

• • •

Tiger's plan was to play the four days of the tournament and then attend the Super Bowl, New England–Seattle, that Sunday night in Phoenix. But after missing the cut, he flew east and home. Once there, he turned off his phone and went to work in his backyard. He drove his kids to school, to soccer, to their other activities. Then, after a long weekend home, he was out the door again, this time flying to San Diego for the next event, at Torrey Pines. Golf always offers a fresh start, at least on paper. He played eleven holes before withdrawing.

On it went. A first-round 80 at the U.S. Open at Chambers Bay. A third-round 85 at the Memorial. A golf year that ended in mid-August. A back surgery in mid-September. A follow-up surgery in October. A birthday at the end of December, his fortieth, Darius Rucker performing at Tiger's restaurant. Blessedly, 2015 came to an end. The new year had no precedent for Tiger in his professional life. For the first time since 1991, Tiger went an entire year—the whole of 2016—without playing once on the PGA Tour.

He wasn't completely AWOL. In April, he went to the Champions Dinner at the Masters and sat with Jack and Arnold. It was

Jordan Spieth's first Masters dinner, and it turned out to be Arnold's last. In July, Tiger went to the Congressional Country Club in Bethesda, Maryland, for a Tour event he hosts, the Quicken Loans National, a fund-raiser for the Tiger Woods Foundation. In late September, he was an assistant captain at the Ryder Cup in Hazeltine, won by the United States. In October, after the murder of a former Tiger Woods Foundation scholar named Marcus Edwards, Tiger wrote a letter to the foundation's employees and volunteers, remembering Marcus's promise and acknowledging "the division, violence, and racial tension in many of the communities where our kids live." Earl was a believer in education, and Tiger was picking up where Earl had left off. His letter for Marcus is powerful and moving, and it doesn't matter whether somebody helped with the writing. It carried his signature and the weight of his status. (It was also a reminder that a letter is not a chip shot at TPC Scottsdale, thousands watching. You can rewrite a letter until you get it right.) What he owned, for sure, was the letter's hurt, its don't-quit message, and the heart in its kicker: "This is our stand." None but a fool would underestimate this guy. He contains multitudes.

•   •   •

In early 2017 Tiger played the Torrey Pines tournament. He missed the cut. From there he went to Dubai, to play in an event where major American stars collect major appearance fees, and when Tiger goes, it's like he's hit a gusher. On his way to an infomercial interview being conducted on the roof of the tallest hotel in Dubai and the rest of the world, Tiger greeted his interlocutor, Peter Dawson, the very proper former secretary of the R&A, with this: "Peter, hey, man."

"Very good to see you," Dawson said.

You can imagine the accent—John Gielgud in *Chariots of Fire*. Nearly half a century earlier, Dawson had been the captain of the Cambridge University golf team.

Tiger looked bloated and tired. "You, too, brother," he said.

He played one round in the Dubai tournament and withdrew.

Two surgeries, a full year of rest, and nothing had changed. His back wasn't keeping its end of the bargain.

He didn't enter any more tournaments in February and none in March. For the second straight year, he bowed out of the Masters.

But Tiger went to Augusta anyhow, just as he had in 2016, to attend the Champions Dinner, the first he had ever attended without Arnold at the table. Billy Payne, the club's chairman, was there. Everybody else in the room, except the club's discreet staff, was a former Masters winner. The defending champion, Danny Willett, a young Englishman, put prime rib and Yorkshire pudding on his menu.

Tiger was in professional golf's most intimate setting. He was in pain, but he was with his people, all showered and cologned and in their green coats. And it was there that Tiger shared something intensely personal: His days as a competitive golfer were over.

In that setting, among those people, he never could have expected his revelation to become public. But sixteen months later, it did.

Nick Faldo, who helped Woods into his first green, said in an interview with Dan Patrick of ESPN, "I know he whispered to another Masters champion two Masters dinners ago, 'I'm done. I won't play golf again.'" Faldo didn't identify the other Masters champion. But ten months after that, Jack Nicklaus did: "He did not say it to me," Jack said. "He said it to Gary. And Gary's the one who told me." Gary Player. Before that week was over, within a tiny group, the word was out: Tiger thought his career was over. It would end with fourteen majors and seventy-nine Tour wins, three short of Snead's record.

The 2017 Champions Dinner was on April 4. About two weeks later, Tiger flew to Dallas and had spinal fusion back surgery. It was performed by Dr. Richard Guyer of the Texas Back Institute, a vastly experienced orthopedic surgeon in his late sixties with David

Letterman's gap-toothed smile. In his three previous back surgeries, Woods had had procedures in which his offending bulging disk was shaved, to try to prevent it from rubbing against a nerve. It was the rubbing that brought the pain. When those surgeries didn't work, when a year of rest didn't work, Woods signed on for spinal fusion in desperation. In the surgery, Tiger's bulging disk was removed, and two vertebrae from his lower back were fused into one. It's a common surgery but not a guaranteed life-changer. Roughly three-quarters of the patients who had gone through the surgery had reported some pain relief. That was enough for Tiger. Playing world-class golf again wasn't even a thought. His main goal was to play soccer with his kids and sit through a dinner without pain.

"I wasn't confident," Woods told Bob Harig of ESPN long after the surgery, describing his thoughts as he went into the surgery.

Harig is one of the few reporters, along with Steve DiMeglio of *USA Today* and two or three others, to whom Woods will speak outside of press conferences. Woods occasionally has "walk-and-talks" with Bob and Steve and those few other reporters, answering a question or two and sometimes more while playing in a pro-am.

"At the time, I needed to try to get rid of the pain," Woods told Harig. "I tried everything. I tried stem cell. I tried lidocaine. I tried Marcaine. Nerve block. Nothing took the pain away." Lidocaine is a topical anesthetic. Marcaine is an injectable anesthetic. A nerve block is a medical procedure that promotes numbness. Tiger can sound like a doctor.

Nicklaus is similar. When you talk to him about medical issues, he sounds like he's on the staff at the Cleveland Clinic. Tom Watson, the same. Arnold was the opposite. In a Pittsburgh hospital and preparing for surgery at eighty-seven, he said to his doctor, "Should I be worried?" When the doctor said no, Palmer said, "Then I won't be." He died that day, on the eve of the 2016 Ryder Cup.

Tiger didn't go to the memorial service. He loved Arnold, he often said, but he felt if he went to the service, he'd be a distraction. Well, the Ryder Cup was there. The actual trophy.

Tiger's back surgery was on April 20. On May 24, he offered this report on his website: "It has been just over a month since I underwent fusion surgery on my back, and it is hard to express how much better I feel. It was instant nerve relief. I haven't felt this good in years." Good to hear, but if you had experience in these matters, you knew not to take Tiger at his word on many things related to his health. Five days later, on May 29, Officer Matt Palladino of the Jupiter police found Tiger in his car on the southbound side of Military Trail at two in the morning, completely wasted.

∙ ∙ ∙

The results from his Breathalyzer tests, taken that night at the Palm Beach county jail, were immediate. Woods blew, in the vernacular, zeroes, indicating that there was no alcohol in his blood system. When that result became public, it surprised some people because of Tiger's reputation as a drinker, and because Memorial Day is a drinker's holiday. But he had told Officer Fandrey that he hadn't been drinking, and the test results confirmed that what he had said was true. Everything he said that night was true.

Six weeks later, a toxicology report from the Palm Beach County Sheriff's Department cited five drugs in Tiger's system, listed here by their most common names: Vicodin and Dilaudid, both addictive opioid painkillers; Ambien, a sleep drug; Xanax, an anti-anxiety medication; and THC, the active chemical in marijuana. Five drugs, but no alcohol.

The absence of alcohol didn't surprise one acquaintance of Tiger's, a person who, as a recovering drug addict and alcoholic, has been where Tiger was, a person who is an expert at getting high. "With those drugs, you can mix and match to get the exact high you want without using alcohol," the acquaintance said. "You get to a point where you're like, 'I'm good.' You've got the balance just right."

Vicodin and Dilaudid are notoriously addictive and are almost never prescribed for simultaneous use. More commonly, when one of these two drugs becomes ineffective—often because the patient has built up too much tolerance to it—then the other is prescribed. Drinking even moderate amounts of alcohol while using opioids can be fatal.

The Ambien was not surprising, as Woods has often acknowledged his poor sleep. Over the years, he and Mark Steinberg have had many conversations by text in the small hours of the morning. Ambien has caused all manner of odd behavior, and it is easily abused.

Xanax, one of the most commonly prescribed medicines in the world, is frequently given to patients who suffer from anxiety and insomnia. When used in combination with an opioid, Xanax can be lethal. For sleep issues, Xanax and Ambien would almost never be prescribed to the same patient. But people desperate for sleep will sometimes use the two together without medical approval. That practice alone would constitute substance abuse, as outlined in the *Diagnostic and Statistical Manual of Mental Disorders*, the bible of the American Psychiatric Association.

THC is a drug that is commonly prescribed for pain relief, but it can affect mood much as alcohol does. People have been known to trade alcohol for THC. When John Mayer shelved booze in favor of weed, it made *Rolling Stone*.

So Woods, a fit and disciplined man, had five drugs in him that night, each a psychotropic. That's not a bad night. In medical terms and in plain language, that's drug abuse. If he wasn't an addict, he might have been on the path to becoming one. Being famous doesn't make addressing drug abuse or addiction easier. It makes it harder. Tiger was not just one man with issues in his life, one man among billions, although he was surely that. He was also an industry, and the crisis-management people in his life could not sit idly by.

Later on that Memorial Day, a "statement" was released, supposedly from Tiger: "What happened was an unexpected reaction to prescribed medications." Try saying those words out loud. *What happened was an unexpected reaction to prescribed medications.* It sounds robotic, doesn't it? You might as well be saying, "Raymond Shaw is the kindest, bravest, warmest, most wonderful human being I've ever known in my life." (From *The Manchurian Candidate*, repeatedly.) That sentence, from Tiger's Memorial Day statement, was the opening salvo in the name of damage control, a dark art best left to trained professionals. The PGA Tour took the "unexpected reaction" theme and ran with it every which way it could. But a press release can't whisk away a mental-health problem, no matter how many people follow you on Twitter.

· · ·

The wheels of justice may turn slowly under usual conditions, but they speed up when the defendant takes all the blame, and that's what Tiger did.

He hired a vastly experienced Palm Beach County lawyer, Douglas Duncan, one who knew how a case like this one would play out. Duncan was a lawyer with a working relationship with Dave Aronberg, the state attorney for Palm Beach County. Not that this simple DUI really needed to reach Aronberg's level. Palm Beach County prosecutors handle fifty thousand misdemeanor cases a year, and Tiger's was among them. But Tiger's case also provided Aronberg with a teachable moment for the millions of people following it. The message from Aronberg and his office was a humane one: *We don't want to put a DUI first offender behind bars if nobody got hurt; we want to change the driver's behavior and try to make the roads safer.* Hard to argue with that, and it might help you get reelected. For Tiger, and therefore for his lawyer, the main thing was to make sure a bad situation didn't become worse.

As a matter of law, the case had no complicated issues. Tiger had all but offered a guilty plea right there on Military Trail. Once the tapes of the arrest were made public, there was nowhere for Woods to hide. What happened in 2009, when he crashed his SUV and police officers and EMTs came rushing in, was different. Tiger's behavior hurt his wife and his family, of course, but it was uncovered by an act of tabloid spying, not by a police officer checking out a dangerous roadside parking job. No police report from the Thanksgiving event listed SOCIETY as the victim.

Tiger's mug shot, and especially the dashcam and jailhouse tapes, paved the way for everything that followed. The Jupiter Police Department made the tapes public because Florida has broad court-tested laws that protect society's right to inspect all manner of government documents, including police evidence. The public availability of evidence in Tiger's DUI case would apply to any DUI case in Florida. Yes, Robert Kraft staged a fight in a similar area, trying to stop the spread of Florida's sunshine laws as they were creeping at his front door. Kraft, the owner of the New England Patriots, didn't want anyone to see the police surveillance tapes that recorded his visits to the Orchids of Asia Day Spa in Jupiter, Florida. Yes, same Jupiter Police Department, same Palm Beach County prosecutors' office. But Kraft was fighting and Tiger was not.

Woods wasn't required to appear at his arraignment, and he didn't. His lawyer entered a plea of not guilty for Woods, but that was almost a technicality. Duncan and the county prosecutors were working out a plea deal by which Woods would perform fifty hours of community service at a school, participate in a workshop (via the Internet) where he would hear the horror stories of DUI victims, and go to rehab, which he had already done. None of this was special treatment. It was part of a state program for first offenders. Had Tiger's kids been in the car, or even a pet, the program would not have been an option for him.

How deep any of this went, what kind of impact it had on Tiger, is hard to say. An administrator at the school where Tiger did his volunteer work said nobody at the school was allowed to talk about his time there without his permission. Tiger had little to say about his rehab experience, seven years after his stay at Pine Grove, except to call it an "out-of-state private intensive program." That news nugget landed on July 3, which meant that the longest Tiger could have been at this out-of-state, private, and intensive program was for a month. That's not very long. On the other hand, a life can be reconstituted in a day, if the person is of a mind to do it. Then come all the days that follow.

As part of his plea deal, Tiger had to agree not to drink alcohol or use drugs in unprescribed ways for a year. He had to agree to make himself available for random drug and alcohol tests. He had to give up his car for ten days. He had to waive aspects of his Fourth Amendment rights, which protect against unreasonable search and seizure, for a year. How disquieting, to have a constitutional right taken away. But Palm Beach County had all the cards.

Dave Aronberg saw Tiger only once in person, at a Palm Beach County courthouse, not the main courthouse in West Palm Beach but a satellite one on PGA Boulevard in Palm Beach Gardens. Woods was there to enter a guilty plea for reckless driving. He arrived wearing a suit, a collarless shirt, and large, dark Nike sunglasses. By the time he stood before the judge, in her courtroom and under its fluorescent lights, those glasses were dangling from his neck. The proceeding took seven minutes. Tiger never sat.

It was an ordinary crime but not an ordinary defendant. The state attorney saw in Tiger's eyes what many people have seen over the years, his opponents especially—his focus. The defendant's goal, Aronberg said, was to avoid the scarlet letter of DUI. It can be done. It takes discipline, along with some other things. "He was all business," Aronberg told me. "He was there to get the job done."

That comment brought to mind something Earl used to say when he and Tiger went to junior tournaments together. Taking his inspiration from Julius Caesar, Earl would say, "We came, we saw, we conquered. We got the fuck out of town." Outside the courthouse, there was a big black SUV waiting to take Tiger home.

• • •

The back of Officer Christopher Fandrey's patrol car wasn't anything like a regular made-in-Detroit sedan. Instead of seats, it had a solid, molded hard-plastic bench. The raised back windows were locked in place. There was a mesh metal gate separating the front from the back. There were no door levers. Tiger was sitting in a cell.

Fandrey was ready to leave the scene of the crime and head south to the Palm Beach county jail, a twenty-minute ride away. But before he started out, Fandrey asked Woods who could retrieve his car, which would require towing, with two tires that were flat. Mangled, really. "Kathy," Woods said. He did not use a last name, but Woods had a longtime employee at his company named Kathy Battaglia. A moment later, Woods had a change of heart and cited his girlfriend, Erica Herman, in Delray Beach, about a thirty-five-minute drive south of Jupiter.

The ride to the jail was largely silent. There was a moment of police talk over the patrol car's radio. Tiger would moan, nod off, stare straight ahead.

Fandrey and Woods arrived at the jail's sally port—its staging area—which can be entered only after two heavy sliding mechanical doors are opened. A harsh yellow light flooded the car. Fandrey walked Woods in for processing.

At the jail, Woods had his fingerprints taken and stood for a mug shot that would be seen by the world before the day was out. As an artwork, that color snap must be in the public domain, because before long, it had appeared on posters sold at Walmart, on T-shirts sold by Etsy, on coffee cups sold on Amazon. It's a shocking photo.

The night had already been long for Tiger and for everybody in contact with him. Officer Palladino stopped his patrol car behind Tiger's Mercedes at 2:06 a.m. Woods was placed under arrest at 2:49 a.m. He arrived at the jail in West Palm Beach with Officer Fandrey at 4:02 a.m. At 4:24 a.m., he was asked to recite his full name. He said it slowly and carefully: "Tiger. Tont. Woods." (Tont is his given middle name.) He completed his breath test at 4:31 a.m. He was read his Miranda rights at 4:34 a.m. He provided a urine sample at 4:40 a.m. He was "incarcerated"—the term used by the Palm Beach County Sheriff's Department—at 7:18 a.m.

Woods then spent about three and a half hours alone in a cinder-block holding cell with a glass door, a toilet, and a phone. He wasn't offered anything to eat or drink, and he didn't ask for anything.

The jail's holding cells are a tiny part of a fifty-acre detention complex in West Palm Beach. The population is generally about two thousand inmates. They're housed in three towers, the tallest of them twelve stories. The complex abuts the Trump International Golf Club. When the weather is nice, golfers playing the fourth hole can hear the low hum of congregated men, inmates playing basketball and hanging out on the rooftop of the tallest tower.

Tiger told Fandrey at the jail that he didn't want a lawyer. He was semi-cogent at best, but he seemed to understand Fandrey's question. Maybe Tiger knew on instinct alone that there was nothing to fight, that he had been exposed as never before, that something would have to change.

Back in the day (a Tiger phrase), local cops, in cherry tops, would sometimes take pity on the famous and the drunk and drive them home. It still happens. The Jupiter police didn't do that on that Memorial Day night. They did everything by the book, and that made all the difference. They threw Tiger a birthday party, not that it looked like one, and taped it via dashcam. The second life of Tiger Woods had begun.

Tiger left the Palm Beach County Main Detention Center late on Memorial Day morning. No hat, no glasses, paperwork in hand. There were men playing basketball on the jail's roof and golf on the Trump course next door. *Inmate release*. Every subworld has a vocabulary all its own to separate the pros from the ams. Tiger exited the jail's heavy glass doors and walked down the long elevated, sun-baked catwalk, over a murky canal, to the visitors' parking lot, where the working lawyers and the waiting cabdrivers and the visiting girlfriends park. It was nearly eleven a.m. The day was already sunny and hot. He surely needed a shower, coffee, fresh clothes. Daylight must have never looked so good.

DAY-O!

Tiger celebrated the new year early, by declaring himself ready to play tournament golf again. In December 2017 he played in an event he hosts in the Bahamas with just eighteen players. He was rusty, and he didn't play well. But he did have a good second round. Anybody trying to come back from anything is looking for good news somewhere, and for Tiger at the Hero World Challenge, one good round was better than no good rounds. By Sunday night, when it was over, Tiger had beaten only two golfers. But his back didn't hurt. That's what he said. That didn't make it true.

He turned forty-two on December 30. A ball dropped and it was 2018. Tiger hoped that, for the first time since 2013, he'd be able to play a full schedule. In late January, he played at the old Tour stop in San Diego, at Torrey Pines, where he has won repeatedly. There were stretches where he had to play through a cold fog. He was hitting it all over the map. Still, he managed to make the cut on the number and finished in a tie for twenty-third. At the end of it, he told reporters that his feet were sore but his back was fine.

In mid-February, Tiger played at the old Tour stop in Los Angeles, Riviera. His mother followed him. He played two rounds, his driving game was hideous, and he missed the cut. But not, he said, because of a bad back. It was hard to know where he was and where he'd be going, in terms of his back and everything else.

Then in late February, Tiger played in the Honda Classic at the PGA National resort, the one Tour event where Tiger can play by day and sleep at home by night. And that's where you could see for the first time that Tiger's career might be new again.

He did two extraordinary things there. For four straight days, he hit a series of majestic iron shots. Immense speed through impact.

Superb distance control. Crashing-wave rhythm. The purest, quickest *pa-choomp* sound at impact you ever heard. There were sawed-off follow-throughs, shoulder-high follow-throughs, hands-to-neck follow-throughs. You'd look up, and his golf ball was climbing, then drawing or fading per the flight plan, landing hole high and stopping quickly on firm greens. He had to be, once again, the best iron player in the game. His driver swing was notably different, all oomph, little finesse, and his driving was erratic. His putter and his short game looked good. The irons, though, were at the highest possible level.

The other remarkable thing he did came at the conclusion of his fourth round, with reporters gathered around him. He was less imposing, more relaxed. He was asked a boilerplate question about his Sunday playing partner, twenty-one-year-old Sam Burns, another talented kid trying to find a home in professional golf. Tiger had seen hundreds of them. If form held, Tiger would offer some semi-impersonal scouting report about the kid and his eighth-place finish. Instead, Tiger said this: "He played beautifully. Top ten is big for him because it gets him into Tampa, the next full-field event. He's trying to build momentum and build his exempt status. Today and this week was a big step for him."

Who would have imagined that Tiger even knew anything about the pages of PGA Tour fine print that spell out how a player gets exempt status? But he did. Tiger Woods, walking in Sam Burns's shoes. Amazing.

You felt like asking somebody in Tiger's camp: *What have you done with him—what did you do with Tiger Woods?* Because the old Tiger Woods just wasn't going to worry about Sam Burns and whether he qualified for Tampa. That was never going to happen.

• • •

And then another weird thing happened. Tiger signed up to play Tampa himself. Tiger, in Tampa. Tiger Woods playing in a plain-Jane

Tour event called the Valspar Championship, staged at Innisbrook, a hard, flat course, one of four at a sprawling housing development alongside a low-key resort for people who know what it's like to save up for a vacation. Joe LaCava had urged his boss to add a tournament that he was not considering and had never played. Talk about a brand-new day.

For starters, in the old days, nobody could talk Tiger into anything. For another, Tiger had always been a creature of habit, a planner, and not at all the kind of guy who would just add an event. His days are regimented and organized. They're busy, with precise times for workouts, business calls, meetings, school drop-offs and pickups. And *still* he signed up for the Valspar Championship with little notice.

A sports columnist for the *Tampa Bay Times*, Tom Jones, assigned himself the task of watching every shot Tiger played through the week. He was rewarded for his efforts immediately. Tiger played well in the first round and had the lead for a long stretch of the second. From that point through the end of the tournament, fan hysteria—the shouting, the running, the craning—was at a level that rivaled the 1997 Masters. There were thousands of fans following Tiger all through his Friday round at Innisbrook. It was a zoo.

"Friday was one of the greatest days in Tampa Bay sports history," Jones wrote when the tournament was at its halfway mark. The pent-up emotion, the desire to see Tiger Woods be great again, was washing over the course like a rising tide. A young resort staffer, assigned to an early shift in the hotel gym, wasn't expecting any predawn business on Friday morning. But then Tiger came in alone, hours ahead of his 7:56 tee time. Tiger Woods, looking to win his first golf tournament in almost five years, was rolling around on a giant exercise ball, stretching his fused back.

The Sunday crowd following Tiger was likely twice the size of the Friday crowd. The fans were practically frothing. I had never seen anything like it, not even at the 1997 Masters. On seventeen in that final round, Tiger made a bomb, well over forty feet, and walked to the eighteenth tee one shot out of the lead. His heart had to be racing. It was, in ways, like old times. He knew what to do, how to breathe, how to think amid the noise. The final hole was a 450-yard par-4. A birdie would mean a playoff.

As he looked down the fairway, reality must have set in. Even though he was chasing, even though the only meaningful score he could make on eighteen was a 3, he decided to play an exceedingly cautious shot, a 3-iron off the tee. Nobody on Sunday had a longer second shot into the green. Tiger's was 185 yards. A good drive might have left him with 110. His putt to tie was from way downtown. He made a 4 on the last and finished a shot behind the winner, Paul Casey, an Englishman and a former Ryder Cupper.

"I was sitting in the clubhouse, watching on TV," Casey told me later. "Tiger in his prime would have hit driver there, maybe 3-wood, and it would have been in the dead center of the fairway. Second shot's going to be close. Birdie putt is going to at least scare the hole. So what I saw that day was not the Tiger I was used to seeing."

Tiger wasn't ready, and he knew it. That's why he hit an iron off that last tee. Good golf, at any level, requires an I-can-do-anything fantasy life, tempered by clinical realism. For the smartest players, realism will always carry the day. Iron off the tee gave Tiger a chance. A poor tee shot with a driver or a 3-wood could have left him with no chance at all. Every shot has a built-in cost analysis.

If Tiger found it uplifting to finish second by a shot, there was no sign of it. He said, "I believe my game is progressing."

• • •

Four months later, the British Open was at Carnoustie, on Scotland's stern east coast. As Tiger made the turn during the last round, he was tied for the lead. The tenth tee at Carnoustie is far from the club-house and practically in town. From there to the house, you're often playing into a sea breeze. The sky is gray as often as not. You try to avoid bunkers that have been there for a hundred years and a crossing burn that has been there far longer than that. Carnoustie is as hard and as pure as golf gets.

Erica Herman, Tiger's girlfriend, was following him, and Sam and Charlie, Tiger's daughter and son, were walking with her. Tiger wasn't just trying to win his first major title in ten years and a month. He was trying to win golf's oldest championship with his kids watching. "I've won a lot of golf tournaments in my career," Tiger said that week. "They don't remember any of them."

The British Open—the Open Championship—is the most major of the majors. The U.S. Open is the harshest. The Masters is the most clubby. But the Open is the most primal. It's the golfiest. You can win a British Open with your putter, but you don't need to. The greens are typically slow and flat, and that diminishes the importance of putting, the game within the game. You don't win an Open with your driver. The courses are usually short and firm, and you don't need to hit driver often. You win an Open by hitting flush irons with a piercing flight. You win by reading the turf and its humps and hollows, and by accepting a round's bad bounces with a measure of equanimity. Tiger had won three Opens but none in twelve years. Finally, another chance had arrived.

But he couldn't keep it going. After an all-world par on ten, he went backward on eleven and twelve. By then it was pretty much too late.

Maybe it meant too much to him. The dream of sharing a win with his children and for them to see the rewards of his hard work. Maybe, like at Tampa, he just wasn't ready; his golf wasn't good enough. Maybe it would never be good enough. It was a noble try.

When Tiger came off the eighteenth green, his mouth was

tight, his neck was strained, and you could see the exhaustion in his eyes. He looked to be in psychic pain. A chance had come and gone. No honest person could promise him a next time. He was forty-two, with a surgically repaired back. "I'm fused," he had said that week. He was different. The non-fused population would never really understand.

Francesco Molinari, Tiger's playing partner, had won a tournament three weeks earlier outside Washington, D.C., where Woods was the host. Tiger had handed him the trophy. They had played each other in Ryder Cups. People wanted to know if Molinari was nervous, playing with Tiger Woods while trying to become the first Italian to win the Open Championship. He wasn't. This Tiger wasn't the old Tiger.

In the scorer's room, Tiger said to him, "Congratulations on winning your first major." The implication, and the encouragement, moved Molinari. *You've won one, and you'll win more.*

"From a man with fourteen majors, it was something," Molinari told me later. Tiger, despite his disappointment, had shown true grace.

Tiger would have loved a mulligan for his tee shot on the eleventh, an iron that went a mile right. After that, he tried to play a series of miracle shots that didn't pan out and ended up making a double-bogey 6. "He almost tried too hard there," Molinari said.

Tiger and Molinari, with his dark, recessed eyes and Italian movie-detective manner, came off the eighteenth green. They climbed a set of makeshift steps, walked over a makeshift bridge, and arrived at a makeshift platform. Tiger's kids were there. Even with everything going on for Molinari—he was about to become the first Italian crowned as the Champion Golfer of the Year—he found himself watching closely and being moved by what he saw. He's an incredible person, understated, intelligent, and straightforward. He said Tiger looked to be on the verge of tears.

Tiger hugged his son and daughter and said, "Hopefully you're proud of your pops for trying as hard as I did."

. . .

A month later, in the last major of the year, the PGA Championship, Tiger was again one of the last players on the course. The heat was appalling long before high noon. Tiger was carrying a spare shirt. The course, at the Bellerive Country Club in suburban St. Louis, was soft and wet. Beer was being served intravenously to fans. They were way into it, and way into Tiger. It felt like Tampa. Tiger shot a final-round 64 and finished second, two shots behind the winner, Brooks Koepka.

Tiger's kids were at home in South Florida. "We haven't talked about golf at all," Tiger said afterward. "We've talked about school, and that's about it. I don't want to talk about golf with them this week. They're interested in starting school, and they're nervous about starting school. So that takes far more precedence than me playing a major." Something had changed since Carnoustie.

Tiger's golf at Bellerive was a study in scrambling. Gary Woodland, Tiger's fourth-round playing partner, said Tiger looked like he was shooting 74 when he shot 64. But the two most memorable things Tiger did that week, both within the space of an hour, did not involve a golf ball.

Seventeen at Bellerive is a six-hundred-yard par-5, and when Tiger got to its tee on Sunday, he still had a slim chance of winning. But his tee shot was a wild push-slice that sailed off into the weeds. His week was done. Tiger then took a second, phantom swing in the direction of the tee marker. That swing might have had even more heat in it. He had the red ass. It was a pleasure to see, and it was memorable.

The other moment was nothing and everything. Tiger waited for Koepka to finish in order to congratulate him, bro-style. In the decade since Tiger had won his last major, that had become a common practice, for friends and runners-up to wait for the winner. A photo op and a nice gesture, emblematic of the kinder and gentler PGA Tour. There wasn't much of that in Tiger's prime. Guys didn't wait for Tiger, and he didn't wait for them. But there he was, at the end of a long day in the office, standing outside an entrance to the clubhouse, broiling heat rising from the pavement. Tiger, waiting on the winner. Incredible, really. When Koepka arrived and saw Tiger, he seemed surprised. They laughed, they shook, they hugged, Nike swoosh to Nike swoosh. If golf ever had two stronger men sharing one square yard, the scene was not witnessed by hundreds and recorded for posterity. What smiles. (What teeth!) Koepka's girlfriend, Jena Sims, was standing right beside them, thunderstruck. She was staring at Tiger, as were hundreds of other fans.

. . .

I have found it useful, over the years, to go deep with fans and players and others who are Tiger Woods true believers. James Tigabasa is such a man.

I met James at Dad Miller, a public course in Anaheim, California, where Tiger played his high school matches. James got there long after that. He grew up in the 1960s and '70s in a mud hut in Uganda. No running water. No *anything*. His mother and father brought him into the world. Tiger Woods, by deed and example, gave him his life.

When James Tigabasa was growing up there, rural Uganda was beyond poor. There was no electricity in his village, and his walk to school took two hours. There were days when he wore only a long shirt. He didn't own a pair of pants. There were boys in his village who were forced to become child soldiers in civil wars they knew nothing about. There were times, when his father was still able-bodied, that James's family ate antelope and sweet potatoes. But at other times

James went to sleep (not to bed) hungry. His father had three wives and a spear. A world most of us could never understand or know.

Throughout Africa, in many of the places where the British established colonies, open fields were turned into golf courses. Ten miles from James's village was a simple nine-hole layout, the Kabale golf course, where James caddied and learned to play. He was about ten when he started, but James can't tell you his precise age for any of the landmark events in his life, since there is no written record of his birth date. He walked to the course. He spent as much time as he could there—it increased his chances of not being conscripted into war. He learned to hit the ball straight because he had only one ball. When he got a golf club with a grip, it was a revelation. He carried the bags of Ugandan sheiks who paid him the equivalent of fifty cents for a round. It was a fortune. Golf was James's savior. His word, and he doesn't use it casually.

About twenty-five years later, James, then in his mid-thirties, was working at the eighteen-hole Uganda Golf Club in Kampala, the capital. On a Sunday night in April 1997, his bosses decided to keep the clubhouse open late and its TV on. Something odd and momentous was happening: A young black man was trying to win the Masters golf tournament. That's when James Tigabasa heard the name Tiger Woods for the first time. "I knew the names Jack Nicklaus, Gary Player, Tom Kite, Tom Watson, Peter Alliss, Ian Woosnam, Ernie Els, Nick Price—but those were white people," James told me. "I thought, *Who is this black man?*"

It was past midnight and into Monday when Tiger won that first Masters. An idea took root in James. More than an idea, actually, and more than a dream. Close to a calling: to work in golf in the country that was able to produce a black golfer who had won such a beautiful tournament on such a beautiful course.

Within ten years, James had shot the course record, 59, at Dad Miller, Tiger's schoolboy course. He got an hourly rate job there, working in the pro shop and the driving range, teaching on the side. When Tiger was in the early stages of planning and building the Tiger Woods Learning Center on land adjacent to Dad Miller, James got hired as a golf instructor for it.

Uganda was not out of mind for him. If anything, he was more aware of its despots and warlords and the hierarchies they imposed. But in a good year, James could make thirty thousand dollars in his American working life and send much of it home to Uganda, where his wife and children continued to live. James was the opposite of a golf bum.

His American life was almost monastic in its simplicity. His car was exhausted but it started most of the time. He seldom took golf trips and none that he had to pay for. He almost never ate out. His life was golf, apartment, Western Union, but he was content. The game was a religion for James Tigabasa, and Tiger Woods a high priest. James was teaching golf, the game he shared with Tiger, to children at a facility that bore Tiger's name. He pinched himself daily.

I had three long interviews with James. In all three—at the Dad Miller pro shop, at an Olive Garden, and at an Ethiopian restaurant—James cited one particular interaction with Tiger. The golf staff at the learning center had been flown to Chicago for a junior golf tournament. There was a tournament dinner. Tiger made an appearance. James was sitting at a round banquet table when Tiger approached, put his hand on James's shoulder, and said, "You're doing a good job, James. Keep doing what you're doing." Those two sentences have been lodged in his head ever since. At first they brought him unimaginable joy. Later, when he was let go from his Tiger Woods Learning Center job, they became an unsolvable riddle. He has never understood why he was fired. He knows Tiger would not have said what he did without meaning it.

He returned to his former job at Dad Miller. He has daily

struggles. I saw a customer in the pro shop flip a credit card at James. An indignity, one in a series. But James's life has meaning. He provides for his family. He finds it satisfying to be around golf every day. He takes particular pleasure from teaching promising young players who work hard at golf and at school. If James knows one thing about Tiger from his days at Western High on Western Avenue in Anaheim, it's that Tiger was a promising young player who worked hard at school. James's passion for Tiger has never abated. It's become more intense. His life is entwined with Tiger's. When he roots for Tiger he feels like he's rooting for himself.

·   ·   ·

Five weeks after the PGA Championship in St. Louis, with the heat of late summer following him around like a loyal dog, Tiger was at the East Lake Golf Club in Atlanta for the concluding event of the PGA Tour season, the Tour Championship. Tiger and twenty-nine others.

East Lake was where Bobby Jones learned to play as a boy, and you can see elements of it in the course he co-designed in his early thirties, Augusta National. The East Lake clubhouse is now practically a Jones museum, and the club itself has been able to preserve at least the appearance of Old South ease aided by large sums of New South wealth. The neighborhood around the fenced-in course is middle-class, working-class, and working poor, but the neighborhood and the club don't have any town-and-gown issues. The club is a not-for-profit that has returned millions to its neighborhood. Each has been good for the other. In the period when Tiger started winning U.S. Amateurs, the course and club, which had been in steep decline, underwent a complete makeover. By the summer of 1996, when the Olympics were held in Atlanta, East Lake's renaissance was one of the happiest stories in golf and in Atlanta. Two years later, Tiger was playing in the Tour Championship there. And twenty years after that, on the last day in the summer of '18, Tiger left the club late on Saturday afternoon with a three-shot lead in the season's last event. One more round.

On Sunday, Tiger arrived at the course wearing a sleeveless workout shirt and a backward baseball cap. (More graveyard spinning for Bob Jones.) By the time he got to the first tee, in the midafternoon swelter, Tiger was wearing a black polyester T-shirt under his red-for-Sunday golf shirt. Red was his power color and his good-luck color, a gift from his mother, a nod to her Eastern traditions that are part of Tiger's birthright.

People were on edge. The prospect of a win meant too much to too many people. A victory would be the burial of a long run that everybody wanted to forget. It would be a coronation, but for what exactly was hard to say. It would be a fresh start. It would be win number eighty, five years after number seventy-nine. There would be a party, maybe.

Tiger was paired with Rory McIlroy. They went off at two-thirty. Tiger made a birdie on the first hole. His lead was four. Tiger hadn't forgotten how to do this. He knew how to close. Or so it seemed for most of the day. But then he made a bogey on fifteen and another on sixteen. Then he hit his second shot on the par-4 seventeenth over the green. He had the kind of lie that, for someone recovering from the chip yips, could trigger a relapse. Everybody was nervous, starting with Tiger.

Much later, when Tiger described the shot, you had a glimpse into how his mind works. His use of *bounce* here refers to the heavy, rounded sole of his wedge.

"The lie was tough," Tiger said. "Most of the lies at East Lake were in pretty high grass. There really wasn't a bottom, so we were playing splash shots. But that one I hit to a sparse part of the rough. My bounce was going to get exposed, and I just didn't want it exposed too much. So I used a little bit more leading edge on that shot than normal. That was tough. I only had a two-shot lead. If I don't get this up and down, it's a one-shot lead. Playing the last hole with a one-shot lead is a little different. Playing with two, I can handle that. And that's why it was important to get that up and down. I had just bogeyed the last two holes. The last thing I wanted to do was make three straight bogeys and have a one-shot lead on the last hole and make a mistake again. There were a lot of things going through my head, a lot of different scenarios, like there always are. I'm just running through the different scenarios. The easiest scenario was, Get this thing up and down and go win it on eighteen."

Can you imagine doing that, weighing all those different scenarios forty or sixty times a week on every unusual shot you have? John Daly and Arnold Palmer didn't have to do all that long division. But Jack Nicklaus and Ben Hogan did. And Tiger does. All that thinking, and then playing with such emotion and athleticism.

Tiger got it up (the delicate chip) and down (the ensuing three-foot putt). He came to eighteen, a par-5, with a two-shot lead. He ripped his tee shot and smashed his second into a greenside bunker. And that's when the dam burst, late on that hot Sunday afternoon.

It was the fans first, storming the eighteenth fairway, most of them men in their twenties and thirties, cell phones raised high, desperate for their own taste of Tiger in full. Moments later, it was Tiger's turn as he approached the final green and allowed himself a passing and premature thought about the end of his barren years. And by the time he holed out, it was everybody. All that stored energy, finally finding an escape valve. It was raucous and out of control, a weird blend of relief and joy. There was so much to bury. The many invasions Tiger had incurred, by surgical knife, by police report, by tabloid stories. But more than anything, it was a big bash, open to all.

During the awards ceremony, Tiger was holding a silver replica of Calamity Jane, the blade putter that Bobby Jones used all through his golfing prime. Tiger didn't hoist it or kiss it or do anything with it except grip it absentmindedly, as if he wanted to take it out for a test run. Off on the side by himself, as he often is, Johnny Miller was watching intently.

"I knew my own career, in broadcasting, was getting near the end, and I was just thinking, *I've seen this guy's entire career from start to finish,*" Johnny told me later. "I saw him win at Newport over Buddy Marucci, I saw him win the U.S. Open by fifteen at Pebble. I saw everything. I'm tied to Tiger. His whole life has been like one long movie, with all these ups and downs. He was trained by Earl to be almost a deity. But there were costs. We all saw them. And he was coming back from them."

Bob Jones IV, our Dr. Bob, was in the East Lake clubhouse when Tiger won, surrounded by some of his grandfather's memorabilia. Tiger's final putt dropped, and the roar was so loud the clubhouse shook. Jones could see ripples in his water glass.

"When Tiger won his first Masters, he was a specimen in a glass," Jones said later. We were at East Lake, sitting in a baking tent. "People would shout his name and he would walk right by. The East Lake win was different. It was a shared experience. I watched him warm up before that last round and then walk to the first tee, and he was actually making eye contact with total strangers. I felt connected to him for the first time, and he was connecting with us for the first time. We were seeing the transformation of an athlete into a man. It wasn't just a sporting achievement. It was a human one."

I asked Jones about the thousands of young people around the final green—many of them about the same age as Jones's own children—standing there with their mouths open and their hands up, phones in them, recording for posterity.

"Those young people are just thrilled to be a witness to something so exciting," Jones said. "But years from now, when they see some of the twists and hardships that life can present? Then they'll see this same event in a much deeper way."

Jones has never met Tiger, but he's watched his life unfold and done it through the prism of his paternal grandfather's experience. He's had hundreds of patients and has read hundreds of case studies. He regards Tiger's life and times as sui generis.

"He might have done it with a counselor, and he might not have," Jones said. "Either way, he's the one who did it. I have a lot of people who come to me because they want to stop hurting. But there are fewer people who want to stop hurting and are willing to make changes in their lives." Tiger, Jones was certain, was making changes in his life.

"There's an old joke in my profession," he said. "How many psychologists does it take to change a light bulb? One, but the light bulb has to be willing to change." Enter Tiger.

ACT I.

In any given April, there are two distinct events with the same dateline: Augusta, Georgia. One is the Masters, the actual tournament, an often exciting sporting event that is work to watch on foot but offers good opportunities for social intercourse and business schmoozing. The other is a reality TV series called the Masters-on-CBS. Its showrunner, for almost forty years, was a profane perfectionist from Philadelphia named Frank Chirkinian. Frank's nickname was "The Ayatollah." Chirkinian didn't invent Arnold Palmer in the late 1950s and early '60s, but he figured out how to portray him on TV, to both men and women. Ever since, watching the Masters has been family entertainment, and if it overlapped with Easter supper, the box stayed on.

Chirkinian, aided and abetted by Augusta National, had an auteur's knack for revealing character, whether his protagonists were winning, losing, or hell-bounding to a playoff. His deputy, Chuck

Will, used to say Frank's gift was how he framed the golfer and how long he stayed before cutting away, and in hiring broadcasters who used words like they were paying for them. Frank's viewfinder captured Arnold's roughneck glamour by way of his muscular, awkward finish position. It caught Jack's intensity in the ongoing staring contest he had with his golf ball. It caught Tiger's amateur-years promise in his flowing follow-through and baggy windbreakers. It's astonishing, really, that one director started with Arnold (in 1959) and went out with Tiger (in 1996). The career of one director bookended by the game's two greatest leading men.

In the color-TV era, three Masters tournaments stand alone. There's the 1986 tournament, when Jack Nicklaus, considered ancient at forty-six, shot a back-nine 31 on Sunday and won by a shot over Greg Norman and Tom Kite. There's the 1997 tournament, when Tiger won by twelve shots at age twenty-one. And there's the 2019 tournament, when Tiger won his first major in eleven years, with one memorable Thanksgiving and one memorable Memorial Day in between. One stage, three dissimilar stories.

Chirkinian believed that you could travel the world, in sport and out of it, and not find better live theater. For some years, in his late middle age, Frank lived in a suburban development near Augusta, opened a restaurant, became a member at the Augusta Country Club, and harbored a fantasy about joining its neighbor. He venerated the Augusta National course, its membership, the clubhouse, the club's history. If you think Augusta National is hallowed ground, Frank got to you.

Somewhere in the playbill for the 2019 Masters, The Ayatollah should get a mention. He was the first producer fully devoted to telling the story of both the golfer *and* the human being lurking within him. At Augusta in 2019, those two stories came together as never before.

· · ·

Chirkinian's greatest insight into the Masters was to see it as a play in three acts. You don't need to be a dramaturge to identify the lead player or to break down the 2019 spring production into three tidy acts. In the first, there were Tiger's four practice days, one more than normal for him—Sunday, Monday, Tuesday, and Wednesday. In the second act, there were the first three rounds. And then the third and final act, Masters Sunday.

You may already know the stage and its many props, the various water hazards, the sloping greens, the inconvenient trees. You know how the play ends. (The morning after Masters Sunday, Tiger's picture was above the fold in *USA Today*, the *New York Times*, the *Wall Street Journal*, and every other American daily with a midsection and a pulse.) But it was Tiger and his backstory—and all the supporting actors and *their* interesting choices—that got this teleplay nominated in the category of outstanding drama.

• • •

For years, on the Sunday before Masters Sunday, there was a sleepy changing of the guard during which the club morphed from ultra-private playfield to the public epicenter of the sporting world. On that Sunday, members could find themselves playing in the vicinity of various former winners: Jack Nicklaus, Tom Watson, Bernhard Langer, José María Olazábal, various others. In more recent years, the day has become more crowded because of the finals of a tele-vised children's knockout competition called the Drive, Chip & Putt Championship, which concludes at Augusta National on the Sunday before Masters Sunday. Just as preteen ballplayers imitate the mannerisms of big-leaguers each August at the Little League World Series, these DC&P golfers behave like mini-me pros each April in Augusta. You'll see children who weren't even born when Tiger won his fourteenth major showing off Tiger-model fist pumps. The win-ners get the full treatment, and you could say too much treatment:

Golf Channel close-ups, expert swing commentary, post-round interviews, trophy ceremonies with former Masters winners distributing the hardware. If any of these kids ever turns into the next Tiger, they'll have their Mike Douglas moment, with Adam Scott and Bubba Watson, regulars at this annual festival, in the Jimmy Stewart and Bob Hope roles. A person you don't see there is Tiger.

Tiger's MO at Augusta is to avoid distractions and time commitments. He often eats in his rental house. He seldom plays in the Wednesday Par-3 Tournament. He doesn't hang out in the club's so-called caddie shack, as many of the players do, although he would like it if he did. He can't *stand* waiting for food, and the caddie house, right on the practice tee, has good food available all day long, hot, cold, and in between. Also, there are no reporters, and the few members who do come around the players actually like. Some of the international golfers—Rory McIlroy, Francesco Molinari, Tommy Fleetwood—will stay there for an hour or two or more, watching soccer on TV. Tiger likes soccer, but sitting around is not his thing.

Tiger, at any tournament but especially at the Masters, has limited patience for social niceties. Every year at Augusta, you see former winners, white-haired gents in their green coats, doing business entertaining, of a kind, all through the week. Fuzzy does it at a steak house called TBonz on Washington Road. Billy Casper did it on the upstairs veranda, wearing his club coat. Seve Ballesteros would be inside, enjoying long lunches, the wine bottles on the table adding a distinctly continental touch to the scene. Tiger's move has been to turn the entertaining over to others. You'll see executives from companies that sponsor him following him around as he plays. Some of the gents from Hero MotoCorp, an Indian motorcycle manufacturer that sponsors Tiger's annual December tournament, are easy to identify, as they are among the few spectators wearing turbans at any given Masters. A tour guide from TGR Ventures, Tiger's company, leads the way. *And we're walking.*

In 2019, on the Sunday before Masters Sunday, Nick Faldo was hanging around the DC&P competition in the morning. In midafternoon, he and his son, Matthew, went out and played. It was an unusually warm, calm day. The course was empty and quiet. While coming off the eighteenth green, at 6:40 p.m., Faldo saw something that made him do a double take. It was Tiger, on the ninth hole, with two men. One was Joe LaCava, Tiger's caddie. The other was Rob McNamara, a vice president at TGR Ventures and a former college golfer. It was a surprising sight in part because Tiger usually starts his workday as early as possible, and Augusta National isn't really a slip-out-late kind of place. But what struck Faldo was the stillness of the scene.

Joe carried the full bag, but Tiger used only three clubs over those nine holes, two wedges and a putter. He was out for a pre-tournament course walk. It had been years since Woods had been at Augusta on that quiet Sunday before Masters Sunday. The last time he had been there so early, a local reporter had asked him why, and Woods said, "So I don't get bothered by people like you." It was the kind of mean-spirited comment Woods has made often over the years, but he meant it. The Sunday before Masters Sunday was a chance to commune with the course in peaceful solitude.

Tiger took his time on those nine holes. Tiger, two of his employees (with matching shaved heads), a Sunday afternoon with nothing else going on. Woods doesn't get a lot of that. They spent over two and a half hours trying and noting this and that. Faldo saw a golfer getting himself into a dream state. The PGA Tour produces a mountain of statistics under headings like Strokes Gained Putting and Strokes Gained Ball Striking. What nobody can measure is Strokes Gained Thinking, Strokes Gained Preparing, Strokes Gained Imagining.

Tournament weeks, at any major, only get more hectic on the way to Sunday afternoon's grand finale, at least for the contenders. Ten days before the first round of the 2013 U.S. Open at Merion, Justin

Rose played the course by himself. "It's nice to be out here early, without ten thousand people around sticking Sharpies at you, and getting a chance to fall in love with the course," he said then. He fell in love that day. Soon after, he won the U.S. Open at Merion. Later, he joined Merion and named a racehorse Master Merion. The relationship that golfers have with the course they're playing is part of the mystery of golf. When Ben Crenshaw was in his prime, the caddies would say he couldn't play a course he didn't like, at least not well. He won his two major titles on a course that figured in his childhood dreams, Augusta National. He won his first jacket, in 1984, while splitting up with his first wife. He won his second, in 1995, days after burying his golf mentor, Harvey Penick. Talk about strange confluences and peak experiences. Crenshaw looks at a golf course as a poet. Tiger looks at one as an engineer. It's not all or nothing for them or any golfer, but every golfer is ultimately either a poet or an engineer. You don't have much choice in the matter. Being a poet is more fun. Being an engineer is more reliable. On that Sunday walk, Tiger was both.

The poets, the less original among them, will sometimes describe Augusta National as a "cathedral in the pines." Tiger does not. It's refreshing, and it brings to mind what Mark Calcavecchia used to say about his trips to Augusta: "Can't wait to get there, can't wait to leave." To Tiger, it's a golf course and an opportunity. He's impatient by nature, and Augusta National seems to exacerbate his impatience. He once gave an absolutely withering look to a club member who dared to interrupt him while practicing, even though the jacketed man's only purpose was to tell Tiger when he was due back on the course after a rain delay.

Tiger has an interesting eye. While he would never ooh and aah about the club's flowers or its trees or its famous driveway, he's intrigued by the mechanical bollards at the foot of it, five dark, heavy metal cylinders that go up and down at the touch of a button. One of those bollards once rose through the bottom of a member's car as he waited for the gates to open. There's a lot of that at Augusta, strange tidbits that will never get in the paper. Tiger comes to Augusta with only big questions in mind: What's the forecast? How's the course playing? Who do I have to worry about?

Tiger has made more money from his wins at Augusta than anybody could say. There's the purse, and then there's everything that comes with being a Masters champion. It would have to be at least $100 million. It's likely far more. But that's a conversation nobody will engage in. Part of the Masters tradition is not to talk about the purse or the price of anything, except the sandwiches. (Cheap.) It's actually one of the best-paying tournaments in golf. The winner's share for 2019 was $2 million. In 1997 the winner (Tiger) received $486,000 from the club. The winner's check went up 4.1 times in twenty-two years. It far outpaced the rate of inflation. But that increase is consistent with the growth rate of the S&P 500, which grew 3.8 times over those twenty-two years. It's become fashionable on Tour for players to thank Tiger for the increase in their paychecks, but Henry Paulson, Alan Greenspan, and Bill Gates (an Augusta National member) should probably get some credit, too.

Tiger is a numbers guy. His ability to remember anything numerical is dazzling. If you're an acquaintance of Tiger's and you tell him your routine for morning push-ups and the distances of your afternoon runs, he'll remember it for months, if not longer. He has a head, and a memory bank, for pictures, too. He can tell you how a ball was sitting in the first cut of rough for a shot he played a decade ago. He can reproduce giant scoreboards in his head long after Sunday night, and tell you who stood where with how many holes to go. He processes words with unusual speed and can respond to complex questions after a nanosecond of thought. When Joe LaCava, bag on his shoulder, gives Tiger front, middle, and back numbers from some funky, unexpected lie, Tiger absorbs the information instantly and never asks to hear the distances again. He can remember the weather when he plays and where he sat during a rain delay. He can recall what a player or a broadcaster or an official said that annoyed him. He's impressive far beyond his physical gifts. Augusta National tests both your mind and body. A golfer's memory bank helps immeasurably there.

He'll talk, if asked, about his hug with his father as the 1997 tournament concluded. His second hug, with his mother, gets much less attention, but it has to be prominent in Tiger's mind and memory. Two hugs, each with a shelf life of forever. His parents were already living independent lives, but Tiger's golf got them to the same place, with the same rooting interest, for one brief shining moment. The march of time. By 2019, that 1997 tournament had been over half a lifetime earlier for Tiger.

At the 2018 Masters, his first after the Memorial Day arrest, Tiger's overall game was still a work in progress, and it would have taken a near-miracle for him to have won. But one year later, the air was warm, his back was cooperating, and his game was better. He was driving it well enough to win. His iron game was the envy of the free world. His putting game was harder to know, as there's no lab test to predict what will happen on a downhill must-make Sunday four-footer, not on that course. But in every visible way, Tiger was in a good place.

And there he was, on the Sunday before Masters Sunday, playing a pitch shot from over the ninth green, because over is a good place to miss on nine, unless the pin is in the back. No fans, no TV cameras, no pressure. Just Tiger and his caddie and his wingman, walking the course, taking mental snapshots, adding to his vast institutional memory of the place. He had played ten thousand shots, in practice and competition, at Augusta National. Ten thousand and counting.

• • •

There are often changes, subtle and not, on the Augusta National course, though the club's preferred word is *improvements*. Greens get rebuilt, bunkers are made deeper, trees are planted, new back tees are constructed. Rough is grown, though at Augusta National it's called *the second cut*. When Tiger started preparing for the 2019 Masters, the main thing he wanted to see was the new back tee on the par-4 fifth.

Everybody did. The hole had been stretched out by forty yards and now measured 495 yards. Tiger had made an earlier reconnaissance trip, playing a full eighteen holes, holing out and keeping score. That's a common practice for the game's top players, to come to Augusta long before the Masters to check things out, but it's not entirely useful. In February and March, the course usually pays slower and softer than it will for the tournament, and the players will hit the ball much farther when the bell goes off, owing to game-day adrenaline. Still, Tiger's practice-round 65 that day must have been a good thing. If that's not going to get you in the mood, what will?

Tiger played that day with Rob McNamara, one round among the hundreds they have played together, going back to their junior-golf years in Southern California in the late 1980s and early '90s. If you click on McNamara's photo on the TGR website, a Walt Disney quote pops up: "All our dreams can come true, if we have the courage to pursue them." (When you click on the photo of Tiger, the company CEO, you see one from his father: "You get out of it what you put into it.") McNamara played college golf at Santa Clara, a Jesuit university in Northern California. He went to work at IMG, the talent agency that originally represented Woods, when he and Tiger were both in their mid-twenties. He has worked with Tiger, and for him, ever since.

When Woods returned to the PGA Tour in 2018, McNamara became a much more visible part of Tiger's public life. In 2018 and 2019 the five people you saw most frequently around Woods were Joe La-Cava, Tiger's caddie; Mark Steinberg, Tiger's longtime agent; Glenn Greenspan, Tiger's spokesman until he was let go late in 2019; Erica

Herman, Tiger's girlfriend; and Rob McNamara, Tiger's "brother by choice," as Erica once described him. But brother or not, friend or not, Rob had a job to do, and his job was to serve Tiger. (Tiger pays him, not vice versa.) Really, aside from Tiger's children, it would be hard to name anybody in his circle of trust who does anything other than serve the man. That's not unusual. In the star-maintenance business, it's the norm. Compared to many other star athletes, and many other stars period, Tiger travels light. One reason Rob became more visible at the start of 2018 was because Tiger, for the first time, didn't have a swing guru in his life, and he actually trusted Rob to look at his ball position at address.

In the Jones era and the Hogan era, in the Palmer-Nicklaus-Watson era, the game's best players almost never had their teachers on public display. That changed for good when Greg Norman became the world's top-ranked player, with Butch Harmon at his side, and Nick Faldo, with David Leadbetter. By the time Tiger, with a swing shaped and refined by Butch, had pushed Norman off the mountaintop, almost everybody had a swing coach. Some of these swing coaches, hardwired to sell themselves and their ideas, were irresistible by the time they finished their Golf Channel bits, and you knew lower scores were coming if you could wrangle the last spot in their next school.

In 2018 and 2019, Tiger was guru-free. To see him on a driving range with a bucket of balls and no swing coach was every bit as retro as the hard-collar shirts Arnold liked to wear right to his end. Rob was on the scene, always, "a second set of eyes," as Tiger described Rob's role. Rob wasn't in Tiger's ear. He didn't have his hands on Tiger's hands as Tiger worked on his takeaway. But their golf chat was right in Tiger's comfort zone: shaft-tip measurements, ball position on uphill pitch shots, spine angle at impact with the driver. The things that could maybe make a difference between shooting 71 and 70.

But Rob also had a growing role in Tiger's off-course life. It would fall to Rob to tip the locker-room attendants, a seemingly simple and human act that didn't come naturally to Tiger, who is frugal by nature. (There was Rob, on a Sunday night somewhere in 2019, giving the fellas $500 and a sleeve of balls. One attendant told me Phil's number was $2,000, no golf balls.) It was Rob who orchestrated the delivery of new clubs for Tiger to test. It was Rob who regularly rode shotgun from Tiger's rental house to his reserved parking spot. Along the way, they could talk about pin positions or wind direction or anything else either of them might have seen in the morning TV coverage. It was Rob who chatted up the deputy sheriffs assigned to walk with Tiger for the week. Rob was all in, and in on everything.

Also, Rob was . . . *nice*. Yes, E. B. White dismissed *nice* as a shaggy word, but it's an apt summation of Tiger's aide-de-camp. With his dad-at-the-mall appearance and manner, Rob wasn't going to steal any of Tiger's thunder, and had no interest in doing so. (Butch Harmon, Hank Haney, Sean Foley, Earl Woods, Lindsey Vonn, the caddie Mike "Fluff" Cowan, and Steve Williams, in varying degrees and in different ways, enjoyed basking in Tiger's glow.) Rob's manner with Tiger's public—with fans, tournament officials, reporters, security officers, players' wives, tournament sponsors, others—was polite, for starters. He was engaged. He'd stop, consider what he was hearing, look the person in the eye, and say something real in response. He understood that was all most of these strangers and semi-strangers wanted, some kind of meager connection. Tiger was horrible at it. For Tiger, the starting point was often "What does *this* guy want from me?" Insert profanity as you see fit. There are two easy spots.

Rob's rising visibility coincided with a diminished public role for Mark Steinberg. Steinberg is a fit and intense man, a lawyer by training and combative by nature. He's an early riser and a hard worker. He bites his nails. He was briefly, in the late 1980s, on the University of Illinois basketball team as a walk-on. That takes drive. It predicted his adult life.

In Tiger's second year as a pro, he was looking for a new agent at

IMG during a time when Steinberg was developing IMG's client list with notable women golfers, including Annika Sörenstam. Alastair Johnston, the vice chairman of IMG and the person who most recruited Earl and Tiger to the agency, suggested to Woods that Steinberg might be a good fit for him. "Yeah, I knew you'd give me the basketball guy," Tiger said to him, in Johnston's telling of it. At that point, Johnston and Tiger were neighbors at Isleworth and would see each other on the range there. Johnston knew that Steinberg's skill at basketball would make him seem less effete than his predecessor, Hughes Norton, who got to IMG by way of Yale and the Harvard Business School. Tiger was more likely to connect with the guy who sat on the bench as a walk-on of a Big 10 team that made it to the Final Four. Basketball is significant in Tiger's life. Magic Johnson (as an icon of his boyhood) and Michael Jordan (as a role model for domination) are seminal figures to him.

After almost two decades at IMG, Steinberg became a partner at Excel Sports, a small management company with a roster of all-stars from the NBA, baseball, and the PGA Tour. In addition to Woods, Steinberg oversees the management of Matt Kuchar, Justin Rose, Justin Thomas, and Gary Woodland, among others.

His clients swear by him, and some people who have seen him with a contract in hand say he's easy to negotiate with. "Gives you a number and doesn't play games," Mark King, a former CEO of TaylorMade, once told me. But Steinberg is also a case study in (one man's opinion) myopia, suspiciousness, and rudeness. He's a busy guy, and one group he doesn't make much time for is reporters. (There are exceptions.) He can be comically dismissive. When Tiger ruled the world in the early 2000s, Steinberg's press-tent nickname was Dr. No. At least he was fast about it.

I should point out that my friend Alan Shipnuck and I wrote a satirical novel some years ago called *The Swinger* that featured a biracial golfer named Tree Tremont, tended to by his agent, Andrew "Finky"

Finkelman. Steinberg was, to say the least, not amused. When I tried to explain this book to the real Mark Steinberg, four months before the 2019 Masters, he walked off midsentence. Tiger is never just flat-out rude like that, or almost never.

We all learn as we go. Many golf fans have observed that Tiger became far more patient and open with reporters after Memorial Day 2017. I would agree with that. It's as if he had started to see sportswriters for what we are, representatives of the fans who pay for Tiger's jet fuel and everything else, and often immersed in the game ourselves. There's also this, not original to me: Tiger's kids had reached the age of Google, and that gave Tiger an incentive to change the narrative. (Tiger once said of his kids, "I don't let them go on social media." Good luck with that.) An easy starting point for Tiger was the pre-tournament press conference and the post-round Q&A. Tiger was fourteen years old when he asked the writer Jaime Diaz, "Why do they have to know everything?" Maybe young Tiger saw TMZ coming, along with the banality of modern celebrity. In any event, he eventually figured it out: You might as well talk, and create your own narrative.

As for Mark Steinberg, I'm not pretending to know him. Once I had a brief phone interview with him as he offered encouragement to one of his children during a kiddie swim competition. It was a window into his world away from Tiger. As Gabriel García Márquez once said, "Everyone has three lives: a public life, a private life, and a secret life."

• • •

Terry Holt, Bernhard Langer's caddie, had the same idea as Tiger on that Sunday before Masters Sunday, to take a look at the front nine in the quiet of late afternoon. Holt, a slender Englishman who lives in northern Florida, has been traveling the world as a touring caddie since the late 1970s, and he worked his first Masters in 1984, for Andy Bean. He knows every hump of the course, but he also knows the course is never the same from one year to the next. Neither, of course, is the caddie's player. So Terry's first order of business, upon arrival each year at Augusta, is to walk it alone, with a few golf balls and his yardage book.

He was on the par-3 sixth hole, rolling balls on the front left part of its deep, sloping green, when he saw a surprising sight: Tiger Woods, Joe LaCava and Rob McNamara beside him, heading toward the shelf on the back right part of the green, where the hole is usually cut for the fourth round.

Terry figured he'd let Tiger and Joe get ahead of him, then continue his course walk behind them. Tiger did some putting and some chipping, which Terry expected. What Tiger did next was unexpected. He walked down the green's slope toward the veteran caddie, extended his hand, and said, "Hi, Terry. How's it going?"

Terry had had no interaction with Tiger since the second round of the 2001 Buick Classic in Westchester, New York. Terry was caddying for Paul Azinger, who had played with Tiger in the first two rounds. Terry had talked to Tiger about Tiger's fishing trips with Mark O'Meara, some down-the-fairway small talk started by Terry. Now Tiger was initiating a conversation and calling Terry by name.

They shook hands, and Tiger said, "I heard that this is it, that Bernie's playing in his last Masters this year."

Bernie. Terry was amused. Tiger loves to add a vowel to a given name whenever he can. (But he calls Rickie Fowler Rick.) Terry was also surprised.

"Really," he said. "I haven't heard that."

Langer, who was sixty-one, is the poster child for the golfing benefits, and the general benefits, of diet and exercise. Except for the lines on his face, Langer seemed to have barely aged since his second Masters win, in 1993. He continued to be one of the best players on the Champions Tour, for golfers fifty and older. For diet and exercise,

Tiger is trending in Bernhard's direction. Tiger could be long done at sixty-one. But if his body holds up, you could see him still ranked among the top two hundred in the world.

Tiger didn't seem to be in a rush to go anywhere, and that made an impression on Terry. Over the years, Tiger has typically looked like a man afraid to stop, worried that a crowd would form around him if he did, holding him prisoner while asking questions about his favorite courses in Arizona and forcing him to smile for phone snaps.

"Bernhard retiring, that would surprise me," Terry said. He could see that Tiger was listening, so he went on. "Three years ago we were two shots out of the lead Sunday morning." That was in 2016, one of the years Woods did not play, but Tiger surely knew. If golf is on TV, he watches, with the volume off.

"Then last year we made the cut," Terry said. In 2018 Bernhard finished only two shots behind Tiger, despite spotting Tiger eighteen years.

Terry and Tiger talked about the Masters tradition by which former winners could continue to play in the tournament until the player decided he could no longer play to his standards, to use a Hogan phrase. (He once said, "I am the sole judge of my own standards.") In 1967, at fifty-four, Hogan finished in a tie for tenth, and never played in the tournament again. Other former champions have played into their seventies, shooting scores far higher than their age. It's a sensitive subject at the tournament, for the club chairman and for the former winners who are in their sixties and seventies. For Terry, sixty himself, it was interesting to realize how attuned Tiger, at forty-three, was to the issue. But in the year Tiger won his first Masters, Arnold shot 89-87 to miss the cut by twenty-seven shots. Doug Ford, the 1957 winner, shot 85-94.

They agreed that the course, now more than ever, had a way of telling a player when it was time to call it a day. When Tiger first started playing in the Masters, the course was much shorter and wider.

"But there are certain years when veteran players can still contend on this course, because they know how to play it," Terry said.

"I would agree with that," Tiger said.

A firm, fast course is more playable for more players. But 2019 would not be such a year, they both knew, as the course was playing long and slow after a soaking winter and spring in Augusta. Even with all the underground apparatus—there's a SubAir system to drain the course—it would play soft. Suddenly, they were two golf nerds, comparing notes.

"I think some of these players retire too early," Terry said. "Look at what your friend Mark O'Meara did just last month."

After missing the cut at the 2018 Masters, O'Meara had decided to call it a day. No more Masters. But then he started playing better, and in March 2019, at age sixty-two, he won on the senior tour. That win made him the fourth-oldest winner ever on that tour.

"I saw that," Woods said. He knew about O'Meara's win in the three-round Cologuard Classic, held in Tucson, and about the eight consecutive birdies O'Meara had made. Tiger will meet the age requirement for the 2026 Cologuard Classic, if the event still exists.

Terry was wearing the heavy white overalls that the club requires caddies to wear. The original purpose was to cover the ratty clothes that some of the caddies wore. Tiger had his putter in hand. Joe and Rob were at the back of the green. Before long, Tiger went back to work, and Terry did, too.

The whole conversation might have been three minutes. But it was memorable for Terry. He had never seen Tiger so personable, so relaxed, so warm.

Tiger went to seven. Terry gave him some space, then went there himself. Tiger walked the eighth hole; he walked the ninth. It was 6:40 p.m. Nick Faldo was on the eighteenth green.

Rob and Tiger mapped out a schedule for Monday, Tuesday, and Wednesday. There were three things Tiger had to do. There was a Tuesday-afternoon press conference in the club's press building, a Taj Mahal for the typing class. There was the Tuesday-night Champions Dinner. And there was the Golf Writers Association of America dinner on Wednesday night. Aside from that, he was a free man. On Monday morning, he'd pick up where he had left off on Sunday.

Before that night was over, Tiger and Rob looked at the long-range weather forecast. Thursday, Friday, and Saturday were all expected to be unseasonably warm, with highs in the mid-eighties. Passing rain was likely on Friday, but other than that, the first three days were mostly dry and not windy. That was excellent news for Tiger's back, and for the rest of him, too.

. . .

On Monday morning at eight, Tiger stood on Augusta's tenth tee beside two of his favorite people in golf: Justin Thomas, who was twenty-five, and Fred Couples, who was fifty-nine. Two months earlier, Tiger had named Fred as an assistant captain for his Presidents Cup team, which would play in Australia at the end of the year.

Fred and Tiger were an odd couple. For pure natural talent, Fred, along with John Daly, is probably as gifted as anyone who has ever played, yet he won only one major title, the 1992 Masters, with Joe LaCava caddying for him. And he might not have won that one had it not been for the improbable way his ball stayed on the sloping bank that separates the twelfth green from Rae's Creek, which fronts it. He made par there, pitching it stone dead from the bank with exquisite nonchalance and bare, tanned hands. (Fred is one of the few golfers after World War II to win a Masters without wearing a golf glove.) His next move is part of the legend of Fred: he fished out a drowned ball from the creek in one easy gesture. Even though he was playing in the last group on Sunday at the Masters, he was at heart a public-course golfer, and he couldn't just walk away from a free ball staring him in the face. It's almost impossible to imagine Tiger doing anything like that. Lost in the telling are the five practice swings Fred made, four of them carefully made outside the yellow hazard line. Fred only made it look easy in the end. It wasn't. Tiger had won way more often than Fred, and often by ridiculous margins, but somehow Tiger's wins, and his life, never looked easy. For Fred, it was the opposite. Nonchalance was his art form.

"I'm not trying to be mean, but Tiger isn't as helpful as Freddie," Justin Thomas said after those nine holes on Monday. He wasn't being mean, he was being truthful. Whatever Justin got from Fred, he'll likely remember it forever. Tiger was once that kid, playing with Greg Norman, trying to figure out all the better layup positions. The march of time.

• • •

Tiger's Tuesday-afternoon press conference was a clinic in efficiency. The club holds these sit-down interviews in an auditorium that looks like a university lecture hall, a wide, cold, windowless room, far too formal and imposing for its purpose. There's a fifteen-foot gap between the raised stage, where the interviewee sits, and the first row of scriveners. There are four rows behind that. Everybody's on their best behavior. There are fine oil portraits of the club's president in perpetuity (Mr. Bob Jones) and chairman in memoriam (Mr. Cliff Roberts) on either side of the stage. No press room could be more decorous.

Reporters, in a custom that began with the opening of the new press building, don't raise their hands high to ask questions. If you get the cap of your Marriott pen to midchest, you're pushing things. You know it's your turn when the moderator-showrunner, an Augusta National member seated beside the player but not too close, calls you by name. (Tiger is given an especially wide berth.) The moderators know every reporter by name because they have an electronic seating chart that's linked to the reporter's press credential through the magic of wireless technology.

Tiger's Tuesday session lasted twenty-five minutes, its prescribed length, and it was a slice of pecan pie for him. No family questions, no business questions, no political questions, no meaning-of-life questions. It was all golf. As it should be, you could say, except there are never any opportunities to ask him anything that goes much beyond his swing, the course, and his back.

Tiger explained that the reconnaissance-trip 65 he shot was nice but "doesn't really matter." He said the mock turtlenecks he planned to wear during the tournament were a throwback look from "back in the day," meaning 2005, the year he won his fourth Masters title. He noted that the tournament "patrons" (he used the preferred ANGC term) were the most respectful fans anywhere. He talked about the "non-glued hosel" on his driver. He said how impressed he was by the quality of the golf played in the inaugural Augusta National Women's Amateur. He said the first tee shot at Oakmont was harder than the first tee shot at Augusta National, which he described as plenty hard, particularly when the tee is back and even the long hitters are hitting 5-irons into the day's first green, which is a terror. It must sound painfully banal, but it's actually strangely pleasurable to hear Tiger talk about golf. He's an expert on the subject, and when he goes deep on some golfy thing (the difference between the old balata golf ball and the modern urethane ball, for instance) he's especially interesting, provided you like golf. He can't go deep like Lee Trevino can, or Jack Nicklaus. They're golf-talk gods, with insights into every aspect of the game. They're also plus-four storytellers. Maybe all that will come later for Woods. Anyway, he didn't come to the 2019 Masters to entertain anybody, not in the press building, not on the course.

The best question of the session was asked by Steve DiMeglio of *USA Today*. "Tiger, couple of quick ones," DiMeglio said after his name was called. "What's the logo on your shirt?" DiMeglio is the

Einstein of the short question. He once asked somebody, "What's your vice?"

Tiger took a quick peek at the logo on his shirt, as if to remind himself what was there, like a Hollywood star on a talk show needing a prompt to set up a movie clip. Tiger was wearing, most atypically, a brown polo shirt with a curling collar and a little orange-and-black logo on the left breast. The only Nike swooshes in the house that day were in the peanut gallery.

"Oh," Tiger said in mock surprise. With a single word, he had turned his performance up a notch. "Frank."

"It's what?" DiMeglio asked.

"Frank," Tiger said, his mood suddenly playful. "My headcover."

"Oh," DiMeglio said. "O*kay*."

Frank the Headcover was a star in old Nike spots, a furry tiger puppet with a voice supplied by the actor Paul Giamatti.

DiMeglio had what he needed. He asked about the newly lengthened fifth hole.

Tiger looked and sounded good. He had no signs of sinus issues, which he sometimes has at Augusta. He didn't appear to be tired or frustrated or bored. Really, he hadn't looked or sounded that good since 2007. We were in a different building then, and Tiger's life was in a different phase. At the 2007 Masters, Tiger was looking to win his third straight major. Every single thing he said and did was magnified and intense. He was Babe Ruth, Secretariat, Michael Jordan— an athlete of almost incomparable greatness. The moderator called on one reporter by the color of his shirt in that pre-tournament press conference. The press badges were still analog. Tiger had complete ownership of that room. He was at the height of his powers.

The 2007 tournament turned out to be a wild one, with nasty weather on Saturday. Nobody broke par for the week, and Tiger finished in a three-way tie for second, two shots behind the winner,

Zach Johnson. Even on Sunday, after all that third-round misery, the tournament czars showed no mercy. Tiger was asked about the course setup. With the rising heat of lost chance in him, he said, "Whatever it is, I don't care, as long as I come out on top." He was outside, standing on his cleated feet, his game mask very much on. *As long as I come out on top.* That wasn't let's-play-nice. That wasn't acting. That was the actual man. He had finished second and he was pissed. It was intense.

The pre-tournament press conferences have turned into glorified infomercials. It's the questions, the answers, the setting, the pins-and-needles vibe. There was a time when these sessions gave reporters a chance to get to know something about the players. They were a starting point. There was some give-and-take. The mood was often playful. The players would typically linger afterward. Over the years and under various bylines—Dave Anderson, Furman Bisher, Dan Jenkins, Sally Jenkins, Bill Lyon, Jim Murray, Ed Pope, Bob Verdi, many others—scores and scores of players were brought to life in tidy 750-word stories datelined Augusta. If you expand the pool to include all the stories about surprise Thursday or Friday leaders, it's in the hundreds.

That world is gone. There might be one reporter who has Tiger's phone number. Players *enjoyed* having dinner with Jim Murray, deadline poet of the *Los Angeles Times*. That was then. Today the few reporters who have a good rapport with Tiger have never had a meal with him. Everything with him is at arm's length. It's a shame.

Dan Jenkins, who knew Hogan intimately and many of the game's legends well, once wrote a column about Tiger under a headline written by his own self: NICE (NOT) KNOWING YOU. Jenkins came to his first Masters in 1951 and covered every one afterward until he missed the 2019 tournament, on account of his being newly dead.

Jenkins feasted on the local patois. *On account of. Fixin' to. Reason being. Love her to death. Now driving. Toonamint. He enjoyed birdie 4.*

Jenkins would have enjoyed the 2019 tournament, but he would have skipped Tiger's Tuesday session.

The last question posed to Tiger was about the importance of the first round. It was right in his wheelhouse. He answered at length and walked out a side door to a waiting golf cart. The scriveners filed out the back. A near-verbatim transcript would be available soon enough, but there might be time for some high-end grazing first.

Tiger's press conference represented a half-hour of live programming for Golf Channel, more with all the post-conference analysis and replays. That little moment, when Tiger sneaked a peek at Frank, played better on TV than it did in the room. On TV, it looked intimate. There was just one camera, and it was tight on Tiger. In real life, Steve DiMeglio was about forty feet from Tiger, and it took Tiger a couple of seconds just to figure out where Steve's amplified voice was coming from. Still, twenty-five stilted minutes is better than nothing, right?

Nike sold out its limited supply of Frank the Headcover golf shirts like *that*.

· · ·

If you ever attend the Masters on a Tuesday, and you have the right credential, you might want to take a seat on one of the benches by the clubhouse entrance that faces Magnolia Lane, right around half past six. Consider bringing a newspaper or some other prop to look less conspicuous. You'll be in for a treat: the march of the Masters champs, one after another, showing up for their annual dinner. Cocktails start at 6:45 on the second floor. To get there, they have to enter the clubhouse first, and that's why you've staked out that spot. You won't believe how good that Gary Player looks. Like a movie star.

In April 2019, there were thirty-three living Masters champions, and thirty-two of them were in the house on Tuesday night, freshly laundered, showered, and cologned, in their green coats, dress shirts on, ties neatly knotted. A sharp-looking crowd. Jackie Burke, ninety-six, was at home in Houston. But Bob Goalby, the '68 winner, age ninety, was in the house and right on time. Tiger was, too. He parked his car (he's not a valet guy) and walked right in, his gait slightly pigeon-toed, different than it was when he was a kid starting out, before his surgery count started mounting. He had on pressed pants and a pressed shirt, a knotted tie, no coat. His club blazer was sitting in his locker, the one he shares with old Jackie Burke. Tiger likes to travel light.

In came Jack. In came Faldo and Phil. Twelve coats among those three. Olazábal, Langer, Crenshaw, T. Watson, B. Watson. (All members of the two-timers club.) Charles Coody and Tommy Aaron. Charl Schwartzel and Trevor Immelman. Raymundo, Ángel Cabrera. Adam Scott. Fuzzy and Walrus. Fred. The others. The new guy, Patrick Reed, keeping the Texas count up.

A lot of Texans have won at Augusta. Jordan Spieth. Hogan and Nelson and Jimmy Demaret (a three-time winner). Crenshaw and Coody. Ralph Guldahl—*GOOL*-doll—from Dallas. Talk about a legend. He won the U.S. Open in 1937 and again in 1938 and then the 1939 Masters. He wrote the hard-to-find *Groove Your Golf*. He gave lessons to Howard Hughes. Look him up and say goodbye to your afternoon. Guldahl enjoyed the Tuesday-night dinners, hanging with Wardrobe. (Demaret. He could dress.) What's not to enjoy? The food and company are good, and they don't make you sing for your supper. Tiger has never missed one. At his first dinner, he served milkshakes as his dessert course. The host was twenty-two and weighed 155 pounds.

Hogan, the 1951 winner, started the dinner in 1952. He was not at all an extrovert, but he liked the company of golfers, and some of the former winners were close friends, especially Henry Picard. "I wish to invite you to attend a stag dinner at the Augusta National," Hogan wrote to the other former winners. "My only stipulation is that you wear your green coat." Hogan paid that year, and the winner has treated ever since.

Vijay Singh, in his year, went all out, bringing in a Thai chef from Atlanta. Olazábal and the few other foodies among the former champs still talk about that dinner. But the main job of the reigning champ is to select the entrées and everything else, top to bottom. The club prints the menu, and the club chairman presides. By tradition, the former winners make the chairman an honorary member of the Masters Club, the guild of former winners. *Honorary.* In other words, *Don't get carried away here, sir.*

Golf could not have a better stag dinner, and a lot of the status enjoyed by the Masters is because of it. The names, the setting, the occasion, the stories. The mystery of it. Golf's Skull and Bones. The dinner gives the players a chance to talk about the tee shot on eighteen with the tournament on the line in the company of others who actually understand.

You feel for the men who had one hand on the door, some Hall of Famers, others almost famous for what they almost did. Tom Weiskopf, Greg Norman, Johnny Miller in the first category; Ed Sneed, Chris DiMarco, Len Mattiace in the second. Johnny. He had three second-place finishes at Augusta. The club should give him a green vest, he likes to say. Len Mattiace lost to Mike Weir in a one-hole playoff and ever since has referred to the week as "ninety-eight percent great." What would either of them or any of them give to have a seat at the table? Tiger caught the last few years of Sam Snead, on his feet, hat off, telling dirty jokes. Tiger is a student of the genre himself.

Tiger's first dinner, in 1998, was the final one for Jack Stephens as club chairman. He was a relaxed old gent, funny and assured. Tiger was on hand for all eight dinners hosted by Hootie Johnson. The players liked his bluntness but not (to generalize) the rough he grew and the trees he planted. Tiger was there for the eleven dinners presided over by Billy Payne, the Robert Moses of Augusta National.

Payne's swan song came in 2017, the same year Tiger said his playing days were over. Tiger's spirits were better in 2018, Fred Ridley's first dinner as chairman, and they were better yet a year later, when Patrick Reed came in from the cold. Fred is a golf guy. They like that.

Three deaths—Snead's, Seve's, and Arnold's—were jolts to the dinner, and some of the champs feared that the dinner had started to feel mechanical. *And now we'll sign the menus. And now we'll tell the jokes.* But the 2019 dinner was a good one, and a return to its Texas roots. Crenshaw told a long story about meeting Nicklaus in a second-floor loo at the Merion clubhouse in 1971 and attempting to shake his hand, and everybody roared.

This is amazing: At Tiger's first dinner, Gene Sarazen was there and completely with it. Gene Sarazen, who invented the modern sand wedge, who won the 1935 Masters wearing woolen knickers when they were in style, was in the Augusta National clubhouse in 1998 to welcome Tiger to the club within the club. The Squire attended close to fifty Tuesday-night dinners. His preferred dessert was a scoop of ice cream "the size of a golf ball," as he put it. A master of portion control, and ninety-seven when he died.

Sarazen's Masters win made him the first player to complete the career grand slam, not that any of the Golden Age scribes used the term that way then. The modern, professional Grand Slam—the Masters, the PGA Championship, the U.S. and British Opens—wasn't a thing yet. Eventually, Hogan did as Sarazen had done, winning all four professional majors over his career. (Hogan played in one British Open and won it.) The next to do it was Player, followed by Nicklaus, then Woods. Nicklaus was the first person to do it twice, and then he did it a third time. Tiger matched him in 2008, when he won his third U.S. Open. Two men with three career grand slams, and nobody else has two. That tells you something about modern transatlantic air travel and how dominating Jack Nicklaus was in his era and how dominating Tiger Woods has been in his.

Tiger, the only player to win the four modern majors in a row, knows all that. He won the 2000 U.S. Open, British Open, and PGA Championship, and the 2001 Masters. The Tiger Slam, in some circles. Tiger's retort: "Call it what you want. I got the four trophies on my mantel." He had the trophies, and he knows every name on them. He's not a true historian, as Crenshaw is. But he knows a lot. He knows about the golfers before him like Mike Tyson knows the great boxers through time. Golf does a good job at handing down the game, one generation to the next. There are members of the Tuesday Night Supper Club who know the story of Beau Jack, an Augusta caddie and shoeshine man in the 1930s who, staked by Bob Jones and other members, became the lightweight champion of the world in the 1940s. The fellas don't go to the dinner intending to preserve the game's oral tradition. It just happens.

Sushi and seafood are served on the second-floor porch as appetizers, and the first course of dinner is served at half past seven in The Library. There's a fine portrait of Cliff Roberts done by Eisenhower and there's Jones memorabilia on the walls, and a collection of golf books. Everybody eats at one long rectangular table. There's no assigned seating, not even for the winner, but guys tend to sit in the same spot each year, with allowances for new arrivals and RIP departures. After Arnold died, Tom Watson moved beside Nicklaus. Tiger sits to Jack's left. Mark O'Meara sits next to Tiger.

In Tiger's early years as a pro, he and O'Meara were close. They both lived at Isleworth, where they wore out the range and the course together. Many pros had a fantasy of having what O'Meara had: a perfect backswing. He also had a pretty wife, a big house, a refrigerator filled with food, TVs with working remotes, and fun kids who treated Tiger like an older brother. (Tiger and Mark's son Shaun, who grew up to be a deeply bearded sales director for a deeply funky clothing line, have continued to be friends.) When Tiger was in his twenties and early thirties, he and O'Meara compared notes on investment strategies and swing thoughts and fishing lures. It was a period in their lives, and lives change. Tiger got married. O'Meara got divorced and moved to Houston. Tiger ran over a hydrant, got divorced, and moved to Jupiter. He and O'Meara drifted.

In the telling and the retelling—in the fishbowl of Tour life—it became more than that, especially after Woods didn't go to O'Meara's induction into the World Golf Hall of Fame. The induction was timed to coincide with the 2015 British Open at St. Andrews. It was held in a magnificent concert hall a half mile from the eighteenth green of the Old Course. Tiger was in town for the Open, and he knew how much it would mean to O'Meara for him to be at the Monday-night ceremony. He no-showed, and O'Meara didn't mention him in his speech. It says a lot that Tiger had no one in his life to tell him he had to be there. As for O'Meara, nobody had to explain to him what everybody knew, that Tiger can be as cold as Fargo in February. O'Meara knew that Tiger's game was AWOL, that he was in pain, that he despised the staring that came his way at any public outing. Still, O'Meara was hurt. How could he not be?

But the following April, there they were at the Tuesday dinner, sitting side by side. And the year after that and the year after that and the year after that. Golfers are creatures of habit. To get good at golf, you have to be. When O'Meara won the 1998 Masters, it was Tiger who slipped the coat on his shoulders.

If the past holds, and it usually does in golf, Tiger and Mark will continue to sit next to each other at that dinner until the day comes when one of them is no longer there.

• • •

Down the table from Woods and O'Meara is the praise-the-Lord, pass-the-biscuits section, where Larry Mize, Bernhard Langer, and Zach Johnson sit together. Olazábal sits near some of the other European players. Woods is across the table from him on a diagonal.

The players are invited to tell the chairman their candid feelings about anything related to the course or the tournament. (Seve, especially, never held back.) The chairman listens and nods and takes various matters under advisement. He offers remarks.

Tiger is a fast, head-down eater, and he's never been one to linger at these dinners, even in the best of times. At the 2017 dinner, he was so uncomfortable that he could barely sit, and he was out the door early. He had a plane waiting for him, not that anybody knew. But at the Patrick Reed dinner, Tiger didn't seem to be in any rush at all. The main course was bone-in cowboy rib eye. *Good choice, Pat.* Tiger served cheeseburgers one year, steak fajitas another, porterhouse steaks twice. He was enjoying himself. What a difference two years can make. He was old at forty-one and reborn at forty-three.

When Jack was forty, he won the U.S. Open and the PGA Championship. At forty-one and forty-two, he played in all eight majors and had five top-ten finishes. He was going strong. Tiger's body in 2017, at forty-one, was crying uncle. He was in pain when he told Gary Player he was done. When Player told Nicklaus what Tiger had said, sorrow washed over Big Jack. Nicklaus wanted to keep his records, of course: the only player with six green coats, the only player with eighteen majors. But he also wanted Tiger to have the chance to go down swinging.

Tiger flew off for a medical consultation that night. Then came surgery, an arrest, a reckoning. The win at East Lake, Bobby Jones's childhood playfield in Atlanta, followed by a Ryder Cup in Paris where Tiger was running on fumes and the Americans got trounced. A January, February, and March with a normal, full schedule for the first time in six years. And now it was April again, and Tiger was seated beside Jack Nicklaus, right on schedule, in their customary seats, at their once-a-year dinner. Jack was struck by how positive Tiger was, how confident. "Almost, *almost* cocky," Jack said later. "And I have never seen him cocky."

"You're swinging so well," Gary Player said on that Tuesday night. He's prone to hyperbole, but Tiger knew those words were true.

"I'm not finished yet," he said.

•   •   •

Tiger was on the range Wednesday morning and it was hard not to gawk. It's not just that Tiger's swing had far more majesty to it than, say, Alex Noren's, one spot over. It's his physique. It's knowing his history in golf intimately. It's the distinctive roundness of his swing. It's how his divots fly toward eleven o'clock because his clubhead comes from the inside, is square at impact, and then closes and turns left as the ball gets launched. Grass blades rise and fall like a pale green firework. The strength and speed Tiger brings to his driver swing is mesmerizing, but once the ball is launched it sails incongruously like a runaway balloon—it floats. Then there are his midirons. With Tiger, and almost nobody else, you'd rather watch him hit a 5-iron than any other club. One clipped shot after another, with metronomic rhythm.

But the biggest impression from watching him, what lulls you into a golf dream state, are the intangibles. Tiger catches a golf ball tossed to him by Joe LaCava, and it looks particularly effortless. It happens a thousand times a day, up and down the range, but it's only with Tiger that you take special notice. As you do, the mind drifts. LaCava suddenly becomes Jerry Grote, and Tiger becomes Tom Seaver. (You can supply your own names, of course.) Tiger sips coffee and a mental snap of Nick Foles shows up, in a stadium tunnel, his large right NFL hand overwhelming a Styrofoam cup. Tiger has an easy chat with John Wood, Matt Kuchar's caddie, and now John McEnroe is saying hi to Mary Carillo at Vitas Gerulaitis's funeral. (I've always been drawn to backstage ease.) Tiger catches a ball from Joe, tees it up, launches another drive. We don't know, and we likely never will, what all he had to do to get there. But there he was.

You knew he could contend, the way he was swinging, with so much speed, balance, and swagger. If you didn't know, you'd never guess that the author of those swings was a middle-aged man with a bad back, flying solo (no teacher) for the first time in his life. Yes, he was using many of the bits and pieces he had absorbed through his life in the game, lessons from his father, from his childhood teachers, from Butch Harmon and Hank Haney and various others. But for the first time in his life, Tiger could say he owned his own swing. To every trophy-hoisting golfer who came before Nick Faldo and Greg Norman, that would sound like New-Age nonsense. Own your own swing? How could you *not?* Jones, Sarazen, Hogan, Snead, Palmer, Nicklaus, Trevino, Watson et al. owned their own swings, and when something went wrong, they could fix it themselves, even during a round. There was once a time when motorists could fix their own flats, too. But Tiger had come up in a different era. On any PGA Tour practice tee, from the mid-1990s and on, you could cut through the fog of teacher-student codependence with a 1-iron, if you could find one. So much young-adult talent, so much arrested adolescence. Tiger's present was golf's past.

Tiger was once Exhibit A for teacher dependency. While on the practice putting green before the first round of the 2007 Masters, Tiger, struggling with his short putting, said to Hank Haney, "You better fucking figure something out before we get back here." (From Haney's excellent book, *The Big Miss*.) It's a surprising comment, because there has never been a better fast-green, short-range putter than Tiger.

The mere presence of an instructor at tournaments was newish. Jack Nicklaus, in his life, never had a teacher anywhere near him when he was preparing to play a tournament round. And here was Tiger, forty-three and trying something new, at least for him: DIY golf. *No swing coach.* Tiger's new status as an independently owned and operated golf pro was a significant development, for him and maybe for the game.

The best moment of that Wednesday on the range came when Tiger and José María Olazábal gave impromptu master-class lessons to each other on how to pitch a golf ball. Not just how to pitch a golf ball but how to do so at Augusta National, which is slightly different than pitching a golf ball anywhere else, because the Augusta turf in mid-April is tight and grainy, and the Augusta fairways, and especially the greens, have so much slope and movement in them. Also, those pitch shots sometimes have to carry wide, deep bunkers with raised lips. Nobody has ever won a Masters without pitching the ball well. Augusta National is the opposite of a traditional U.S. Open course. At a U.S. Open, you can keep score by counting the number of fairways and greens you hit, but at a Masters you cannot. Ever since his first trip to Augusta, Tiger wanted what Olazábal had: pitch-shot magic.

As an amateur on the cusp of prodom, Tiger was greedy. He wanted John Daly's length and Fred Funk's accuracy. He wanted Davis Love's long-iron game and Jeff Sluman's bunker game. And he wanted Olazábal's pitching, chipping, and putting game, which he ranked ahead of even Phil Mickelson's. Once, while waiting on a tee at Torrey Pines, Tiger said, "Phil can do more spectacular stuff, but day in and day out, he can't hold a candle to Ollie."

That Wednesday, Tiger was watching Olazábal, older by a decade, play pitch shots in the short-game area on the clubhouse side of the tournament range. It consists of several greens and bunkers surrounded by a half-acre of perfect turf. The conditions mimic exactly what the players find on the course.

Olazábal pitched one exquisitely. Tiger watched and said, "I don't think I have that shot, Ollie."

"Don't try to bullshit me, Tiger—I know who you are. You've got every kind of shot."

There is an underlying closeness between them, even if they aren't in each other's lives on anything like a regular basis. Golf has a lot of that, another by-product of the private nature of the game. It rarely produces extrovert superstars. Yes, Walter Hagen, Arnold Palmer, Phil Mickelson, and Greg Norman were extroverts. But close to the vest is more common: Bobby Jones, Ben Hogan, Mickey Wright, Billy Casper, Tom Watson, Nick Faldo, Nick Price, Curtis Strange, Bernhard Langer, Vijay Singh, Annika Sörenstam, Brooks Koepka. Lee Trevino, believe it or not. Tiger Woods.

Tiger responded by dropping a ball from the spot where Olazábal had just played and practically holing the shot. Olazábal's nod said it all. *Of course.*

They then spent twenty minutes talking shop. They talked about how pitch shots and chip shots at Augusta are different than they are anywhere else in the world. They discussed how sticky and grainy and tight the fairway turf is at Augusta. How you seldom get a level lie. How the grain is typically against the player. How the margin for error is zero. They talked about ball position, about the steepness of the downswing, about holding off the follow-through. They talked about how you have to read the grain twice at Augusta when playing a pitch shot, once at address, a second time where the ball will make landfall. They talked about wedges: their leading edge, their bounce, their scoring lines. There on the range were two of the best wedge players ever. Two magicians, each performing for the other, unaware that they were drawing a crowd.

· · ·

In his thirties, Tiger started getting wistful about his two years at Stanford, remembering how he'd bonded with his teammates, noting the pleasure he took from being exposed to Western Civ. There must have been some revisionism going on. He was raised as a child soldier, trained to do only one thing, which he did with lethal efficiency, reporting to the lieutenant colonel, retired. You don't just bury your lone-wolf training at the first team meeting. Those college kids in the 1990s loved the path to adulthood that *Animal House* captured. Tanks on beaches, out. Sofas on frat-house lawns, in. But you were never going to find Tiger on that sofa. You can't expect to keep up with Otter all night and shoot 66 the next day with Nike and IMG watching.

Tiger owes his life to the Vietnam War. No American military presence in southeast Asia, no Tiger. His tough immigrant mother came out of it, and his doting retired-colonel father. Tom Watson went to Stanford in the late 1960s as a midwestern aristocrat. Tiger went as a first-generation American. He wasn't going to go to Stanford to *hang*. But nothing could have prepared him for being on the team bus with this Notah guy, with his hoop earring and his great black hair and all his dripping charisma, giving Tiger shit about something—and like *that* everybody's having the *best* time and using the word *classic*. Days at U. But for Tiger, it was all fleeting, and not connected to the larger task at hand. Do you think any of us can really understand his early years, his high school years, his college years? Not likely.

In April of his freshman year, Tiger was the only player in the Masters field wearing a Stanford hat. He was in Butler Cabin on Masters Sunday, the low amateur in the year Ben Crenshaw won his second green coat. Tiger was wearing a Cardinal Red shirt. Jim Nantz asked him about his college plans, and Tiger said, "I'm going to go all four. I feel it's right for me to live it up a little bit. You're only young once, and college is such a great atmosphere, and I really love it there." It was as if he were reading off a teleprompter.

That was the 1995 Masters, Tiger's first. He was the reigning U.S. Amateur champion, and José María Olazábal was the defending Masters champion. By tournament custom, they played the first two rounds together. Olazábal saw Tiger's extraordinary length. Tiger saw Olazábal's short-game magic. Length is length and hard to teach. Olazábal had Augusta's real money shots. They're more learnable. Tiger stayed close.

"I remember a practice round with Seve and me," Olazábal told Juan Luis Guillen, a Spanish golf writer. "We were hitting balls on the range and Tiger asked us if he could play with us." This was in 1996, Tiger's second and last Masters as an amateur. "Tiger had a lot of questions for us. We spent a lot of time hitting approach shots around the green and putting. He asked about technique, how we control the trajectory of the ball. He was particularly interested on how we put spin on the ball, the physics behind it." Tiger had found his people. They didn't want a thing from him, and Olazábal and Seve knew things that Tiger did not. Does this Tiger Woods sound anything like a kid who is going to wander a campus at midnight trying to find Theta house?

Tiger was back at the Masters a year later, as a pro, and that was when he won by twelve. The hug shot made the cover of *People*. That didn't make it easier for him to find a peer group. It made it impossible. There was no peer group. At least Ollie and Seve understood Tiger's desire to pitch it better. They could bond over that.

When Seve died in 2011—fifty-four, complications from a brain tumor—Woods immediately recalled that long-ago practice round at Augusta. "To hear him explain how to hit shots around there, it was just artful," Tiger said. He was at the Players Championship, at TPC Sawgrass, a course for which Seve had no use. "How much spin you need to put it here, and where you need to land it," Tiger said. "He looked like he didn't try to do anything mechanical. He just understood it." In his short eulogy, Tiger showed how much *he* understood. There was so much humanity in it. Seve was a friend. Not in the conventional sense, but more than we know.

. . .

The Golf Writers Association of America has an annual dinner on the Wednesday night before the first round of the Masters in a county-owned catering hall, practical but charmless, called the Savannah Rapids Pavilion, on the Savannah River, with South Carolina on the other side. It's about a fifteen-minute drive from the club in normal conditions, but Washington Road is hard to predict during the Masters. There are about a thousand members in the association (most of them not active writers), and about three hundred people, members and guests, attend the dinner. The night starts with a long cocktail hour and is followed by a long dinner, and before the night is out, a hundred different people will get shout-outs for something. One of Rick Reilly's patented moves was to run to the stage on his slippery loafers, to minimize the dead time between his name being called and the dreadful silence after the last clap has been clapped.

Tiger has won the GWAA's Male Player of the Year Award ten times, and one year he won the Charlie Bartlett Award for "unselfish contributions to the betterment of society." You could write a book about the Tiger Woods Foundation's good works. For starters, about eight thousand kids are part of its after-school programs. Earl Woods understood from childhood that education was the great societal equalizer, but when he and Tiger started the foundation in 1996, its main focus was junior golf, particularly exposure to the game for kids who didn't come from traditional golfing families. It was Tiger, in the aftermath of the September 11 attacks, who redirected the foundation's emphasis toward the classroom. Selling that to Earl was easy, as Earl was a believer. One of the first things Tiger did as a pro, Earl beside him, was to start the foundation. Tiger's Charlie Bartlett Award was a long time coming.

Tiger doesn't stay for these Wednesday-night dinners, not even for the salad course. Typically, he arrives deep into cocktail hour, collects his hardware early in the proceedings, makes some quick and often bland remarks, and leaves. Really, it's surprising he comes at all. He starts work early on Thursday, no matter what time he goes off.

Still, if his name is on the program, he does his part. He shows, he grips, he grins, he splits.

He might have skipped the 2010 dinner, as he was returning to public life with the spotlight of his scandal still on him. He was invited to that dinner to accept his award as Player of the Year for 2009. After all those *New York Post* covers, and the lunchtime sermon earlier that day from Billy Payne, the Golf Writers dinner had to be about the last thing he wanted to do. But he showed.

Tiger had no reason to attend the next eight dinners. Despite his five wins in 2013, the GWAA voted Adam Scott as its Male Player of the Year, even though Tiger's year, in terms of wins and near-wins, was better. But that was the year of the rule book for Tiger. That was the year Brandel Chamblee gave Tiger a report-card F for being "cavalier" with the rules. When all the ballots were tallied, the GWAA voters revealed their collective conscience.

For half a decade Tiger went dark. Not getting a GWAA dinner invitation was the least of his concerns. Joe LaCava was home in Connecticut for most of it, looking for a wall to paint, making an occasional inquiry about a job outside of golf, surely worried about health insurance and tuition payments and the normal stuff of middle-class life. Who knows what Tiger was doing. By mid-December of 2017, there were 1,198 players in the world better than Tiger, according to the official world-ranking list. That's what happens when you're a professional golfer not playing professional golf, even if you're Tiger Woods.

Then came 2018.

It wasn't like he flipped a switch. There is no switch. But in the excessively hot summer of 2018, Tiger contended for those two major titles, the British Open and the PGA Championship, fused back and all, before winning the Tour Championship at East Lake. He had played frequently and well. He was carrying himself in a different way. At the end of the year, the Golf Writers voted to give him the Ben Hogan Award, presented annually to the person "who has continued to be active in golf despite a physical handicap or serious illness." Tiger's bad back was one of his qualifying credentials.

Tiger drove himself to the Savannah Rapids Pavilion, right on time, as per usual. He watched the Brooks Koepka highlights video and listened to Koepka's Player of the Year remarks. Then Bob Harig, a former GWAA president, introduced the Hogan winner. Tiger came to the lectern. Trim blue blazer, black button-front shirt. Blue curtains behind him. No tie, easy manner, looking up. He gripped, he grinned, he opened with a joke: "How come I didn't get a video? I got Bob Harig."

And then he did what he almost never does. He told a story straight, from his life, without a moment of sarcasm, in no rush to go anywhere. Along the way, he expressed appreciation to Rickie Fowler, Justin Thomas, and Dustin Johnson. To Johnny Miller, newly retired from NBC, getting a GWAA award that night for contributions to the game. To Doug Ferguson, the AP golf writer, getting the PGA of America's Lifetime Achievement Award in Journalism that night. To Mark Steinberg and Glenn Greenspan. He talked about the Presidents Cup played at Liberty National in September 2017, where he was an assistant captain. He spoke for five minutes, without notes, and here, edited slightly, is what he said:

As Bob so eloquently put, I was done—at that particular time.

In order to actually come to the Champions Dinner, I had to get a nerve block. Just to be able to walk and come to the dinner. But it meant so much to me, to be part of the Masters, to be part of the Champions Dinner. I didn't want to miss it. And it was tough. It was uncomfortable.

I ended up going to England the next day—actually, that

night, after the dinner. I saw specialists there. And they recommended that, unfortunately, the only way for me to get rid of the pain was to have spinal fusion surgery. And so we decided to go to Dr. Richard Guyer, in Texas. And I had the surgery.

It was not a fun time. It was a tough couple of years there.

But I was able to start to walk again. I was able to participate in life. I was able to be around my kids again and go to their games and go to their practices, take them to school again. Those are all things I couldn't do for a very long time.

Golf was not in my near future, or even the distant future. I knew I was going to be a part of the game, but playing the game again? I couldn't even do that with my son, Charlie. Couldn't even putt in the backyard.

After the surgery, lo and behold, I started to feel a lot better. I was able to start putting. Dr. Guyer gave me the okay to start chipping.

At the Presidents Cup, my spine hadn't fused yet, so I had to wait another couple of months before it was fully fused. And he gave me the okay to start swinging.

He says, "You can start ramping up."

"Yeah, okay. What does that mean?"

"You can start hitting drivers here in probably about two weeks."

Tell you what: I hit driver in two weeks. Let's say that first driver carried maybe ninety yards. I was a little apprehensive about going after a driver. I didn't want to go back into that situation I had been experiencing for a couple years there. But I started ramping up. I started playing. I started getting the feel for the game of golf again.

Being around the young boys at the Presidents Cup was a blast, and their energy was infectious.

I was then able to start playing some practice rounds at home with JT, Rickie, DJ. And they were fantastic. They really helped me along and got me into the process of playing competitive golf again. Eventually, I started gaining confidence. I started playing tournament golf.

Lo and behold, I put myself in contention in Tampa. I put myself in contention in a couple major championships. And I finally put it together at the Tour Championship.

I wouldn't say this is an amazing story.

But I do have to say that in order to have had the success I've had, I've had a lot of support. From Steiny and Glenn over here. From people who have been close to me and have really supported me.

As I've come back and started playing again, and being a part of the game of golf at this elite level again, it's good to see all of you, and all the writers who have followed me and have written some really nice articles, and really supported me, and have given me just some great words over the past year and a half. I can't thank you enough.

It's meant a lot to me, to be able to receive this award, after its namesake. What Mr. Hogan went through, and what he did, what he was able to accomplish post-accident, is truly remarkable. And just to have my name on this list of recipients is truly special.

To all the recipients here, for all the work you have done—either serving the game, participating in the game, growing the game of golf—I say congratulations to all of you.

And to all the golf writers who voted for me to be a part of this: Thank you for all the hard work and the dedication that you have all shown over the years. Promoting the game. Growing the game of golf. We are so thankful to have all of you in here.

Johnny, what you have been able to accomplish in the booth. Fergie, what you've done, receiving a lifetime award. These are very special people in this room. And I'm so honored to be here. Thank you very much.

I didn't get to hear Tiger speak live that night, but I watched a video of it later. The blue drapes behind him brought to mind the ones in the background of the clubhouse at the TPC Sawgrass, when he gave a painful mea culpa after leaving the rehab facility in Hattiesburg. That speech, nine years earlier, was an exercise in scripted damage control. This speech was Tiger, the actual man, as he was that night. It brought me to tears. The candor in those five minutes, at least by Tiger's standards. (It doesn't come easily to him.) His willingness to speak about his physical pain. His ability to convey other things—anguish, gratitude, peace—in other ways.

What Mr. Hogan went through. He blinked slowly through the words, and you knew he understood what Hogan had endured, likely in ways we cannot. *It meant so much to me, to be part of the Champions Dinner.* Tiger's gratitude. *I wouldn't say this is an amazing story.* His modesty.

You listened to Tiger and you could tell, maybe for the first time, the extent of his effort to get to the 2017 Champions Dinner, to those back specialists in England, to Sam's middle-school soccer games, to the last hole at East Lake, his fans swarming him.

Tiger, on that Wednesday night at the Savannah Rapids Pavilion, surely was not Lou Gehrig at Yankee Stadium, Independence Day 1939. The Iron Horse was in the early grip of the disease that claimed his life, and still he was able to say these words: "Yet today I consider myself the luckiest man on the face of the earth." Tiger wasn't Bob Jones at Graduation Hall, St. Andrews University, 1958, slowed by spinal disease and still able to tell the townspeople, "I could take out of my life everything except my experiences at St. Andrews and I'd still have a rich, full life." Tiger's remarks were not a study in eloquence. But they were his words, and they were him.

The effort he made in those five minutes, in a room that's always big and typically cold, was moving. The effort to connect with people who have been, as he has been, deepened by the game. To connect with the people who cover him, who celebrated Tiger's end-the-drought win at East Lake with deadline write-ups and smartphone tweets. To connect with people, period.

ACT II.

Tiger was seeing a lot of Bernie. He saw him Tuesday night at the Champions Dinner. He saw him Wednesday night at the Golf Writers dinner, where Langer was collecting the Senior Player of the Year award for the fifth time. He saw him on the leaderboard on Thursday afternoon, in the first round of the tournament.

Bernhard began his round at 12:10 p.m., about an hour after Tiger, and he was on the leaderboard most of the afternoon, mostly because of his front-nine 34. Tiger, on those same nine holes, shot 35, enjoying a birdie 4 on two (common enough) and a birdie 3 on nine (decidedly uncommon). Through the day, he played the kind of conservative golf that has defined the vast majority, and the less telegenic part, of his career.

Tiger's first bogey of the tournament came on that newly lengthened fifth hole, a par-4 that was playing almost like a par-5, if you didn't drive it long and in the fairway. He didn't.

Golfers of every stripe wish they could say they love each of their fourteen clubs as they love each of their children, differently but equally. It's a fantasy. When Tiger turned pro, his driver was the club that gave him the biggest advantage over the field. Since then, the ball has become harder, shafts have lost half their former weight, and the heads on drivers have doubled in size. Tiger's advantage was stripped from him as golf went through a technological revolution in the name of publicly traded profit that has hurt the professional game. (Imagine major-league baseball with metal bats.) Along the way, Tiger's driver, among his fourteen clubs, had become his greatest liability.

The bogey on five began with a pulled drive, left from the get-go. The shot was in the air for all of a nanosecond before Tiger tried to direct it: "Get down." But his golf ball, like an untrained dog, defied its master and finished in the left side of a left bunker. Its lip was so high Tiger couldn't even think about reaching the green from it. He made 5.

He had a different kind of driver problem on the par-4 seventeenth. The hole is wide and straight and only 440 yards, but Tiger has always struggled with the tee shot there, even after the burial of Eisenhower Tree, a grand loblolly pine that had stood menacingly on the left side of the fairway from the day the course opened, though it earned its name only when Eisenhower started hitting it regularly. By the 2014 Masters, just its ghost remained. The club issued an obit for the tree. Death by ice storm, February 16, 2014. For whatever reason, Tiger played the hole like the tree was still there.

A well-designed par-4 is one where good players are forced to think about the hole position as they stand on the tee. Seventeen is a classic example, with a green about as hospitable as the Boo Radley house. It's often sunbaked, and it's sloped like a ski-resort bunny hill. Over is heinous, and short's no picnic, either. A golfer in the Masters needs to hit driver on seventeen to have the shortest possible second shot into it, and with Ike's tree gone, it's wide enough that there's not much to worry about anymore. Tell that to Tiger. He held on too long with the driver, keeping the face open at impact and beyond. The shot had no chance. Every alert playing partner is also an air-traffic controller, and Jon Rahm, one of Tiger's two playing partners, had his right arm up and pointing right almost immediately.

As Eskimos have dozens of words for snow, golfers have a long vocabulary list to describe their worst shots, and under *S* you will find *shank*, *shove*, *skank*, and *skull*. This was a high-order shove job, and you wondered what choice response Tiger might have to it. Where some golfers might mutter, "Fuck you, golf ball," Tiger never does. His admonitions, profane or not, are always and tellingly directed at himself. A mild and amusing one: Tiger, sixth hole, tee shot, Friday round, 2010 Masters, back from the scandal, pulled 7-iron: "Tiger Woods. You *suck*, goddammit." But on seventeen that day, Tiger suffered in silence as his drive scattered fans before settling on a patch of packed mud in a meager forest. As he addressed the ball, the fairway was to his back, wide, sun-drenched, and inviting. Tiger made bogey, his second of the day.

A recurring Augusta nightmare for Woods is the bogey-bogey finish. He did it once, famously. That was in 2005, in the last round, and it resulted in a two-man playoff for the title, which Woods won over Chris DiMarco. On this Thursday, Tiger was third off the tee on eighteen, a humorless par-4 that goes straight up a hill. He hit a good drive, but it took an unlucky bounce and trickled into a fairway bunker on the left. Golf is filled with unlucky bounces and far fewer lucky ones. Tiger has said for years that to win, you have to get lucky. That's true if you win by one, but not when you win by twelve.

It was time to bear down. You're not going to make 3 from where Tiger's ball finished in that bunker. What you want to avoid is 5. Tiger's ball, stamped with his name, was surrounded by bright white sand trucked in from North Carolina. The rules don't allow a player to touch the sand, so Tiger got a feel for it as all golfers do, through the soles of his shoes. Getting a read on the sand is especially important at Augusta, where the top layer is fluffy, with firmer sand underneath. He dug in, he bore down, he hit a solid one. Incredible, really: From 180 yards, and going straight up the hill, he smashed a 7-iron and his ball carried the bunker's tall lip and flew to the safety of the back right part of the green. Could there be fifty people in the world with enough strength and ability to hit that shot on anything like a consistent basis in their mid-forties? Not even close. From the fringe of the green, Tiger made a careful two-putt par from thirty-five feet.

He took off his hat, first to acknowledge the fans, later to shake hands with his playing partners, Jon Rahm and Haotong Li, a twenty-three-year-old pro from China. Playing tournament golf comes with a lot of social responsibilities, no matter where your mind is, no matter how dismissive a golfer may be of the game's social niceties. Tiger has little use for them. But he has figured out how to play the role assigned to him.

He had just shot 70, two under par. Twelve pars, four birdies, two bogeys. It could have been better, it could have been worse. That's always the case.

His two bogeys were born of his two poorest drives, one that went way left, one that went way right. Tiger is nothing if not realistic about his golfing weaknesses. Maybe not in public, but to his camp and to himself. He knows what everybody knows, that a golfer can't win the Masters making guesses about where his miss will settle. A golfer's goal is to turn big misses, unpredictable and unplayable, into playable, predictable misses. Do that, and you have a chance. Golfers are always fiddling, always working on something. Tiger's Friday-afternoon tee time was 1:49. He had some time to fine-tune.

You could say, given where he had been two years earlier, that Tiger's first-round 70 was some achievement. Tiger did not. His thing is now and next. Tiger already knew what he'd be doing Friday morning. Live tournament coverage began on Masters.com at ten, and Tiger would want to know how the course was playing. He'd want to see exactly where the pins were located. You can't know too much. Not every golfer believes that, but Tiger does.

He made the three-hundred-yard walk from the eighteenth green to a room in the clubhouse repurposed for scoring. Ropes went up to create a pathway and a parade route. Tiger nodded to the spectators. He made eye contact. Nothing for most, but something from him.

He came out of the scorer's room wearing a Rolex and a beaded bracelet made years earlier by his daughter, both on his left wrist. He did a quick series of interviews—the car wash—as if he were on a conveyor belt, a member standing beside him and moving him along. Domestic broadcast. Foreign broadcast. Print and Internet reporters, many holding little old-style recording devices, as club rules prevent reporters from bringing phones (with built-in recorders) out of the press building. (You don't want to know what happens on the second offense.) Tiger said, "There's a sixty-one-year-old up there on that board; he knows how to play this golf course." Bernie.

Except for the age reference, Tiger could have been talking about himself. He knew his path to Sunday-afternoon contention was not going to be what it was in 1997, when he drove it twenty-three yards longer than the field average and hit short irons into the back-nine par-5s, thirteen and fifteen. To contend in 2019, it would have to be because he knew how to play the course, and how to read the leaderboard.

Tiger trailed the first-round leaders by four. When Tiger won in 1997, he shot a first-round 70 and trailed by three. When he won in 2001, he shot a first-round 70 and trailed by five. When he won in 2002, he shot a first-round 70 and trailed by three. When he won in 2005, he shot a first-round 74 and trailed by *seven*. He didn't need a perfect first round. He needed a good one—and that's what he had.

Hogan had a recurring dream in which he played a round of golf with seventeen consecutive holes in one, then lipped out on the last. The pursuit of perfection, in golf as elsewhere, is a fool's errand. Tiger shot 70. He wasn't looking for much more.

•　•　•

The first bogey a professional golfer makes in a round is a peculiar thing. After it, the golfer is fallen. In some ways, it's an easier place to be. That's what Jon Rahm saw with Tiger in the second round. "He made a bogey on five, and after that something clicked. He hit fade shots, draw shots, beautiful putting—he was so in control of his ball," Rahm said.

Tiger and Rahm, who looked far older than his twenty-three years, have always had a nice rapport. They know each other because they both play TaylorMade clubs and see each other at ad shoots and at the company's club-testing center in Southern California. Earlier in the year, Woods had asked Rahm what the loft was on his 5-wood. Rahm examined the club's head, where the loft is stamped. Tiger, amused, said, "You have to look?" Tiger knows all his numbers, shaft weights and swing weights, his lofts and lies and everything else. He knows his swing speeds, his launch angles, his spin rates. What Jon Rahm knows is that there's a golf ball near his feet and that it needs to be hit.

Rahm speaks precise, beautiful English, and Haotong has excellent command of his second language. Still, there wasn't a lot of chit-chat over those first two rounds. The stakes were too high.

A half year earlier, when the Europeans had a dominating win at the Ryder Cup in Paris, Rahm had played against Tiger, his boyhood hero, in the Sunday singles. It was the first time he had ever played with Woods, and he couldn't make eye contact with him. When the match was over, Rahm cried. He had grown up on Tiger Woods, and now he had played against him in a Ryder Cup, and he had won. The man-child was a child again.

Friday afternoon was warm and humid in Augusta, with rain clouds and thunderstorms slowly moving in. For Tiger and his back, that was all good. Humid and warm is the weather that greets him more often than not at home in South Florida, and it loosens him. Loose (to a point) is the starting point for length. Speed in golf does not kill. It wins. Tiger's tee shot on the tenth was nearly 330 yards. Yes, it's downhill. Still.

Tiger made a birdie on eleven, the most difficult hole on the course, with three outstanding shots. It only sounds easy on paper: driver long and in play; iron hole-high; ten-foot uphill birdie putt. Bingo, bango, bongo. Three shots that were years in the making.

It took Tiger's threesome about forty-five minutes to play the par-3 twelfth. Tiger stuffed his tee shot, and right after he and the others had to sit in a shelter for a half hour while a thunderstorm came through. Fans were required to clear the course. When play resumed, he missed his five-footer for birdie.

A few years earlier, on the cusp of forty, Tiger told *Time*, "My only peace has been in between the ropes and hitting the shots." Now he was three months into forty-three. He played those last six holes, after the storm, in two under par and in a state of conspicuous peacefulness. There was something so mellow and controlled about Tiger and his play. He drove it great on seventeen, his nemesis tee shot. His birdie putt on eighteen was uphill and turning left and nearly dropped. He could have been mad. He was anything but. He had shot 68.

By the end of the day, he was one shot out of the lead, which was shared by five players. (A big number.) There were three players tied with Tiger and two who were one stroke behind him. For anybody who followed golf closely, ten of those eleven players were famil-iar names. More than familiar. You knew their swings, their stories, some of their wins. The one outlier was Justin Harding, a thirty-three-year-old South African who had made the cut in a major for the first time. Big tournaments tend to have that, an outsider looking to bust on in. "Chuckles and giggles just being here," Harding told reporters. It's possible that Tiger has never used the word *chuckles* in his life, and he definitely wasn't using it that Friday. He was on the leaderboard. He was in the mix. This was getting serious.

Tiger finished at dusk that Friday. The last rain, a sprinkle, had come through as he played sixteen. By the time he came to the eighteenth green, the air was still and the sky was orange. The five p.m. fan evacuation, when Tiger was on twelve, and the lure of happy hour had left the course close to deserted by the time Tiger's workday wrapped up. Those who were still there were all about the golf, and they hugged the man, in a sense, not with hooting and hollering but with sustained applause. Tiger, leaving the eighteenth green for the scorer's room, was smiling like a schoolboy getting a yes for prom. In the nearly twenty-four years I had been watching Tiger play golf, often in person, I had never seen him happier.

· · ·

Golfers try to hide their competitiveness, or that was the old tradition. Tiger didn't and couldn't. On any Saturday, at any tournament, Tiger wants to beat the guy he's playing with. If he's playing well and winning is within grasp and reason, beating his Saturday playing partner becomes even more important. And if his Saturday partner is somebody he doesn't like, that suits Tiger just fine. Golf at Tiger's level requires mechanics, but it requires emotion, too. All competitive golf does.

You almost had to feel sorry for Ian Poulter, paired with Tiger for Saturday and starting the round one shot behind him. Tiger was playing well, and he finds Poulter, as some do, annoying. (Too cheeky, too loud.) Then Poulter had the audacity to show up at Augusta on Saturday wearing lilac pants. Had he not read the pre-tournament memo from Nike that Tiger had already claimed lilac for Saturday, as his color for his third-round mock turtleneck? That meant he owned lilac for the day. Poor Poulter. Tiger likes to beat everybody, but some golfers he likes beating more than others.

The first two days at the Masters are different from its Saturdays, and the Saturdays are different from the Sundays. On Thursday and Friday, the players go off in threesomes. On the weekends, after the thirty-six-hole cut, they play in twosomes. Table setting is done. Play is faster. By Sunday, when there might be twenty players left with a chance to win, the mood is tight and tense.

By Saturday, Tiger knows the course, as it's playing that year, much better. He has adjusted to the speed of the greens and the length of the fairway grass. He knows where his game is and what he can and cannot do. He knows that the better he plays on Saturday, the more judicious he can be on Sunday, and he's a judicious golfer, much more so than it might appear. He starts his Saturday with a number in mind, what he wants to shoot. He's hinted at that many times over the years. What he doesn't acknowledge is a secondary goal, which is to bury his Saturday playing partner. That we can see for ourselves. The greater the beating, the better. One less guy to worry about on Sunday. Tiger invented that mentality. Hogan never had it, and neither did Arnold, Jack, Watson, or Norman. To win a tournament by one or two is fine, Tiger once told Charlie Rose, "but it's a lot better if you win it by five or six."

Saturday's all right for fighting. In one corner, in the lilac T-shirt, the former heavyweight champion of the world. In the other, in lilac trousers, Kid Poults, all the way from England. The first tee at Augusta National—the tee box, in the game's descriptive jargon—is a dead-flat perfect rectangle of green. It was open on one end and lined three deep by spectators on the other three sides. There was a dampness in the rising warmth, the smell of spring earth with it, everybody hatted and lotioned. *Fore, please.* A hushed quiet. *Tiger Woods, now driving.* A round of applause, a moment of silence. The violent click of a graphite driver head smashing into a plastic golf ball at 120 miles per hour. Tiger looked pleased enough. *The sounds of a switchblade and a motorbike.*

·   ·   ·

The 2019 Masters was the seventy-fifth major that Tiger had played in as a pro. In the first forty-six of them, Tiger had won fourteen. In the third round of each of those wins, with one exception, Tiger shot a lower score than his playing partner. That's some burial program. Along those same lines, as an amateur, Tiger won *thirty-six* consecutive USGA matches over six years. That's why Nike gave him that giant payday when he turned pro. As a pro, Tiger won eleven of his first twelve playoffs, which told you that his match-play knockout mentality was alive and well. All those Saturday rounds told you the same thing. He was going to beat the guy in front of him.

At the 1997 Masters, Tiger was paired with Colin Montgomerie on Saturday. Tiger shot a 65 to Monty's 74. Before that round, Earl told Tiger, "Go out there and kick some butt." After that round, Monty told reporters in his authoritative Scots-English accent, "We're all human beings here. There's no chance humanly possible that Tiger is just going to lose this tournament." That was the year Tiger won by twelve.

In 2001 Tiger shot a Saturday 68 to Chris DiMarco's 72. That meant on Sunday, DiMarco would be playing with Mark Calcavecchia, and DiMarco, after what he had just been through, was relieved. "He's a Gator, I'm a Gator," he said that Saturday night, referring to the mascot of their alma mater. "Go out and have fun." A common Tour attitude, but foreign to Tiger.

In 2002 Tiger shot a third-round 66 to José María Olazábal's 71. "It was the easiest sixty-six at Augusta I have seen in all my life," Olazábal said years later. "He dissected the course. I remember the Spanish media started asking me after the round whether I felt I had options for Sunday. I said, 'What options? Haven't you seen this guy play? This tournament has an owner.'"

In 2005 Tiger shot 65 to David Howell's 76. Howell, an Englishman, said afterward, "Tiger is lovely to play with." It was a genuine compliment. It meant that Tiger went about his business, expertly and courteously, and that he gave Howell the room he needed to play his round, even if it meant shooting 76.

On one level, winning a seventy-two-hole stroke-play golf tournament is simple: Just shoot the lowest score. That's the genteel way to look at it. Then there's the Tiger approach: Beat everybody. And if you want your U.S. Open win in June to help you at the British Open in July, *pulverize* them. That's boxing, and that's match-play golf, once you make an allowance for all those *good putt* shout-outs. Stroke-play is the right side of a golfer's brain. It's logic and proportion. Match-play comes out of the left, from the capital of controlled emotion. It's Marvin Gaye singing "Sexual Healing."

Tiger is wired for match-play. He showed his mastery of stroke-play golf, the pro game, when he won that first Masters in 1997 by twelve. Later, sometime in his mid-twenties, with Y2K in the air and his college buddies in grad school, it must have dawned on Tiger: He had both the match-play gene and the stroke-play gene; he was a left-brain golfer and a right-brain golfer; he could simultaneously seize the day and pace himself. In other words, he was like no golfer before him. He had it all.

On that Saturday at Augusta, Ian Poulter, his visor and shirt dotted with endorsement deals, played a nearly flawless round of golf, a sun-drenched 68. He stood right up to the man and played as well as he could. It wasn't enough. Tiger shot 67. Tiger's lead over Poulter had been one. Now it was two. Sunday was coming, and Ian Poulter would be the least of Tiger's worries.

ACT III.

Sunday was strange from the start. On a normal Masters Sunday, the last group of the day is a twosome that plays off the first tee at 2:40 p.m. But with storms moving into Augusta, the tournament's overlords did something unprecedented. They arranged for Sunday's play to be in threesomes, not twosomes. The last tee time was 9:20 a.m.

A normal Masters segues into *60 Minutes,* and the new winner pops into the clubhouse for a toast from the members as they eat their Sunday supper. This Masters would end before the close of lunch service.

Francesco Molinari had ensured a spot in the last group because he was the leader of the tournament, at 13 under par for three rounds. Tony Finau and Tiger were in a tie for second, at 11 under par. In a normal year, Molinari would have played with Finau in the day's last group, and Tiger would have been in the penultimate twosome with Brooks Koepka, who was the only player at 10 under. But the bad forecast changed the fourth-round math, which was a break for Tiger. It's always best to see at close range what the competition is doing. Plus, the winner usually comes out of the day's final group. That's part of the majesty of the whole thing, the winner as the last man standing, long shadows creeping toward him, a bloodless duel, the victor holding not a Wogdon & Barton pistol but a Ping putter destined for a glass-enclosed cabinet.

Brooks Koepka was playing with Webb Simpson and Ian Poulter, going off eleven minutes ahead of the Molinari group. You had to think of the final threesome as the Molinari group, despite Tiger's presence. Molinari had the Claret Jug. He had the two-shot lead. He had played three steady-Eddie rounds. There was only one catch. It was Masters Sunday.

Molinari is from Turin, an hour (by train) to the east of the bright lights of Milan. He is the opposite of flashy. His monotone brings to mind Bernhard Langer or Henry Kissinger. In interviews and in exchanges with other players, he never exaggerates anything. He's the son of a dentist (his father) and an architect (his mother), and his older brother, Edoardo, a trained engineer, is a professional golfer who played on the 2010 European Ryder Cup team, as did Francesco.

When Francesco won Arnold Palmer's tournament a month

earlier at Bay Hill, he was given a red six-button cardigan, modeled on a sweater Arnold practically lived in. (Arnold would push those sleeves up to get the cuffs out of his hands at address. It turned into a style statement.) Asked if he would ever wear the sweater in public, Molinari said, "No, I'll keep it hidden away with the other trophies. I don't need to show off what I've won."

Waking up on Masters Sunday in the house he had rented for himself and his family, Molinari put on a pair of dark blue pants and an off-white shirt with pale blue stripes. A passing and uninvited thought (he told me later) came barreling through: How would the blue and the white go with the green? Did he want that question in his head? Of course not. But we all know how these stray thoughts work. They don't even knock.

Molinari played first off the first tee, followed by Finau, then Tiger, who rose at four a.m. to start his long road there. Molinari's opening tee shot was long and straight, but he made an anxious swing with his second shot, pulling the ball long and left. His third shot, a chip, was poor, and his putt for par nearly died at the front door before falling in. It was a 4 on the card, but not all 4s are equal. You wouldn't call it a rousing start. Anybody could see that, Tiger especially. The applause for Molinari's par putt was merely polite.

Few foreign players have received a warm embrace from the Augusta fans over the years, so Molinari knew he'd be on his own except for the presence of his Spanish caddie, Pello Iguaran. British Open fans are the most worldly in their appreciation, in part because you can get good odds on foreign players at the local betting shops, but also because they just love golf. Masters fans are the most provincial. Tournament tickets—the vaunted badges—are often handed down from one generation to the next, family heirlooms with Augusta roots.

Polite applause was all Seve and Olazábal ever received in their primes. Ian Woosnam, Sandy Lyle, Bernhard Langer, Nick Faldo, the same. Charl Schwartzel and Trevor Immelman, too. Woosnam, on the Sunday of the 1991 Masters, was paired with Tom Watson in the day's last twosome, and there were moments of passing nastiness, by golf's civil code, between the fans and Woosnam. Molinari wasn't getting that sort of treatment. But this was a Tiger show.

Molinari opened with six straight pars, but he was scrambling, and you knew something had to give. On seven, Tiger saw his children for the first time. They had flown up from South Florida that morning. On seven, Molinari made his first bogey. No, that was not cause and effect. It was an old golf adage with Texas roots: "Two things ain't long for this world: dogs chasin' cars, and pros with putts for par." Molinari, looking stressed, missed a fifteen-footer for par on seven. He didn't "undo" that bogey with his birdie on eight. His bogey on seven was a 5 forever. Greg Norman used to talk about that. Bruce Edwards, Tom Watson's old caddie, worked for Norman briefly. Bruce was upbeat by nature, and once, after a bogey, Bruce said, "C'mon, Shark, we'll get it back on the next one." Norman said, "There is no getting it back." That exchange is golf: flights of fancy, baseline realism.

Nobody was watching Molinari more closely than Tiger, except maybe Valentina, the tournament leader's elegant wife. But she's diminutive, and the crowds around the last group overwhelmed every tee and every green, so her view was often obstructed by an XXL Nike shirt and a cup of beer. It's work, trying to watch a golf tournament in person. Valentina could see almost nothing of what Francesco was doing. Tiger could see everything.

"I can see body language," Woods said much later. He was responding to a question from the AP's Doug Ferguson, and he wasn't talking about Molinari at the Masters, at least not specifically. "I can see how well they're hitting it. Guys may hit the ball in the fairway, they may hit the ball on the green, but they've hit two hollow shots. And you know over the course of time they're going to make a mistake. If you get a guy who's flushing it, then we know that sound, too. He's not going to go away." *Hollow* is among the most derisive words in the Woods vocabulary, and there are few words more dear to him than *flush*. Those press-conference comments from Tiger, by the way, are insights he never would have said when he was twenty-three or thirty-three. They were revealing and honest, and they made the game more interesting for any fan.

Molinari had a one-shot lead over Tiger as the final threesome went from the ninth green toward the tenth tee, up a hill and across a mowed greensward, Tiger leading the way, followed by two players and three caddies, along a wide corridor created by gallery ropes. The players get space at the Masters.

The morning was cloudy but not threatening, neither warm nor cool, not gloomy but not *not* gloomy, either. The day was blah, and when Tiger made a bogey on ten to fall two shots behind the leader, it just didn't feel like a day when something thrilling was going to happen. Yes, people always say that the Masters doesn't begin until the back nine on Sunday. But now it was the back nine on Sunday. There was something slow about the course and the golfers on it. Playing in threesomes, which had never happened on a Sunday, was part of it. Everywhere you looked, you saw guys slugging putts and not getting the ball to the hole. The grass on the course's sloping fairways was not bright and blinding, as it typically is, and there was no spring wind whistling through the pines. The spectators were slow to rise to the occasion, their body clocks thrown off by the early start, almost as if it were the first morning of daylight saving time.

It was not a normal Masters Sunday except for this: At the end of play, a golfer would go to Butler Cabin and get a green club coat dropped on his shoulders by the previous year's winner, Patrick Reed.

The last player to win back-to-back was Tiger in 2001 and 2002. In 2001 Vijay Singh got Woods into his boxy coat. The following year, the club's chairman, Hootie Johnson, helped Tiger into the jacket so that Tiger didn't have to do the lifting himself.

"Tigah," Hootie said, "I think we might wear this jacket out, putting it on you, before your career is over."

Hootie struggled in his effort to deliver the coat's right armhole to Tiger's right arm. "Sorry," he said.

"Hey, no problem," Tiger said. "I did the same thing to Mark." Mark O'Meara in 1998.

That coat. It makes people nervous.

. . .

Coming off the tenth green and the bogey Tiger made there, Joe gave his boss a new ball. "Bogey doesn't necessarily mean new ball, but at that moment, it was time," Joe said later.

As the final group gathered on the eleventh tee, up a hill and in the woods, Molinari and Tiger stood as they had at the first, at 13 under and 11 under. Finau had dropped one shot and stood at 10 under. As Tiger watched Molinari, Molinari watched Tiger. A standoff.

There were the other chasers, Brooks Koepka most notably, one group ahead. Koepka had established himself over the previous two years as the brawniest man in the game, in every sense. He was tied with Woods, with the two par-5s to play. A short par-4 and a medium-length par-4 for Koepka, with his extreme length. Molinari and Woods both had an eye on him when he was within eyesight. When they couldn't see him, they listened for him.

At the Masters, you play in a bubble. The fans have no cell phones, so they can't offer real-time scoring information to the players. Rules officials at the Masters stay back and don't talk. Leaderboards are scarce and are not updated in real time. Still, they're critical. Tiger knows the locations of all of them and never misses the chance to study them. When he's between leaderboards, he listens. A birdie roar is more like a group squeal at a second-grade pizza party. An eagle roar is low and rumbly. He tries to figure where the sound is coming from and who did what to create such frenzy.

The final threesome was heading down eleven. To say that eight holes remained would be crass. Tiger knew better than anyone: This play's lengthy (two hours) denouement was just beginning. All the while, an intensely personal real-time documentary was being shot, with the help of seventy-five CBS cameras, about a man, private by nature but famous by deed, trying to reclaim a lost life while starting a new one, and doing so with millions of people watching.

. . .

For those who don't know Augusta well, there are five holes in a six-hole stretch on Augusta's back nine where any shot, including some good ones, can finish submerged in water. Water is in play on eleven, where there's a pond to the left of the green. On twelve, where Rae's Creek runs in front of the green. On thirteen, with a creek running all along the left side of the fairway and then in front of the green and along its right side. On fifteen, where there's one pond in front of the green and another behind it. And on sixteen, where there's a pond in front of the green and on its left side. There are shaved slopes leading to all this water, and every year you see balls trickling down these itty-bitty hills, gaining speed as they plop in and sink to their premature deaths.

Rees Jones, a second-generation course architect, once told me, "Water is the only thing the pros can't recover from." Rees's father, Robert Trent Jones, did work at Augusta National starting in 1947 to make players more worried about water on more shots. He deserves a hand. The Masters wouldn't be the Masters without all those watery graves.

When the contenders get to eleven, you start hearing more references to Amen Corner, Herb Wind's two-word poem. Herb first used it in a 1958 story in *Sports Illustrated* about Arnold's first Masters win.

Herb was a music buff. He took a song title, "Shoutin' in That Amen Corner," and dropped it into his piece as "the Amen Corner." The song is a swing spiritual, if such a category exists, brought to life most notably by a Native American singer named Mildred Bailey, who was encouraged in her career by Bing Crosby, who was a friend of Herb's. (Kevin Bacon must be lurking here.) Herb moved the phrase out of church and into the great outdoors, as it went from church ladies to sportswriters. His prose signpost describes the southernmost corner of the club's property, where the eleventh green, the twelfth hole, and the thirteenth tee are crammed into a nook. The amen part comes if you can keep your ball dry when approaching the green on the par-4 eleventh, when playing the par-3 twelfth, and when playing the par-5 thirteenth. By Herb's strictly kosher definition, Amen Corner ends with the tee shot on thirteen. Still, lots can go wrong from there to the hole, so if you want to stretch it to the bottom of the hole on thirteen, that's okay. Regardless, they should put a collection plate on the fourteenth tee.

Herb revered the Masters and had meaningful relationships with three of its iconic figures, Bob Jones, Ben Hogan, and Jack Nicklaus. He prized his letters from all of them. Herb wrote letters and received them. On a wall in his telephone-booth office at the *New Yorker*, his longtime writing home, Herb had a framed one from Bing Crosby. One part (through the fog of memory) read: "You ask me if I'm playing much. Only days." When Herb retired in 1990, I gave him a CD with "Shoutin'" on it. Poor choice, format-wise. I should have found an LP.

Herb was fascinated by Tiger but never had the chance to write about him. One of the last U.S. Opens Herb covered was the 1985 edition, when T. C. Chen of Taiwan finished one stroke behind the winner, Andy North of Wisconsin. Near the end of a long piece, Herb wrote, "Naturally, I would have liked to be present when a golfer from the Orient first broke through in our championship."

Fifteen years later, in the U.S. Open at Pebble Beach, Tiger, who by background is more Thai than anything else, sort of became that golfer. Herb was living in a nursing home outside Boston then, following the game as best as he could. The U.S. Open was a holy week for Herb, and the Masters was even holier.

. . .

Many observers have focused on how important it is to avoid three-putt greens at Augusta in order to win there, and it is. However, keeping your ball dry on the back nine on Masters Sunday will make or break your day, too. Granted, it doesn't sound like the most exciting of goals, but consider the year when Warren Buffett invested in brick and other durables and said, "Try to contain your excitement."

Since 1948, only three golfers have taken Sunday penalty shots from the back-nine creek and ponds and gone on to win the tournament: Gary Player in 1961 and Tom Watson in 1981, both on thirteen, and George Archer in 1969, on fifteen. In 1948 Claude Harmon hit it into the creek on thirteen but was able to play it out and save par. He won by five shots, then a record. His son Butch was four years old and was being raised in a house that was all golf. Claude is an important piece in the puzzle of the 2019 Masters. Claude begot Butch, and Butch, you could say, begot Tiger. Butch's understanding of Augusta National is in his bones, and he passed on to Tiger what he could.

Today the best description of how to play Amen Corner comes straight from Tiger's mouth, in an interview he did for the club. "God help you if you ever have a little wind blowing through there," he said before breaking down the pieces (slightly edited here). "It's gusty and it's blustery, and you don't know what direction it's coming from. Anything can happen, and it has happened, and it will continue to happen."

On eleven: "I've seen balls hit off the big slope, short and right of the green, and actually go into the water. If you play it in sixteen for the week, you're doing great."

On approaching the twelfth tee: "People appreciate their past champions, and the ovations we've gotten over the years—it's pretty incredible. I'm trying to appreciate the ovation, but also, out of my left eye, I can sometimes catch which way the wind is going. I like watching guys hit on twelve when I'm on eleven, if we get a chance. See how they hit it, how they react, how high the ball was, and where did it go. If I'm able to get three looks at it, I usually have a pretty good idea. But a lot of times I think it's useless, because the wind's going to change by the time I get over the golf ball."

On playing the tee shot on twelve: "There's a lot of times you just hit it and you think, *Do I say get up? Do I say get down? Do I say be the right club?* A lot of times you just look at it and you know what it's going to do. The traditional Sunday pin is on the far right. We all know the water's in play if you're short. Anything short, it's coming back. And if you go long, it's a tough par. The back bunker is no joke. You've got to be committed to your location, to where you want the ball to end up."

On playing thirteen: "Man, it's a good par-five, but it's the length of a par-four, in the modern game. It just happens to turn a little bit too much, I think, for a par-four. From the tee, you hit three-wood or driver to the corner, or around the corner. I've seen guys just pull out driver, tee it up a little higher, and bomb it over the treetops. It can be done, but it's a risky tee shot. Once you have that ball in position, you're presented with a hanging lie. It feels like I'm in Little League, hitting some high inside fastball that I have to turn on."

On finishing Amen Corner: "You can play it well and just get the wrong wind gusts and you'll walk out of there thinking, *I just hit what I thought were perfect golf shots into each hole, and I got the wrong gust and I'm over par playing these holes.* And then there are times when you can go birdie, birdie, eagle, and play them four under par. And that changes the whole round and changes the whole tournament."

Those comments were recorded and posted before the 2018 Masters. They held up brilliantly for the 2019 tournament.

. . .

The last two water holes at Augusta are the par-5 fifteenth and the par-3 sixteenth. They're not part of Amen Corner, but they're a little two-step dance of their own, dangerous and exhilarating.

The pond in front of the fifteenth green is shaped like a stretched heart, but that has to be ironic. No water hazard at Augusta National is the final resting place for so many good shots. Sergio García once made a 13 on the hole—the octobogey—with five balls in that pond, and not one of the five shots was really downright bad. On the tee, a long hitter is thinking about stuffing his second shot and making an eagle 3. But 6 is more likely.

The sixteenth is only 170 yards, and the one thing you have to do is keep your tee shot dry. In 1996 Greg Norman was leading the tournament Sunday morning, six shots ahead of Nick Faldo, who was in second place. By Sunday night, Faldo had won by five shots, with Norman in second place. It was an all-day funeral. Standing on the sixteenth tee that afternoon, Norman trailed Faldo by two. All hope for him was not completely dead, until his tee shot on sixteen went into the pond.

On the eighteenth green, Faldo and Norman, despite the years of antipathy between them, hugged. Frank Chirkinian, in the final moment of his final Masters, framed the shot perfectly and cut off the mikes. There was nothing to say. Faldo and Norman were completely different in manner and style and personality, but all that vanished in the moment. A golfing tactician from England (Faldo) and a golfing pirate from Australia (Norman) were suddenly long-lost brothers far from home, and they were the only two people in the world who could understand the cruel and lonely beauty of their game. That was Faldo's third coat. Norman never got the one thing in golf he really wanted, but there's something gorgeous about unrequited love. They didn't know it then, but for both men, the serious part of their playing careers ended that day.

None of the amateurs made the cut in 1996. Tiger returned to Stanford and turned pro four months later. The plan laid out in Butler Cabin a year earlier—"I'm going to go all four"—had been ditched. By the time Tiger returned to Augusta for the 1997 Masters, Norman and Faldo, the last of the old guard, had cleared the stage. Golf had changed.

There weren't all that many players for Tiger to beat. Ernie Els, Phil Mickelson, Vijay Singh, Payne Stewart, and a few others were going to have good tournaments. But Tiger was going to have a good tournament at nearly every tournament. "Tiger never let anybody win," Jack Nicklaus once said. Tiger was so dominant for a while that he made winning look easy. He kept reminding us it was not.

• • •

Molinari, Tiger, and Finau were out of position as they stood on the eleventh tee. The three golfers in front of them—Brooks Koepka, Ian Poulter, and Webb Simpson—were already on the twelfth tee, struggling to read the wind. There was barely a ripple on the pond beside the eleventh green, and Rae's Creek, in front of the twelfth green, was still, too. Yet the tops of the trees beyond the twelfth green were heaving to and fro. The air was heavy, and rain was starting to fall. As the forecast said, isolated storms. Amen Corner was about to get one.

Koepka, Poulter, and Simpson were looking up and down and all around. A golfer in conflict, unsure about what to do, is painfully easy to identify. Koepka and Poulter put their tee shots into the wide, still creek.

Play can get out of rhythm on Augusta's back nine, with all those water holes and all those drops. Tiger and Molinari and Finau each made pars on eleven. Tiger was done acknowledging his past-champion reception on the twelfth tee, while Koepka and Poulter were grinding their way to double bogeys on the twelfth green.

The twelfth is a strange, moody, short hole. It produces more sorrow than joy, although that depends on where you're sitting. (As the saying goes, every shot makes somebody happy.) It looks charming and cozy, but with one bad shot, its fangs come out.

Koepka's double was good news for Tiger and Molinari. Big bad Brooks had arrived at twelve tied with Tiger and trailing the leader, Molinari, by two. Koepka left the twelfth green and walked up the hill to the thirteenth tee trailing by four.

Tiger had seven holes left. He was chewing gum, a new habit. You could see his jawline moving with every bite. At times there were beads of sweat on his face, along with a persistent triangle of midchest perspiration on his bright red mock turtleneck. It wasn't the temperature. It was the occasion.

At different times, Tiger was sipping a pink drink from a clear bottle. He was applying lip balm. He was walking with his hands in his pockets to keep them dry. When he wanted the towel on his bag, he either made eye contact with Joe and pointed at it or got it himself. He was a study in conservation.

Molinari had the honor on twelve. He looked tired. He had been at the top of the leaderboard all day Friday, all day Saturday, and all day Sunday. His eyelids were heavy. He was the reigning British Open champion. Now the Masters was his to win or lose.

He stood on the tee of the hole that has, at different times, flummoxed Jordan Spieth, Hubert Green, Jack Nicklaus, Tom Weiskopf, Gary Player, Ken Venturi, and a bunch of others. Tony Lema. Payne Stewart. Greg Norman. Curtis Strange. Curtis once made a hole in one on twelve, plucked his ball from the hole, and then threw it in the creek. Weiskopf used to say he felt naked, standing on the twelfth tee, in front of all those deathly silent fans.

Molinari's tee shot pitched on the slope on the far side of the creek, just as Fred's ball did in 1992. Fred's ball stayed. Molinari's ball dribbled in. The guy standing next to me started clapping. I felt a pit in my stomach. Bob Jones had a written directive to fans about that very thing, a passage that is still given to fans today. That's not golf, clapping for misfortune. I felt ill, and I felt trapped. Everyone at Augusta National that day—the course holds about fifty thousand people—seemed to be standing beside the twelfth tee. Finau played last, and he hit his ball in the creek, too.

Tiger had played his tee shot for the fat of the green, to the degree the green has a fat part. He hit his tee shot on the most conservative line, to the middle of the green. The good news was that it's slightly wider there. The bad news was that you're far from the hole, with the pin on the green's far right. He left himself with a long putt, but his ball was dry. Dry and on the green. Somebody had flipped a switch. The Masters was on.

Tiger crossed Hogan Bridge, a graceful stone arch over Rae's Creek. He did some surveying of the green while his playing partners dealt with their problems on the other side of the creek. The rain and wind had left dozens of little spring leaves scattered on the green. Woods saw some course workers up on the hill beyond the green and asked, "Do you guys have blowers up there or no?" They didn't. Woods started using his putter head as a broom. Every little thing was suddenly so important. Every little thing was suddenly so intense.

Jack Nicklaus, on his bonefishing trip in the Bahamas, was watching. "Tiger was just rejuvenated by seeing those balls in the water," he said later. He looked at Tiger's face and knew what he was thinking: *I can do this.*

• • •

With Molinari and Finau dealing with their problems on twelve and Tiger raking leaves, let's take a quick break in the action and look at how this unlikely threesome came together.

In April 1997, Francesco Molinari was fifteen, at home in Turin, and watching Tiger win the Masters by twelve. He was already a good amateur golfer. That event deepened his interest in the game. Tony Finau was seven, at home in Salt Lake City, and watching the first golf tournament of his life. That summer, inspired by Tiger, he took up golf.

"I was watching and dreaming of one day of playing in the Masters, knowing it would be a hard task," Molinari told me, after the dust of the 2019 Masters had settled. "There were not many Italians in history who had even played in the Masters."

Francesco and Tony were both mesmerized by Tiger. "He was very charismatic. I loved the way he played, the way he changed the game," Molinari said. "He was different. He was like Michael Jordan. He played at another level, another level of greatness. More athletic, more powerful. He could produce the winning shot whenever he needed it. He had a confidence that nobody else seemed to have, and it kept building and building. He was miles ahead of the others. He knew he was going to win, and the rest of the field knew he was going to win. There was an inevitability about it."

As a quick aside to this quick aside, when was the last time you heard a native English speaker use the word *inevitability*, or any word with seven syllables?

At the 2006 Masters, Tiger was the defending champion. By Masters tradition, the defending champion plays the first two rounds with the reigning U.S. Amateur champion. That's why Tiger played with Ben Crenshaw in 1995. That's why Tiger played with Edoardo Molinari in 2006. Edoardo brought his own caddie for the 2006 Masters, his kid brother, Francesco.

Tiger introduced himself to Francesco on the first tee. Francesco, shaking underneath his caddie overalls, almost laughed. He thought, *Everyone knows who you are.* Francesco, a young pro then, remembers a few brief conversations with Steve Williams about who would get the pin. He remembers Tiger's awesome power. He remembers Edoardo hitting a lot of shots that went sideways. Francesco has never reminded Tiger about how and when they met. Not at the Ryder Cups in which they have both played, not at Carnoustie, not in Washington, when Francesco won Tiger's event. "Fate keeps putting us together," Molinari said. "So many of my career milestones are associated with Tiger. For me, it is strange. For him, it is nothing, because he has so many."

On the Sunday of the 2018 British Open, Francesco felt like himself. On the Sunday of the 2019 Masters, he did not. "Probably ninety percent of the people following us were supporting Tiger," he said. "I did have my wife. I understood what was happening, because of who Tiger is, because of his history at the place, because of how much it would mean for him to win another one. It was noticeable for me. They weren't against me. They were for Tiger. I did very well to still be leading after eleven holes."

And then he got to the twelfth tee. Tiger received his ovation as a former winner. Molinari had the honor.

"I was between an eight-iron and a nine," Molinari said. "I decided to take the eight. My line was the middle of the bunker, middle of the green. When you hit one more club, it's easy to take too much off of it. I pushed it a bit. The ball was in the air, and I was looking at it and thinking, *It's not enough.* It's one of the toughest holes in golf. Long and left is not good. Neither is short and right. There's no bailout. I felt the wind was into us from the left, but you don't really know. I wanted to keep it under the trees, to protect it from the wind. It didn't go higher than I wanted. My mistake was pushing it too far right." It pitched on the far bank, it dribbled down it, it died in Rae's Creek. He made 5. Tony Finau made 5. A steady rain was starting to fall.

• • •

The thirteenth tee is up a slight hill from the twelfth green and back in the woods. Spectators aren't allowed there, and for the players, after the claustrophobia of the twelfth tee, it's a moment of blessed isolation. Now Tiger had the honor, and for the first time since 2005, he was in a tie for the lead in the last round of the Masters. He had remained at 11 under par after his two-putt par on twelve, the second a four-footer that looked easy only after it was in. Molinari's double bogey had dropped him to the same score.

That afternoon, at different times, Patrick Cantlay, Dustin Johnson, Xander Schauffele, Brooks Koepka, Francesco Molinari, and Tiger Woods either had the lead or shared it with others. Tiger had two major things in his favor. He was in the last group, so nobody had more holes to play, and he had those four coats. But 11 under was not going to get it done. It had no chance. He'd have to make something happen on his final six. And what was true for him was true for Molinari.

That meant they both had the two short par-5s, the thirteenth and the fifteenth holes, and the par-3 sixteenth, where birdie is a reasonable thought. But they also had the three remaining par-4s—fourteen, seventeen, and eighteen—where a missed fairway or green can easily mean bogey. That's especially true on the final two holes. It's some final stretch, those last six. It really is an artwork, despite all the makeup it requires, and for one week a year, it's a public art installation that brings a lot of pleasure to a lot of people, no matter how much chaos may be unfolding in the rest of the world. It's nice to have the break.

• • •

Tiger hit driver on thirteen. In other circumstances, or at other times in his golfing life, he has hit hard, drawing 3-wood shots there. It's a hook hole with a hook fairway (for the righty). But

Tiger was playing with the body he had, with the swing he had found himself in the back of his closet, with a driver, shaft, and ball designed to optimize *this* Tiger, at age forty-three with a made-by-science back.

He teed his ball about a foot from the right tee marker, a sawed-off pine bough. Scores of other golfers had already been in that part of the tee. The rain was falling steadily now and the turf was damp. There was a hint of rising mud. Finau and Molinari, waiting to play, stood under umbrellas held by their caddies. Tiger was set up for a fade shot, starting it down the middle. Brooks Koepka had teed it up in the same spot with the same idea one group in front of him and smashed one 325 yards, the ball finishing on the right side of the fairway. With the hole in the front right of the green, it was a good place to come in from.

The left side of the fairway is defined not only by winding Rae's Creek but also a dense forest of pines and various hardwoods. Over there is nothing but bad. A ball in the creek or in the trees could cost a player the tournament, and Tiger had warned against left-side flirtation in his *How to Play Amen Corner* instructional video. All through the year, fade tee shots with the driver had been more reliable for him. If his tee shot on thirteen went straight, perfect. He'd be in the flat part of the fairway and have the shortest distance to the hole. If it faded, that would be fine. If it sliced, he could live with that—you can chip it out of the right trees and still have a putt for 4. Anything but left.

Golf is like everything else. You plan. Then real life intervenes.

From the tee, Tiger could see the wide fairway sloping toward the creek, the various trees on the left, the pines on the right, the fans underneath them, standing on a tarmac of fallen pine needles. He made a mighty backswing. He was going to rip it. In his black golf shoes with round nickel-sized plastic cleats, he looked like he was standing in a batter's box. When you're playing well, you can swing as fast as you want. Speed equals distance. On the scorecard, thirteen is a short par-5 measuring 510 yards. The players don't care what it's called. For Tiger—for any of the long hitters, which is everybody these days—it's a chance to be putting for a 3. But the first order of business is to hit your tee shot long and in play. Tiger was at the moment in the round where he had to step on the gas.

He made a powerful transition from backswing to downswing. And as he did, his back foot moved in the mushy turf. "Ahhh, I fucking slipped," he said. His swing path was out of whack. His ball was off its intended path. Tiger was hot.

If you cared—about Tiger, about Molinari, about golf, about second chances—you couldn't breathe.

Finau, with his PhD in these matters, said later that the shot was a toe-hook, starting left and curving left. For two long seconds it was flirting with the tops of the trees high above Rae's Creek. The exact place Tiger said not to go.

If you were watching the CBS broadcast, the yellow and black tracer lines, generated by laser and showing the flight of the ball, showed Tiger's drive sailing left, toward the trees. At the course, the spectators were dead silent.

A CBS camera operator, Paul Padelsky, working his first Masters, was following the flight of the ball perfectly. He was looking at it through his viewfinder, his camera on a swiveling tripod planted on the right of the thirteenth fairway, about 250 yards from the tee. "You know that millions of eyeballs are going to be watching your shot, and it's Tiger Woods, so you have some butterflies," Padelsky said later. "But you're just trying to do your job." Keep that golf ball in your viewfinder. He did, one golf ball amid scores of high-altitude branches.

The tournament likely turned on what happened next. Tiger's ball was at least twenty yards left of where he wanted it. It had toe-hook spin on it, so it wasn't going to suddenly start fading. Padelsky's best reading of his own work was that the ball ticked off a branch, changing its flight plan. Padelsky made a swiveling clockwise turn with his camera to keep Tiger's ball in his viewfinder.

In the space of about five seconds, he could see the three distinct stages of this tee shot: white ball against gray sky, white ball among dark trees, white ball on pale green fairway grass, safe and sound. If you were standing there in the rain, you saw only the finale: the ball landing on the left side of the fairway, taking three small bounces, and coming to rest about 310 yards from where Tiger stood on the tee. Even with earpieces in both his ears, Paul Padelsky could hear the fans erupt.

Tiger was not happy. He took the gum from his mouth with his right hand and gave it a backhanded flip into the azaleas behind him. He knew he had gotten away with one.

He hit 8-iron for his second shot on thirteen from 160 yards. A two-putt birdie. A 4 on his card just the same.

. . .

The Italian Detective, all grit, made a 4 on thirteen, too. He and Tiger both made pars on fourteen. They were both at 12 under par standing on the tee of the par-5 fifteenth. Nobody was lower.

Tiger's birdie on fifteen was out of a textbook. Drive that went nearly three hundred yards, uphill. A crunched 5-iron second shot, full and flowing, 240 yards of pure golfedness, with two yards of draw. He had caught the dead center of the clubface at impact and the heart of the green when it pitched. That's how you play golf. The speed of the swing, his balance through it, the purity of the impact. It was breathtaking. That must sound like crazy talk if you're not a golfer, but it might fill you with longing if you are. He two-putted from forty-five feet. Some 4.

Molinari's 7 on fifteen was a clip from a horror movie. A tee shot shoved into a stand of pines. A rushed layup that went too long and too left, ending on the other side of the fairway. A pitch shot that hit an overhanging tree limb and fell listlessly into the front pond. A penalty shot. A second pitch shot that didn't reach the green. A chip shot for bogey that nearly went in but did not.

Francesco had played so well for so long. Then came twelve, then fifteen. He rushed. He panicked. He shelved for a moment his single greatest tool, his golfing intelligence. It cost him the tournament.

He tapped in for 7 and removed the flagstick. His playing partners still had to finish. A gent through the end.

• • •

Tiger (and his playing partners) made the short walk to the sixteenth tee at 13 under par. For the first time, and by one shot, he was the solo leader of the tournament.

His tee shot on the final par-3 pitched hole-high with draw spin on a green that tilts from right to left, toward the pond. Tiger's shot had a better chance of going into the hole than the water. His commentary, first with the ball in the air, later as it traversed the sloping green and edged toward the hole, was a study in intensity: "C'mon. C'mon. Come on, baby. C'mon. C'mon. C'mon, C'mon. C'mon-c'mon-c'mon." An 8-iron from 170 yards to two feet. Twenty delicious seconds, start to finish.

The lady seated behind Tiger, in a paisley shirt and big white-framed glasses, was going crazy. A bullfrog near the green, bullhorn in hand, was going crazy. In the press building, reporters and food servers and spring-break interns, watching on various screens, were going crazy. On the second floor of the clubhouse, in The Library, a group of men in blazers—including the CEO of the PGA of America, the commissioner of the PGA Tour, and some executives from Rolex—were standing in front of a small, elevated TV. The door to the verandah was open. They heard about the shot, by way of a roar rumbling across the course, before they saw it on that little TV, broadcast several seconds after it actually happened. Then they went crazy.

One floor down, in a corner table of the grill room, Rob McNamara and Erica Herman and Sam and Charlie Woods were watching on TV, going crazy.

Two people were not going crazy. One was Tida Woods, sitting with her grandchildren at that corner table, watching with almost oblivious intensity but showing little beyond that. The other sane person just then was her forty-three-year-old son.

Tiger made his two-footer for 2. He walked to the seventeenth tee, putter in hand. His two-shot lead was about to be posted on a nearby leaderboard, but everybody knew. He looked subdued and alert. He wasn't talking. He was thinking (he said later) about the shot he was preparing to play, one of his least favorite on the course. He was thinking about the final day of the 2005 Masters. On that Sunday, after a birdie on sixteen, he had been the leader by two. Then he came to seventeen and hit a tee shot that was almost off the map. Bogey. On eighteen, he pushed his approach shot into a greenside trap and made another bogey. He had spent his lead. He needed one extra hole to win.

You would really need an unusual mind to take such a nasty flashback head-on and turn it into something useful. But Tiger has never had any use for the happy-talk school of golf therapy, where you try to convince yourself that you like something you actually despise. He's from the deal-with-it school. *Take* that, *tee shot on seventeen!* The golfer as boxer. It was how he was raised.

His drive on seventeen came out of a cannon. No fore-right yells this time. It would have gone *through* Eisenhower Tree, it was hit so hard. A few minutes later, Tiger was standing at his bag in the middle of the seventeenth fairway. He was waiting for Brooks Koepka, on the seventeenth green and 145 yards away, to make his par putt. Tiger suffered in silence, barely moving. He took off his golf glove.

He sipped his pink drink. He put on lip balm. He gave a look to Joe that seemed to say, "Any time now." An impatient man playing a game that requires a reservoir of patience. It can't be easy.

Up in the clubhouse, Rob, Erica, the Woods kids, and their grandmother were escorted by a club staffer from the clubhouse to a clear spot beside the eighteenth green. Mrs. Woods, in her mid-seventies and not a tall woman, walked across the clubhouse lawn and, in a demonstration of her own good balance, stepped effortlessly over a black metal chain without needing or wanting any help.

Tiger made a tap-in two-putt par on seventeen. Some months later, at the end of the PGA Tour golf season, a reporter asked Tiger to name his shot of the year. He quickly settled on his tee shot on seventeen, Sunday at Augusta, when he buried his demons there and the terror wrought by Eisenhower Tree and drove it long and in play. It looked like an excellent drive, for sure, but it didn't look *that* special. It was. "It allowed me to go on to win," he said.

On the eighteenth tee, still leading by two, Tiger hit a poor 3-wood tee shot, a strange second, and a cautious pitch for his third. But he was closing in on it. Near the green, Tiger's gang—Sam and Charlie, Rob and Erica, Mark Steinberg and Glenn Greenspan—were starting to show signs of celebration. It was bubbling up in each of them. They were looking around and at each other. They were making the scene and taking it in. They were two steps ahead. Everybody was, except Mrs. Woods. Her hands were on her grandson, but her eyes were on her son, now well into middle age himself. He needed two putts to win and used them both. Tida Woods was watching carefully. Her son won by a shot. Tiger won.

. . .

Tiger's putt to win was about eighteen inches, and it was the last stroke played in the 2019 Masters. It fell on a Sunday afternoon, getting on half past two, near the normal last tee time at a normal

Masters. Fourteen years after his fourth Masters victory, Tiger had won his fifth. Nearly eleven years after his fourteenth major title, the 2008 U.S. Open, Tiger had won his fifteenth. Tiger's arms went up, and for a moment he looked like a human goalpost.

In golf, as in life, you keep so much pent up, and now he had an opportunity to let loose, with millions watching, and he did. He screamed. It was a scream that cannot be spelled, a scream beyond the confines of language. At the same time, a roar of approval was washing over him, coming at him from all sides in surround sound. Within seconds, despite the continued throaty din of the patrons, Tiger returned to earth and fulfilled his various responsibilities. He picked the ball out of the bottom of the hole—the ball that Joe had given to him as they came off the tenth green—and placed it in his front right pocket. He wiped his lips clean of spittle with his right sleeve. He removed his black baseball cap and repositioned a few wandering hair strands. He wiped the perspiration off his right palm on his pant leg. He gave Finau a soul shake that morphed into a hug. He shook hands with Molinari with appropriate sobriety. ("You're part of a tournament that's going to become part of golf history," Francesco said later, "but at that moment you're just pissed.") Tiger shook hands with their caddies. Then, a half minute into his reign as the new champion, Tiger saw his own man, and he let loose again. Joe and Tiger hugged each other and shoved each other. You know how men can be.

Joe's ultimate contribution to Tiger is not discussing clubs or reading putts. He shows little emotion on the course. He spends a good amount of time updating his yardage book. When it comes to how he's going to play a shot, Tiger doesn't need or want much help. Joe's main contribution is that he's on the team, and Tiger knows it. Joe wants what's best for Tiger. He has no other agenda. He's been practicing loyalty—and its first cousin, stubbornness—all his life, getting in many reps with his various teams: the New York football

Giants; the Rangers; the Yankees in good times and bad. Plus Ryder Cup teams and Presidents Cup teams, and his years as Fred's corner man. Joe knows what it's like to stand in support. Professional golf can be a lonesome business. Ditto for being Tiger Woods. All those people watching him, wanting something from him, trying to guess who he really is, what he really does, where he is, how he thinks. Joe doesn't bother with any of it.

Joe's role in Tiger's life is corporeal. Joe is beside him. He's there. These are physical people who are also smart and practical, driven by numbers and action, not by words, not by intentions. Joe's father and Tiger's father were both schoolboy lettermen who became army soldiers. The fathers knew, as Joe knows, the value of being on a team and what it means to have another man's back. Two weeks earlier, at a Tour event in Austin, an older fan in a crewneck sweater took a photo of Tiger while he was playing a pitch shot. Joe silently pivoted away from Tiger and toward the spectator and ripped the man's hat off his head in one decisive swipe. The man raised his hand. He didn't want more trouble, and neither did Joe. Joe's gift to Tiger is physical. Not as an enforcer (the hat thing was extremely unusual). His gift is his physical presence, and the vibe that comes with it.

In the receiving line on the eighteenth green, Joe was fifth and last. There were thousands of people surrounding the home green, chanting the winner's name. Tiger and Joe looked like a kicker and his holder after a game-winner. "We did it," Tiger yelled above the din. He then walked away, delivering a fierce right-hand uppercut straight into the formerly gloomy air. He exited the stage and lifted his son. He hugged his mother, then his daughter. Everywhere you looked, people were smiling. Mark Steinberg, smiling. Club members, smiling. Camera operators, smiling. There was a waiting line to make eye contact with Tiger. Rob McNamara did and started screaming. Tiger topped him.

When Tiger won the 2006 British Open two months after his father died, he wept in Steve Williams's arms. It was moving, on that warm Sunday night in England, to see Tiger swamped by emotion. And now it was happening again. It would be too simple to say the former was sorrow and the latter was joy. The scream is the great multitasker of human expression. It covers agony, ecstasy, relief, frustration. It's especially useful when you're at a loss for words.

Tiger did a lot of screaming that afternoon. With Joe. Coming off the green by himself. Walking toward the clubhouse, in response to his fans. *His people.* Primal screaming, his mouth so open you could count his teeth. Golf is famously a game for whispering. Roger Maltbie, in the NBC Sports trailers, is the Golf Whisperer. Spectators use their library voices. Players and caddies confer quietly. Golf, Calvinist by origin and reserved by tradition, had never heard such screaming, not from the man at its center. Of course, the game had never seen the likes of Tiger Woods, either. Tiger had won at Augusta, the place where he got the first of his fifteen, and a dam had burst.

If you look at photos of Tiger during that Augusta earthquake, there are some where he looks for all the world just as Tom Brady did, for about two seconds, when the quarterback lifted the Vince Lombardi Trophy at Super Bowl LI, Roger Goodell in the vicinity, the humiliation of Deflategate still circulating in his blood. Tiger and Brady, in victory, both had a look that married satisfaction and vengeance in ways no normal person could.

As Tiger made his way to the clubhouse, the chanting was so loud you could hardly think. Tiger was marching in on a grass boulevard walled in by fans, many leaning in, looking for skin or eye contact but happy enough just to be there. Charlie Woods was trailing his father, until he wasn't. Tiger was making tracks. Forty-three, all those surgeries, all those miles, and if you didn't know, you would have suspected nothing. The adrenaline of euphoria. He was cruising, and his gait was perfect. He slapped hands hard with random fans. There was Bubba, waiting on him. There was Zach Johnson. There was a friend, an acquaintance, a donor, a player, a member. There was . . . who, exactly? It was a blur. He stopped for Bernhard and they shook hands, earnestly. Tiger looked happy. He then went down some steps, made a left, walked through an open door, and disappeared, headed for the scorer's room.

With one signature on his scorecard, swearing to its accuracy, he would become the winner. That's the final act. Not the winning putt going down or the trophy being raised. Not the various post-tournament interviews. Not the arrival of the winner's check by direct deposit.

His final act was to look at the numbers on his scorecard and swear to their accuracy with his signature. The card said 70. A final-round 70. It wasn't perfect, and didn't need to be. What a moment. No cameras, no crowds, no noise. Just a man and his scorecard, checking every number on it, knowing the full story behind every box. Tiger knew what he had done to get there. Nobody else could.

There was a pencil in his long fingers and, at the bottom right of his scorecard, a thin green line waiting for his signature. The only thing left for Tiger to do was sign.

CURTAIN CALL.

Donald Trump didn't waste any time. The first golfer spoke to Tiger the morning after the Masters, which was Tax Day, and a little after high noon sent out this tweet: "Spoke to @TigerWoods to congratulate him on the great victory he had in yesterday's @TheMasters, & to inform him that because of his incredible Success & Comeback in Sports (Golf) and, more importantly, LIFE, I will be presenting him with the PRESIDENTIAL MEDAL OF FREEDOM!"

Had Molinari kept his golf ball dry on twelve and fifteen, Trump's Monday might have been different, and Tiger likely would not have been at the Rose Garden three weeks later for the medal-presentation ceremony. But that's how these things go, at the intersection of politics and sports.

I have written often about Trump and his growing golf portfolio over the years, and have played with him nine times, long before he sought the presidency. (I had something Trump wanted: good write-ups about his courses and their owner in *Sports Illustrated* and its websites. He called the longest of these stories "a B-minus" and said, amusingly, that was the best he could do by me.) He plays quickly and well, but you don't play traditional golf with him. In my experience, matches with him are meaningless, because a real golf match requires precise accounting and uniform rules, even when the real rules are modified. As for the scores he claimed to me, some had to be pure fantasies. (A 68 at Bel-Air? Please.) Golf with Donald Trump is really a different activity, and it needs its own name: TrumpGolf. He's played Augusta National and he's a member at Winged Foot, but he much prefers to play at courses that bear his name. He drives his cart right to his ball, pretty much wherever it is, and he takes mulligans and gives himself putts as he pleases. Innumerable other golfers do the same, except they don't claim to break 80 and to win club championships on a regular basis. He's frequently on his phone while playing, and when he's not, he's selling so hard it can give you a headache. ("Is this not the most beautiful cart path you have ever seen in your life?") Once, while playing in a PGA Tour pro-am, he bellowed into his phone, "I'm here with Tiger Woods," and it was true, in the sense that they were on the same golf course. But he's knowledgeable about golf, and he's an excellent host who is accommodating and warm to his guests. He's also ridiculously entertaining, particularly when making inappropriate observations about various famous people. It's his way of creating intimacy and trying to recruit you. Tiger would likely know this whole routine far better than I.

In my time with Trump, he showed keen interest in three professional golfers: Arnold Palmer ("Now, there's a man"), Tom Watson ("What a man he is"), and Tiger. He said of Tiger, "He has the body of the black man and the mind of the Asian." Yes, it's a racist comment, but my guess is that Trump intended it as a compliment. Trump of course likes him. Tiger is a winner, and Trump likes winners. He named one of his buildings at Trump Doral for him. What was Building 7 is now the Tiger Woods Villa.

Tom Kite was a regular guest in Building 7. Kite played in the Tour event at Doral twenty-three times, starting in 1973, and he liked Building 7 for its proximity to the driving range. In 2012 Trump bought Doral and spruced up the place. Early in 2014, he asked Tiger to come to a ribbon-cutting ceremony to celebrate the rebranding of Building 7 as the Tiger Woods Villa. Later in 2014, Tiger agreed to design a course in Dubai called Trump World Golf Club.

Tiger played with Trump before he was president, when he was president-elect, and during his presidency. Like Arnold and Jack before him, Tiger knows what it's like to play with a president, sitting or otherwise. He's met George W. Bush and logged rounds with his father, and he's played with Bill Clinton, a mulligan-happy golfer, and with Barack Obama, who plays left-handed and with new-convert zeal. A host of famous American golfers have been aligned with the Republican Party over the years, including Palmer and Nicklaus, but Tiger has never revealed anything about his political leanings. Even as he has shown his abiding respect for American military personnel, he has never been political about it.

That's why, during 2018 and 2019, when Tiger—evolving Tiger—said a few things containing trace amounts of political commentary, they stood out.

On one occasion, he answered a question about a Nike TV spot narrated by Colin Kaepernick, the former NFL quarterback who had famously and repeatedly knelt during the National Anthem. Trump was not a fan of either the player or his protest. The Nike ad featured Serena Williams and other athletes, several of whom were missing limbs, and in it Kaepernick said, "Believe in something, even if it means sacrificing everything."

Trump said the spot sent "a terrible message."

Tiger said it was "beautiful."

Another time, asked to name his favorite athlete as a kid, Tiger cited Muhammad Ali, knowing well that Ali is an iconic figure for reasons that go far beyond what he did in the ring.

In late August 2018, Tiger was asked about Trump. Tiger said, "I've known Donald for a number of years. We've played golf together, we've had dinner together." Later, he settled into the normal PGA Tour talking point on the issue, that it's important to honor the office of the presidency no matter what a person thinks of the incumbent's politics. But it remained jarring to hear Tiger refer to a sitting president by his given name. Words don't just slip out of Tiger Woods's mouth. *Donald.*

But in the Rose Garden that night, none of that was evident. Trump was giving Tiger the highest civilian honor a president awards, the Medal of Freedom.

Trump, as president, may never have been more at ease. He read from a teleprompter comfortably, and several times, in unscripted asides, he showed a genuine understanding of Tiger. He noted how Tiger plays the hardest events on the Tour schedule, the historic run Tiger had as an amateur, and how tough Tiger's mother is. Tiger stood beside him, calm and happy.

Before the event, Tiger and Joe LaCava and others visited Trump in the Oval Office. Joe, like Trump, has a rooting interest in the Yankees and the Giants, and they're on the same page in other areas, too—Joe was having a good time. During the ceremony, when Trump offered a shout-out to Joe, Tiger's caddie raised his left hand in a fist.

Joe was sitting in the first row, as were his wife and Tiger's mother; Erica Herman; and Melania Trump. Sarah Huckabee Sanders, then the White House press secretary, sat in the back row, behind Rob McNamara and his wife. It looked like a backyard wedding, with all the guests sitting on plastic folding chairs, except that among the hundred or so witnesses, only about twenty were women. Tiger didn't want anybody from golf's officialdom at the ceremony, so the men who run Augusta National, the USGA, the PGA Tour, and the PGA of America were conspicuously absent. But Trump's list included Eric Trump (son), Jared Kushner (son-in-law), Mike Pence (vice president), and Lindsey Graham (golf partner).

Trump and Tiger were both wearing blue suits with white shirts and red ties, but only Trump had an American flag on his lapel. At the end of the event, when Tiger and his mother and girlfriend and kids joined Trump and Melania for group photos, Tiger was wearing his medal and beaming. Trump pushed down the long microphone stem on the lectern when he realized it was in the photographers' sight line. Charlie Woods, dressed with the preppie ease that was second nature to Bush 41, looked like he was ready to announce his own run for office. Sam Woods, in a dark blue dress with a denim coat over it, showed a shyness and a modesty that her mother and father exhibit, too. On body language alone, you could tell, as you could on Masters Sunday, that Tiger has a true closeness with his kids, one that's unforced but born in effort. He brings them in. He makes extended eye contact with them. He has an unspoken language with them. Erica had selected the kids' outfits. She's a significant figure in all three lives, and she was one of the few people Tiger cited by name in his unscripted remarks.

Erica has led a visible life with Tiger, starting at the Presidents Cup at Liberty National in the fall of 2017. Tiger was an assistant captain, and Erica joined him. It was her first big public outing with Tiger. It was also Tiger's first big public outing since his back surgery and the Memorial Day arrest. He tried to keep a low profile at that Presidents Cup, not that he can ever really do that. The U.S. won, handily, and in victory there were fans chanting for Tiger, the assistant captain.

Trump had helicoptered in for the trophy presentation. He had been president for a little over eight months. When it came time to take pictures with Trump on the eighteenth green, many of the American team members were seeking Trump out, but Tiger was not. During a team picture, Woods was either unaware that the president of the United States was just behind him and about five feet to his left, or he was avoiding him. Trump came over and gave Tiger a big soul shake and they spoke for a few seconds, Tiger leaning his left ear toward Trump's mouth to hear him better amid the noise.

Later, at the winners' press conference, the twelve players, their captain, Steve Stricker, and Stricker's assistant captains all sat on a dais. Stricker and Tiger were conspicuous in their sobriety. (Others had started celebrating.) Tiger was in the yearlong period when he could not legally drink because of his plea agreement with the Palm Beach County prosecutor's office. Karen Crouse asked, "What was it like sharing the stage with President Trump, for anyone who would like to answer?" Tiger closed his eyes for a passing moment and his chin went up. He looked to be in pain. That's what I saw. (He told me later he was not.) Tiger and the others left it to Stricker to raise the flag for respect-the-office.

At the Rose Garden, Tiger had the unmistakable appearance of someone playing a real-life version of *This Is Your Life*. He listened carefully to Trump, who was funny and personable, not bombastic, not caustic. After wrapping up his recitation of Tiger's achievements and attributes, Trump said, "These qualities embody the American spirit of pushing boundaries, defying limits, and always striving for greatness." That was from the script. This was not: "That's what he does." Nobody would disagree with that. Tiger Woods has pushed boundaries, he has defied limits, he has strived for greatness. He has paid for it and prospered from it. He's led a uniquely American life.

Tiger spoke in a low, calm voice, keeping it together, though only barely at times. Golf Channel and C-SPAN covered it live. (More footage for his life on camera.) Tiger thanked Erica, Joe, Sam, Charlie, his mother, his late father, unnamed others who were present. "You've seen the good and the bad, the highs and the lows," he said of that small group. "And I would not be in this position without all of your help." Every word had meaning and subtext.

The whole event, from "Hail to the Chief" to "What a Wonderful World," played by six players from the Marine Band, was barely twenty minutes. Tiger spoke for five. He wrapped up by saying, "I know that I'm the fourth golfer to have received this award: the late Arnold Palmer, the great Jack Nicklaus—and Charlie Sifford. I always called him Grandpa, because he was like the grandpa I never had. And I ended up becoming so close with him that I ended up naming my son, Charlie, after him. And so to have been chosen as the next golfer after Charlie is truly remarkable. So thank you again. And thank you, Mr. President."

He was modest, sincere, appreciative. It was beautiful.

• • •

One challenge of being a reporter on the Tiger beat is the summertime cocktail party. People expect you to say something insightful or original, but it's impossible because everybody knows all about the life and times of Tiger Woods. I've offered, "Tiger's actually more modest than you might guess." More modest, and less comfortable with attention. You can practically hear the gong. Your summertime party people have seen Tiger's half-crazed fist pumps and the aerial photos of his yacht. They've watched him make those slow, look-at-me walks that accompany his can't-go WDs. They know the grand marshal of the stiletto parade was not a study in humility. They're familiar with Tiger's habit of waiting until the last moment—Fridays at 4:59 p.m.—before committing to the following week's tournament, putting all of golf on edge.

Did you say modest?

"For a superstar."

Anybody else need to freshen their drink?

Note to self: Do *not* offer Tiger's Rose Garden remarks as evidence of his modesty. Ditto for his condolence handshake with Francesco Molinari, or his habit of saying "Tiger" upon meeting a stranger for any kind of meaningful visit. People bring a lifetime of experience to their view of Tiger Woods, and any report from the so-called front lines has almost no chance of changing anybody's opinion about anything.

And yet these words are being typed: I believe that, at his core, Tiger Woods is a modest person. Maybe I attach too much meaning to passing moments.

For instance, consider this brief comment Tiger made in Las Vegas the day after Thanksgiving in 2018. It came in the cringy preamble to a pay-per-view, winner-take-all ($9 million) Tiger-Phil match called *The Match.* It was promoted like an old-time title bout. Everything leading up to it was sort of a joke: two rich golfers facing off, the brims of their caps nearly touching. It was painful to watch, especially since

Tiger's first rule of marketing is to avoid the hard sell. (Part of his let-the-clubs-do-the-talking maxim.) Woods wanted the money but not the sales job it required. This was a Phil Mickelson enterprise, and the heavy lifting fell to him, which he performed with his customary zeal. The whole thing was south of meaningless. (Magic Johnson and Michael Jordan were once plotting to play each other in a one-on-one off-season spectacle. David Stern, the NBA commissioner at the time, talked them out of it, on the grounds that it was too tacky.) At a press conference before their match, Tiger was asked what he thought about the odds, which had him as a two-to-one favorite over Phil. The moment called for bravado, in the interest of drawing eyeballs and paying customers. But in a quiet, half-embarrassed voice, Tiger gave a candid answer: "I think they're about right."

Phil won, by the way, on the fourth sudden-death playoff hole. Neither played well. The prospect of playing for nine rocks seemed to leave them both tight. It wasn't great golf but it was entertaining to watch, at least in person. (Home viewers endured a series of technical glitches and were offered refunds.) Tiger did not sign on for a sequel.

Tiger and Phil have a peculiar relationship. Woods has always admired Mickelson's talent, but for years he was crudely and profanely dismissive of Mickelson's physique, his perma-smile, and even his penchant for signing autographs, which Tiger saw as proof of his phoniness. But Mickelson has signed round after round, year after year, just as Arnold did. Whether Phil actually enjoys it or not, he continues to sign and acts like he does. It's been good for golf and good for Phil—but bad for Tiger, faring poorly in the comparisons. Phil might sign one hundred times for Tiger's three. These star golfers are expert marketers, and in marketing your reputation is your brand. Phil's brand is as the witty extrovert who comes at you with a torrent of words that prove his high intelligence. Tiger can't be bothered with any of that. In fact, Tiger seems to have no need to show off how much he knows at all. It's part of his general reticence.

Phil's father, a retired pilot, is reserved. He's as modest as Earl Woods was not. Both men came out of the military. Both were obsessive golfers who raised prodigy sons on public courses in Southern California. But the elder Phil Mickelson was more like Tiger, and Earl Woods was more like Phil. You could imagine Phil and Earl debating the ethics of human cloning or any other subject you might put in front of them well into the night.

Phil would have been jet-rich without Tiger's professional career, but Tiger made him far wealthier, and Phil knows it. It wasn't the prize money—it was how Tiger raised the stakes for endorsement deals, equipment especially, manufactured by publicly traded companies with bottomless pockets. Phil has expressed his appreciation often over the years. Whenever he could, Phil did things to elevate Tiger, but Tiger never returned the favor. He liked the pecking order as it was. They were never sold successfully as a one-two punch, although much was made of their presence together in various team rooms, playing grudge-match Ping-Pong. That didn't make them Arnold and Jack. Arnold and Jack competed in everything and had a deep friendship. They were both rivals and brothers. (Jack was the older of the two, in spirit.) It helped that for some years they shared a manager, Mark McCormack, who kept them on the same page.

But over time, the Tiger-Phil relationship took a turn. In 2016, when Davis Love was the U.S. Ryder Cup captain, Tiger was one of his assistants, and Phil Mickelson was one of the top players. No assistant captain ever had as visible a role as Woods did, and Tiger was impressed by Mickelson's commitment to putting the team's needs ahead of his own. Ever since, Tiger has been going a little easier on Phil. There was more texting between the two of them. But that doesn't mean they were going on ski vacations together.

Tiger, under Earl, grew up engulfed by an ocean of words, many of them profane, funny, or insightful. He could be spectacularly cryptic. (A quickie, from an exhibition Tiger once did, when Earl was getting near his end: Dennis Walters, a legendary trick-shot artist who worked with a dog, batted first, and Tiger third. In between them was Earl. Walters, paralyzed from the waist down, cleared the stage, and Earl came out and said, "I don't have a dog. I don't hit trick shots. I'm just a man.") Tiger grew up on Earl. Earl had theories about everything. Tiger didn't need to hear Phil's.

Phil and Tiger played a rare practice round together at the 2018 Masters. It felt kind of stagy. A few weeks later, at the Players Championship, Phil, Tiger, and Rickie Fowler were grouped together for the first two rounds. A supergroup, golf-style. (Eric Clapton, Jack Bruce, and Ginger Baker, assembled as Cream.) On one hole, Fowler's ball got lodged in a tree. It took him a while to sort through what to do and how to do it. There was a ten-minute period in which Phil and Tiger didn't have much to do. They didn't huddle. They didn't talk.

· · ·

After Tiger's Masters win, he kept a low profile. Tiger and his son, Charlie, a natural athlete with a natural swing, went to Medalist and played out of a cart. It was a father-son outing, but with many stops for Tiger to accept congratulatory handshakes and hugs without annoying requests for signatures or photos. Tiger has a lot of incentive to fly on private planes, to eat in private dining rooms, to stay in private communities when at tournaments, and to belong to private clubs. Hugs are one thing, and phone snaps another.

One night, post-Masters, Tiger and Erica went for dinner with a small group at Tiger's restaurant, and Tiger wore shorts, a black baseball cap with a Frank the Headcover logo on it, a black Nike T-shirt—and a green sport coat that came straight out of Augusta.

One day, Tiger—no hat, jacket on—did a half-hour interview with Henni Zuël of GolfTV. He gets paid by GolfTV—owned by the media company Discovery, Inc.—to do interviews. That is, to "provide content." This is a growth industry for a select group of golfers. (The towel on Tiger's golf bag at the Masters was stamped *GolfTV.*) His interview with Zuël, and all his GolfTV interviews, are not infomercials, but they're not exactly *60 Minutes* in its Mike Wallace heyday, either. Zuël, a young, attractive former touring pro from England, is a superb interviewer, chill and succinct, with a beautiful accent. Tiger signed off on her before she got the gig as his regular interviewer. His ease with her is evident every time they speak. Their half-hour interview was informative and well done, and was one of the very few interviews Tiger gave about his Masters win through the end of 2019. (He declined to be interviewed for this book.) Tiger and his people had figured out yet another way to sell him. Palmer and Nicklaus would talk to anybody about anything, if you timed it right. Yes, it was a simpler time, and the coverage was less intense, but the math was simpler, too. They believed that promoting the game, and themselves, as broadly as possible was part of the job and good all the way around. GolfTV, in spirit and in fact, is a marketing arm of Tiger Woods Enterprises, and will be until the day their contract expires. It's a pure win for Tiger. He gets paid *and* his brand gets enhanced.

· · ·

Tiger was seen walking with a limp after the Masters, looking like an NFL veteran a decade after his final game. He didn't play any tournaments between the Masters and the PGA Championship, held in mid-May at Bethpage Black, a hideously difficult golf course if you're playing out of the rough. Tigermania was bubbling up without an outlet for it. Then, about a week before the PGA, Woods and Joe LaCava, accompanied by Rob McNamara, made a scouting trip to Bethpage, on Long Island, thirty hard LIE miles east of the Empire State Building. To get from Bethpage Black's fourteenth green to its fifteenth tee, this now-familiar threesome had to cross busy Round Swamp Road. A fan caught this passage on his cell phone and offered his own play-by-play in the local dialect: "*Tigah,* we love you, man.

Absolutely love you, buddy. You are the best—*evah*. What a pleasure, man. You are the best, brother." Tiger, buddy, brother, best, love. It was a sonnet, delivered from one man to another. Tiger mouthed his appreciation.

Woods wasn't limping that day or at the tournament, but he was spent from its start. His game was out of sorts, his driving especially, and he looked and sounded tired. He played the first two rounds with Brooks Koepka, who shot 63-65. Tiger shot 72-73. Koepka won. Tiger missed the cut.

The cognoscenti expected him to play better at the U.S. Open, in mid-June, at Pebble Beach. He did, modestly. Gary Woodland shot 271 and won by three. Woods finished eleven shots behind him.

After that, Woods didn't play again until the British Open at Royal Portrush in Northern Ireland, in mid-July. The Open hadn't been played there since 1951, so nobody knew what to expect—not from the course, not from Tiger. Through the week it was often cool or windy or rainy. On one of the practice days, Woods stood on the range, the only golfer on it, hitting balls in a downpour, accompanied by the usual suspects. Steve Williams, caddying then for Jason Day, walked by and offered a group hello. LaCava and McNamara responded in the customary way, but Tiger didn't even look in Williams's direction. Williams was pissed. Another (I would say) instructive mini-moment. Just because Tiger Woods went to jail for a night, followed by rehab for some unspecified time, followed by two wins in Georgia in an eight-month period didn't mean he'd had some kind of total personality makeover. Tiger and his Stevie had enjoyed an unparalleled run together. In his native New Zealand, Steve Williams is both a sporting legend and a philanthropist. But since their 2011 breakup, Williams had done a number of things that Woods didn't like. Most notably, he called a win he had with Adam Scott in a small-field World Golf Championship event in Akron in 2011 "the most satisfying" of his career. At Portrush, in the rain, Steve Williams was making a peace offering, another in a series of them. But Tiger Woods doesn't do forgive-and-forget.

Greg Norman had a similar experience. Two weeks after Tiger's Masters win, he brought a note to Tiger's house. Handwritten, and in all caps, it read:

> TIGER,
>
> JUST GOT BACK FROM A WILDERNESS TRIP.
>
> CONGRATS ON YOUR MASTERS WIN. YOUR JOURNEY BACK TO THE TOP HAS BEEN TRULY IMPRESSIVE.
>
> GO DO A FEDERER.
>
> GREG

Roger Federer, after not winning any Grand Slam titles from 2013 through 2016, won two in 2017 and one in 2018. Woods and Norman are both first-order tennis fans, and both have made stops at Wimbledon en route to the British Open over the years. Norman figured that if Tiger wanted to recognize the spirit in which the note was written and delivered, he would acknowledge receiving it.

· · ·

At Portrush, Tiger missed the cut and told reporters, "I just want to go home." There was something *slightly* sluggish about his speech as he said that. Earlier in the week, he had made comments to a small group of reporters, after flying all night and going straight to the course, and his speech then was slurry. He had sounded similar ten months earlier, at the Ryder Cup in Paris, in an interview with Todd Lewis of NBC Sports after his Sunday loss to Jon Rahm. A few hours after that, at a team press conference, Tiger appeared to be almost falling asleep while sitting upright in a chair. You could understand it, to a point. Woods had played in seven events in a nine-week period, which would be a lot of golf for someone half his age with no back issues. On the Sunday night after his win at East Lake, Tiger and his teammates flew overnight to Paris. He won no points, and the U.S. lost. None of that could have helped. Still, Tiger, playing in rain pants on a Sunday afternoon that was dry and warm, didn't seem to be his normal self.

Jim Furyk, the U.S. captain, had originally named Tiger one of his assistant captains, in a period when Woods was not close to making the team. One day, in a strategy session, Furyk and Woods and the other assistant captains were analyzing how the Europeans might pair their top players over the first two days. There was a lot of back-and-forth until Tiger said, "I've had enough of this. Here's what they're going to do, I guarantee it." At that moment, Furyk could see what kind of team captain Tiger would someday be when he had his own Presidents Cup and Ryder Cup teams: decisive and in control.

Tiger gave up his assistant captain's role when Furyk put him on the playing roster. After Tiger's win at East Lake, it seemed like he would be key to a Ryder Cup victory in France. Furyk played Tiger in four of the five different sessions, twice with Patrick Reed. Woods lost all four times. The Tour Championship and the Ryder Cup in consecutive weeks was too much. Tiger was running on fumes.

But to hear Woods struggle with his speech was alarming, a disquieting reminder of the drug abuse that was so apparent on that Memorial Day night. There are people close to Tiger who worry about relapse. Tiger knows that.

He's an aware person. At the Players Championship, a month before his Masters win, he was making a green-to-tee walk in the third round when he saw a college-aged kid wearing a T-shirt with his Memorial Day mug shot on it. Tiger looked at the shirt with a side glance and almost laughed. "I saw he saw it!" the kid yelled. Celebrity life has never been weirder. A sense of humor helps.

And so does a sense of awareness. About three months after Tiger's Masters win, Thorbjørn Olesen of Denmark, a member of

Europe's Ryder Cup team in Paris, was arrested at Heathrow Airport after a flight during which, among other alleged misdeeds, he reportedly urinated in the first-class aisle of his British Airways overnight flight from Nashville to London. (He was charged with sexual assault, being drunk on a plane, and assault by beating. He offered a plea of not guilty in a London court in December 2019.) Woods heard about the arrest shortly after it occurred and offered his insight in a single word: "Ambien."

If Tiger is in some kind of ongoing therapy for abusing drugs or alcohol or sex, that's his business. Given his reserved nature and his fame, it's hard to imagine his going to meetings with strangers and saying, "My name is Tiger, and I'm—" whatever. He's an inherently private person who leads a massively public life. Contradictory impulses must tug at him every day. Millions of people are fascinated by his public life, and some of those people want a peek at his private one. He has learned the benefits of offering glimpses. It's a tricky business, and a tricky life.

We know close to nothing. Maybe, in Tiger's mind, the most important trip he made in 2019 was not to Augusta in April for the Masters but to Thailand, his mother's homeland, with Erica, his kids, and his mother, in between the U.S. Open and the British Open. Tiger would know, but we don't. Maybe the most significant event for Tiger in 2019 was not getting the Presidential Medal of Freedom in early May but his former wife having a baby in early fall. That meant that Sam and Charlie had another sibling. How could that not be a momentous development in their lives? On that basis, you would guess it would be for their father, too. There are public people who would talk openly about that sort of thing, and Tiger is decidedly not one of them. In mid-October, Elin and the baby were at a soccer game, watching Charlie in action.

• • •

Tiger won an event in Japan at the end of October, his record-tying eighty-second PGA Tour victory. He was never more subdued in victory. He was far from home and from his kids, with a lot left to do before the year was out. The week had been a long one. Maybe he was just tired. It wasn't the Masters.

But it was a meaningful win. (They all are.) The Japan title virtually guaranteed that Woods would pick himself, and appropriately so, as one of the four remaining players to fill out the rest of the twelve-man Presidents Cup team of which he was the captain. The Zozo Championship, played outside Tokyo, was the final event before Tiger had to announce those four picks. For months, he had been coy about the prospect of being the first playing captain on a Presidents Cup team since Hale Irwin in 1994. Had Tiger's play in Japan been downright poor, he might have struggled to name himself. With his win, all debate ended. Earl used to urge Tiger to "let the legend grow." His win in Japan was another LTLG moment in a continuing series.

Nobody could say they saw it coming. Woods hadn't played a tournament in over two months, and he hadn't played well since the Masters. In late August he underwent arthroscopic surgery to repair cartilage damage in his left knee. During his trip to Japan, he wasn't in his usual intra-tournament cocoon. He stayed in the same airport hotel as most of the other players, caddies, officials, and reporters. He made various outings, some social, some commercial. He went to a movie with other players (*Joker*), ate pizza (Domino's), had to wait ninety minutes for a ride (Uber) back to his hotel (a Hilton). Steve DiMeglio broke that story wide open. It was news, because none of this is how Tiger normally operates. And still he won.

Sam Snead is also credited with eighty-two PGA Tour victories, and in victory Woods said the expected things about tying Snead's record. But Snead's total is saddled with asterisks. According to research done by Gary Van Sickle, a former *Sports Illustrated* writer, five of Snead's eighty-two wins were in team events. Another five were against fields with only fifteen or sixteen players in them. One of his wins was in a tournament shortened by rain to one round. Plus, though of course it wasn't Snead's fault, black golfers were prohibited from playing many of the tournaments in which Snead and his contemporaries played. There were probably hundreds of invitation-only events in the 1940s, '50s, and '60s that ignored Ted Rhodes and Charlie Sifford and other talented black players. Earl Woods knew that history inside out. Not all eighty-twos are created equal.

·   ·   ·

Tiger named the last four players to his Presidents Cup roster in early November, a week after the Japan tournament concluded. He announced his picks, an event that was covered live by Golf Channel, from his restaurant in Jupiter. He named Tony Finau, Patrick Reed, Gard Woodland, and himself. Later, when Brooks Koepka said he couldn't play because of a knee injury, Woods added Rickie Fowler to the team. Phil Mickelson was not picked, ending a run of making every national team for which he was eligible going back to the 1989 Walker Cup.

Woods always wanted Reed on the team. He told Furyk before the 2018 Ryder Cup, "He's tough as nails—I'd roll with him anytime." Woods picked Reed because he thought Reed would help the U.S. defeat the Internationals, a twelve-man team comprising players from everywhere in the world except the United States and Europe. But Tiger's selection was also a gift to Reed, a solitary figure on the PGA Tour who had never been one of the boys in his college stints at both the University of Georgia and at Augusta State. After playing poorly and losing twice in two days with Woods at the 2018 Ryder Cup, Reed criticized how the team was managed in comments he made to Karen Crouse. That took chutzpah, Tour-style. And *still* Woods picked him. Tiger likes him and can relate to him. They both, when you drill down into it, started as outsiders. Yes, Tiger became the ultimate insider. But that's not where he began.

•   •   •

Being on the 2019 U.S. Presidents Cup team was always going to be an intense experience for the eleven Americans playing for and with Tiger Woods in the year he won his fifteenth major and eighty-second PGA Tour title. The team would be together not just for one week, which is the norm, but for two. That's because all twelve players were in the eighteen-man field for Tiger's mellow, annual December event in the Bahamas, the Hero World Challenge, held the week before the Presidents Cup at Royal Melbourne in Australia. A crude version of the itinerary: fly to the Bahamas, play the Hero, get on a plane, fly for at least twenty-four hours, arrive in Australia, play the Presidents Cup, fly home.

Then Patrick Reed—picked for the team by Tiger, playing in Tiger's event—made things far more complicated for everybody. In the third round of the Hero tournament, on the eleventh hole, Reed was in a waste bunker near the green, his ball in a depression with a meager but annoying sand hill behind it. He hemmed and hawed about how to play it. He finally set up over his ball and took two practice swings that pushed away parts of that little sand hill with the flange of his wedge. A TV close-up showed it clearly.

It's useful to remember in these situations that the players are super-experts on the subject of how a golf ball sits in its lie. Whatever the camera sees, the player sees better. Whatever the camera knows, the player knows better. As Slugger White—yes, Slugger White, back at it—was reviewing the tape of Reed's actions with Reed, Rickie Fowler saw a replay of the offending practice swings on a TV monitor and said, "I don't even know what you have to review." Paul Azinger, covering the event for NBC Sports after replacing Johnny Miller, said on the broadcast, "If that's not improving your lie, I don't know what is." Even people who have never played golf understand the idea of playing your ball as it lies. It's a commandment.

In my years around the PGA Tour as a spectator, reporter, or caddie, I had never seen or even heard about a rules violation that was so flagrant. Slugger White gave Reed a two-shot penalty for improving his intended line. Coming out of the scorer's room, Reed showed no contrition. The whole episode—what Reed did and how he responded to getting called out on it—was an affront to golf's origin story, to its essence, that you can depend on the player to turn in a *completely* accurate scorecard. One month later, at a tournament in Hawaii, a fan yelled at Reed, "Cheater!" Golf cannot have any tolerance for that kind of outburst, and that might have been just the boorish yell of an overserved spectator. But it might have been more plaintive—that Reed's act had hurt a game that means a great deal to a lot of us. We may not be any good, but do our best to keep it fair, keep it fair.

Patrick Reed should have said thank you to the camera operator for helping him turn in a more accurate scorecard. Instead, preposterously, he said another angle would have shown something entirely different. "I felt like I was far enough away," Reed said. Far enough away? That little hillock was right behind his ball, and his club was in it. He was shoveling. Whenever there's a rules violation, you have to ask why the violation happened in the first place. You have to look to motivation.

Brandel Chamblee, the PGA Tour's most astute and incisive critic—and maybe its only one—went on Golf Channel and talked about the effect the incident would have on Tiger's Presidents Cup team. "Their DNA as a team has been altered," he said. "To defend what Patrick Reed did is defending cheating. It's defending breaking the rules." He missed, as I see it, one point, but it's a crucial one, and it's the reason I've been going on at some length here. I see a straight line from Woods's rules issues in 2013—particularly the one at the

BMW Championship outside Chicago, when he had his finger on a twig and caused his ball to move, even if it was a fraction of an inch—to this event. The custom had been to raise your hand and call the penalty on yourself. *That* is golf. Woods in 2013 and Reed in 2019 were both cases of catch-me-if-you-can. And that is not. Catch-me-if-you-can will be the death of golf, if the game isn't careful. Now, how do I get off this soapbox?

• • •

When he got to Royal Melbourne, Tiger was asked repeatedly about Reed. He said, "I think Pat will be fine. Pat's a great kid. He's handled a tough upbringing well, and I just think that he's one of our best team players and is one of the reasons why all of the guys wanted him on the team."

Tiger must be living under a lucky star. The Presidents Cup comprises five sessions played over four days. Tiger paired the kid (Reed is twenty-nine, with a wife and two children) with Webb Simpson in the first three sessions. They lost three times. The Americans went into the Sunday finale, when twelve singles matches are played, trailing 10-8. They won the event, 16-14. Nobody played better than Woods, who went 3-0. Had the Americans lost, Reed's play and his Bahamian rules debacle would have dominated every serious analysis of the defeat. It wouldn't have ruined Tiger's year, not at all, but it would have put a wet blanket on his final public event. Reed was Tiger's guy.

Tiger's final GolfTV interview of the year was on Sunday afternoon at Royal Melbourne, with Henni Zuël. The Americans had won, and he was floating. He summarized his year of magical golf: "To win a green jacket, to tie Sam, to do this, with all my guys?" He was laughing and smiling, and you could feel his charisma even through the tiniest of screens.

What was it like to be Glenn Greenspan just then, at home in

Florida? After a decade as Tiger's spokesman, he had been let go from his job on the eve of the Presidents Cup without so much as a call from Tiger. There's always life under the hood, with its springs and hoses and sludgy oil. In Tiger's complicated life there are lawsuits, bills, hirings, firings—all manner of things that don't get discussed. But there was Tiger, on a cool afternoon in Australia in mid-December, in his fluffy blue coat and red shirt and white hat, at the end of the best year of his career and maybe his life. It was all good. By the end of the six-minute GolfTV interview—Patrick Reed's name was not mentioned—Tiger had his left arm casually draped around Henni's shoulders, and with his right hand he was holding a microphone under Rob McNamara's mouth. Rob held the winner's large, round gold cup and talked about his role as "the assistant to the regional manager." Everybody laughed. Everybody was happy. Tiger looked so content. He was winning in every way. You know what they say about winning.

•   •   •

In *Golf in the Kingdom*, Michael Murphy captured for eternity the golfer's inner turmoil alongside the game's vague promise of ecstasy. The first half of the book is a gorgeous 130-page golfing fable, filled with the smells of the game and a sort of platonic, drunk-on-golf one-night stand between a callow golfing tourist named Murphy and a Scottish golf professional named Shivas Irons. Shivas is nothing and everything like Ben Hogan, Murphy's real-life early golf hero, going back to the 1940s.

Murphy watched Hogan at close range all through the 1955 U.S. Open at Olympic Club in San Francisco. That experience, at age twenty-four, cemented for life his intense feelings for Hogan. That was the Open when Hogan inexplicably lost in a playoff to a struggling pro named Jack Fleck. Ever since, the mystery of that day and outcome has tapped at Murphy.

Tapped, not hammered. Golf is not at the core of Murphy's life-work, but Hogan was a special case for him. That's because Murphy is a lifelong student of human potential, and Hogan practiced mind over matter as both an art and a science. By all rights, there never should have been a successor to Hogan in Murphy's fertile mind, but of course there was.

Murphy first saw Tiger on TV, and later in person at U.S. Opens and PGA Tour events in San Francisco and at Pebble Beach. In the early 1990s, when I first met Murphy, Tiger was not on our conversational docket. But when I was with Mike at the 2019 U.S. Open at Pebble, all we talked about was Tiger. Tiger and Hogan. Mike was closing in on ninety and improbably fit. He hiked his boyhood links—alongside Alan Shipnuck and me, Tiger in view—with unmasked joy.

Hogan and Tiger both had long paths back to victory after road-side ordeals, no matter how different their two vehicular events might have been. That interested Mike. Tiger, in his return to golf, was figuring out golf for himself, as Hogan had done his whole life. That interested Mike, too. But the main attraction for Mike was this: Tiger had what Hogan had. Each was unlike the others around him.

"On a subliminal level—on a Freudian, subconscious level—I ask myself, 'Why am I so interested in Tiger?' And so I read the algorithms of my own heart, as we all do," Mike told me. "Our bodies often have a strong attraction to something or somebody and we can't figure out exactly why. It's a mystery. And that's how I'm drawn to Tiger."

Mike sometimes has to leave the room when watching Tiger on TV to meditate on Tiger's next shot, "to put a sort of whammy on it—not a negative one, a good whammy." That would have to be the highest form of dedication, fan to player, plebeian to deity. But viewed another way, it's an act of connection. It puts fan and player on the same level, since the spectator is actually doing something useful for the athlete. In theory.

You wouldn't necessarily think that a person who could share such inner-realm notions could also cite Tiger's winning percentages and other stats with nerdy precision, but Murphy can. He's a Tiger Woods generalist.

"My observations are naive," Mike said, "but I would say Tiger swings within the flesh, but also, when he does these supernormal things, *beyond* the flesh. A swing from some other place. He couldn't possibly explain it, but we all know more than we can tell."

I take seriously that a person of Michael Murphy's gifts is drawn to golf, and to Tiger. It makes me think that maybe I haven't completely wasted large chunks of my adult life trying to write about the game and one of its prominent figures.

"Extremely high performers—athletes, artists, writers, soldiers in combat—are doing things that they can't explain and can't be explained, not in conventional Western terms," Murphy said. "Judeo-Christian traditions are often weighed down by notions of law and order. As my friend John Cleese likes to say, 'Western religion is one percent alignment with God, ninety-nine percent crowd control.' Well, there's a lot of that in golf. Golf has this obsession with rules, and it's wonderful. Those rules, even when they're comical, are part of the game's glory. They're necessary. They come right out of golf's Judeo-Christian tradition. And Tiger is of those traditions."

Murphy can speak for ten minutes straight, no water, no pauses. The thoughts are just there, waiting for their release. He continued:

"But at times he also transcends those traditions. That's why Eastern religions and languages and practices are useful when you're trying to get a handle on Tiger. The martial arts have a language for this sort of thing. The notion of *qi*, of *chi*, of *prana*, these Eastern ideas of superphysical energies and actions. Those who are hyper-dimensional, like Tiger, are in a world that can't be contained by normal conventions."

Murphy has athletic gifts himself. When he was in his early fifties, he could run a mile in well under five minutes. But there were always other people who could do what Murphy did better than he. Murphy knew he could not do it all. Tiger, he believed, could. Earl once told me that Tiger, had he not become a golfer, could have been an Olympic high-hurdler, and Tiger has imagined his life as an elite soldier.

"When you look in Tiger's eyes, you see both hyperfocus and re-laxation," Murphy told me. "And it's interesting, because—oh gee, God—in the highest forms of lovemaking, high energy and relax-ation exist side by side. It's that combination that allows for the com-plete engagement of our entire human nature. You see it in every endeavor at the highest levels. A pulling guard in the NFL? He has to have it. He has to have an optimal balance of calm and power."

In his many and sometimes long asides, Mike quoted David Feherty ("Tiger's struggles are more interesting than other golfers' successes"). He noted that both golf and yoga require the "transfor-mation of body, mind, heart, and soul." He talked about how great-ness can come out of hybridity. He remembered how, in the 1940s, other professionals wanted to play with George Fazio for the calm-ing effect he had on them. Murphy is a conversational polymath. At conversation, he's hyperdimensional.

In 1950 Ben Hogan won the U.S. Open at Merion, sixteen months after his near-fatal car accident, in a three-man playoff. The other two players were Lloyd Mangrum and George Fazio. Hogan wrote two books about the swing—*Power Golf* and *Five Lessons*—that will be read as long as people are playing golf, because they're so original. Tiger's first two books—*How I Play Golf* and *The 1997 Masters*—had limited cultural impact on the game. A half year after his fifth Masters win, Tiger announced that he was working on a memoir to be called *Back*. It could be outstanding, if he can open up as Andre Agassi did with J. R. Mohringer in *Open*. It's asking a great deal, as Murphy sees it.

"My supposition is that all Tiger knows is what he does," Mike said. "He has never talked about what he thinks and feels, and he may not be able to express what he thinks and feels. If he doesn't have the language for it, we may never find it out."

That doesn't mean we need to bury all hope. Murphy loves the word *Muggles*, from the Harry Potter novels, for people who lack magical powers, meaning most of us. For Muggles to understand Tiger, we would require a radical paradigm shift (another Murphyism), one that would allow us to figure out things for ourselves that previously we could not.

There are people, Michael Murphy and John Updike among them, who think Jack Fleck, by some act of psychic magic, turned himself into Hogan for a day during their U.S. Open playoff in 1955. Fleck shot 69 and beat Hogan by three. Everybody but Fleck was expecting a different result.

Earlier, I tried to make the case that Tiger had it all, because of his mastery of both match-play golf and stroke-play golf. Murphy is likely onto something far more significant in terms of duality. Tiger Tont Woods has never been just one thing. From the day he was born, he has been an amalgamation of East and West, culturally, physically, and mentally. There could be a book in that, but Michael Murphy might be the only person who could write it.

Murphy reads widely and has, over the years, immersed himself in the Joseph Campbell canon. Campbell was a scholar who spent his life studying mythology and religion and, along the way, shaped George Lucas's thinking during the making of the Star Wars movies. Murphy regularly makes references to Star Wars, as well as the Harry Potter novels, Homer Kelley's *The Golfing Machine*, and occasionally his own *The Future of the Body*. Campbell didn't invent the phrase "the hero's journey," but he helped make it popular. Here is one of Campbell's own descriptions of it, from 1949: "A hero ventures forth from the world of common day into a region of supernatural wonder: fabulous forces are there encountered and a decisive victory is won: the hero comes back from this mysterious adventure with the power to bestow boons on his fellow man."

I asked Mike if he thought Tiger was on a hero's journey. At that moment, we were walking in the rough along Pebble's sixth hole. Tiger was within fifty yards of us. Beyond the green was the Pacific.

"Oh, God, yes," Mike said. "Absolutely!"

• • •

We Muggles don't see much. No matter how much we try, we just don't. At 2:40 p.m. on that Masters Sunday, Tiger slipped into the Augusta National clubhouse and the scorer's room. All that celebration, but nothing is official until you sign for your score.

What was going on in that room? Tiger was in there, with Joe and two tournament officials, plus Francesco Molinari and Tony Finau. Three scorecards were on a table, each of them studied with extreme care. At some tournaments, TV cameras are allowed in the scorer's room, which changes everything, but the Masters, no surprise, is not one of them. So what were they doing, how were they acting, what did they say? And what was *really* going on in there, in the places that no camera could ever reach?

Eleven hours earlier, Tiger had been rising from a bed in his rental house, getting his body ready for work, one section at a time. You might wonder: What was it like to be Tiger Woods *there*, in the predawn dark before one of the biggest days of his life?

On a Friday night in June 2015, Tiger was flying home from Seattle in a private jet after shooting the two worst Thursday-Friday U.S. Open rounds in his life, an 80 and a 76. How about there, on that plane—what was he actually like for those six hours?

There's a fine line between being curious and being a voyeur, but when you've lived as large as Tiger has, people are going to wonder. You can make your guesses about Tiger's public, private, and secret lives, if you're inclined. Or you can, as Joe LaCava does, mind your own business. In the weeks after the win, different interviewers, and even Joe's wife, asked him what kind of gum Tiger was chewing during the Masters. Joe said he didn't know and didn't care. An excellent answer, and likely a truthful one. At his winner's press conference, a writer for *Golfweek* asked Tiger about his gum chewing. "I'm chomping on this gum because I usually get hungry," Tiger said. "I keep eating so much. And it curbs my appetite a little bit, which is nice. Most of the time, most of the issues I have at tournaments, I lose so much weight, as you all know."

Say *what?*

Tiger's recitation of what club he hit into each green on Sunday had the benefit of being understandable. Nine of his approach shots, he said, were with 8-irons. If you had binoculars and were watching him closely, you knew what clubs he hit. As for the gum in his mouth, you could see that, too. One piece went out on the thirteenth tee and was replaced by a new one by the time he was in the fairway.

The gum question was right on the edge of being within the cultural norm for a winner's press conference at the Masters. That's because, by implication, it brought in the real world. There are players chewing gum with CBD in it, legally. If Tiger is one of them, he didn't say. It's no big deal, except those three letters applied to Tiger might get people thinking about his stints in rehab facilities and his arrest. And his victory had further buried all that. We weren't gathered on that Sunday afternoon to discuss any of that old, negative stuff. We were there to celebrate Tiger's win, and his remarkable comeback from his back surgery, and *not* from mental-health issues. Had the winner of the 2019 Masters been Betty Ford or Michael Phelps, that would be different. But it was Tiger Woods sitting on the dais in his green winner's coat. He's private by nature. Secretive, really. Winning can make people forget for a while. On some level, that was part of Tiger's grand plan.

Needless to say, there was no mention of Tiger's 2015 black Mercedes, the one that drew the attention of the Jupiter police officers. What kind of abnormal person would even think of such a thing now, at this feels-so-good moment? Fair enough, but the fact, or at least the notion, remains: Had the Jupiter Police Department not done its job so ably on Memorial Day in 2017, Tiger would not have won that Masters almost two years later. Tiger did the heavy lifting to get there. But Officer Fandrey, who handled that night with both authority and humanity, is more than a bit player in this amazing story.

. . .

Rory McIlroy turned thirty not quite three weeks after Tiger won his fifth Masters. By his example, Tiger showed Rory, and many others, how to practice, how to use the gym, how to handle the heat on Sunday afternoon. Through age twenty-five, Rory was winning at a pace that resembled Tiger's. "My little run," Rory calls it. Four majors in a four-year span. After that, something changed. Rory wasn't Tiger.

McIlroy grew up in a working-class family in the suburbs of Belfast. He was an only child, like Tiger, and his father, Gerry, was immersed in the game, like Earl was. Rory caught Tiger's first fourteen majors on TV. For Tiger's fifteenth, he was much closer to the action. As Rory was signing his card that Sunday, Tiger was making his way through Amen Corner.

Rory wasn't surprised to see Tiger contending, and he wasn't surprised to see Tiger win. What made the biggest impression on him was how Tiger responded to his win, and how the Masters fans responded to Tiger.

"He's vulnerable now in a way he was never before," Rory told me. He was sitting on a bench in the locker room at the Medinah

Country Club outside Chicago. His Nike hat was in the Charlie Brown position, with the brim pointing to one o'clock.

"You have a sore back? Tiger does, too. You've had ups and downs in your life? Tiger has, too," Rory said. "He's on a more human level now. When you show vulnerability, it's endearing. It's the damsel in distress. Our natural human instinct is that we want to support people in trouble. We want to help. With Tiger, people don't feel like they're on the outside looking in anymore."

For a while, Tiger and Rory were the faces of Nike Golf. One of their joint ads, known in the trade as "No Cup Is Safe," shows them hitting golf balls side by side, their shots plopping into distant water glasses and other unlikely places. Through the sixty-second spot, they playfully give each other a hard time. "Just trying to keep up with the old guy, you know?" Rory says to Tiger. "Dude, is that your real hair?" Tiger says to Rory. Their rapport is terrific.

In actual fact, they weren't together when the spot was shot, and at least for Rory, the characters in the ad are not true to type. Tiger often has the needle out with his buddies, but Rory doesn't. He's contemplative by nature. You'll sometimes see him in a hotel lobby or some other public place with his glasses on, serious reading material in hand. As he talked about where Tiger had taken his life in recent years, Rory quoted a favorite poem: "'We never know how high we are / Till we are called to rise.' Emily Dickinson?" Yes, Emily Dickinson.

Golf is fortunate to have some prominent players who are keen observers and commentators. At the top of that list would be Jordan Spieth, Francesco Molinari—and Rory. Rory could write a master's thesis on Tiger.

They see each other regularly, at Tour events, at Ryder Cups, in South Florida, where they both live. They use the same landscaping company at their homes. Rory was amused but not really surprised to learn that Tiger knew the name of his landscaping guy, but Tiger plays close attention to *everything*. Tiger lives in the details.

Rory's view is on the big picture. When Rory was nineteen, we met in Southern California and had a brown-bag lunch, and he talked about going to Mumbai and seeing its slums and the impact that made on him. He sees things another person might miss.

"Empathy can manifest itself in a lot of different ways," Rory said at Medinah. "You can see it in his humbleness. Every time Tiger sees me, he asks, 'How's your mum? How's your dad?' Is that something he would have done fifteen years ago? I don't know.

"When you're as good as Tiger was, your talent can be a burden. It can be a curse. You can't *not* be a slightly complicated person when you've had the life he's had. When you've lived his life, how can you not be become guarded and insular?

"I wouldn't trade places with him. I can walk into Whole Foods, get some groceries, be a normal guy. He can't. But what's different now is that he's putting others in the middle of what he's doing, Sam and Charlie most of all."

Rory had to be onto something, something significant. In 2008, when Tiger won the U.S. Open, he seemed completely self-absorbed. When he returned to golf from Pine Grove, the rehab facility in Hattiesburg, nothing had changed. Since returning to golf after his 2017 surgery and arrest, Tiger has been a case study in human metamorphosis.

Rory spoke of their occasional meals together and how much Tiger's educational philanthropy meant to Tiger. He talked about how good Tiger's relationship was with his former wife, Elin. Rory said that when he sees something off in Tiger's swing, he'll text him about it, and that Tiger appreciates it. What Rory was describing sounded like an actual, evolving friendship.

"What Tiger's doing now is so much more than what he was doing," Rory said. "It's not just that singular mission, to dominate golf."

· · ·

Tiger, unusually, made two trips to Butler Cabin on Masters Sunday. In the second one, he was interviewed by Jim Nantz and Nick Faldo, and he talked about his mother, about her five-thirty wake-up calls to get Tiger to his peewee golf tournaments. Ninety minutes in the Plymouth Duster there, a nine-hole tournament, then back.

It would have been easy in those years to look at Tiger and see him making those swings and collecting those trophies and say he was just doing what came naturally, but there was more going on than that. Tiger's play helped keep Tida and Earl together, or semi-together. Tiger was playing for more than laminate trophies. That's a lot to carry, and to unpack.

In the 1980s, when Tiger was coming up, there weren't many kids of Asian descent playing junior golf in Southern California, and black kids were rarer yet. Combo-platter parents like Tida and Earl were pretty much nonexistent. Tida didn't care. As Tiger rose through the ranks, first as an amateur, later as a professional, Tida was in the first row. Not a hole ahead, like many of the other parents, but right near the action. She wasn't marching those fairways looking to make friends. (When Phil Mickelson's mother introduced herself to Tiger's mother for the first time, it was at the 2012 Ryder Cup.) Tida had a job to do, and glad-handing was not part of the description. She was there to support and to push. When Tiger beat Davis Love in a long-ago match-play tournament, Tida said, "Tiger steal his heart." That four-word game story circulated in press tents for years because it offered an insight into many Tiger Woods victories. In his prime, Tiger was ripping out hearts left and right. In the telling of the Tiger Woods story—Freda Foh Shen played Tida in the 1998 TV movie—Earl gets too much credit and Tida not enough. Tiger is half Tida, if not more.

In her early old age, as she stood beside Augusta National's eighteenth green that Sunday afternoon, she looked like a million other proud immigrant grandmothers whose family had found prosperity in America. Golf was Tiger's ticket, but had it not been golf, it would have been something else. Tida's son, no matter what gifts were assigned to him at birth, was going to make it in something, because the son was going to work. Tida was going to make sure of that. No matter what marital struggles they had, Tida and Earl shared a work ethic. In raising Tiger, that was their starting point.

Tida Woods, graying and serious, was an arresting sight, standing above that green, looking down at it from a little knoll. She, too, is an icon in the game, in her own way. There was nobody anything like her in the vicinity, a woman of a certain age, wealthy, independent, suspicious, surrounded by people—her grandchildren were right beside her—but unmistakably alone, too. In a manner of speaking, she was a widow long before Earl died in 2006.

When Tiger was young, he wondered why people called him black but not Thai. It was a good question. In Thailand, the locals look at Tiger and see one of their own. To whatever degree Tiger practices Buddhism, that's all Tida. None of this is to diminish Earl's role, for good and for otherwise. But Tida deserves more credit for some of Tiger's significant traits: his ruthlessness, his verbal economy, his love of dogs, his solitary nature, his waste-not impulse. When Tiger was a young pro, Tida collected the Nike shirts Tiger didn't want and parceled them out to friends, in their wrappers, as the mood struck her. (Arnold Palmer did the same thing. He stockpiled those hard-collar golf shirts for his own use and gave them to friends as he saw fit.) Tida's old Plymouth Duster was surely long gone by the 2019 Masters, but it was a pleasure to hear Tiger remember it with such fondness and ease.

• • •

I caught up with Tony Finau four months after the Masters. He discussed the event as if no time had passed at all. He described hitting balls that Sunday morning: "You're trying to pretend Tiger's not there and just do your thing. But any player on Tour who ever tells you they can actually do that is lying."

He talks as quickly as he swings, his words tumbling out in long, complete sentences. "There might be a hundred guys who are on Tour because of Tiger, and I'm one of them," he said. "For me, growing up, golf was for rich guys. Then Tiger came. If golf is cool, it's because of Tiger. And I don't know that it is. But I'm glad I play it. And I play it because of Tiger." He was easy and open. He would soon be turning thirty-one. Tiger was difficult and closed at that age.

"Every putt I ever made as a kid was to win the Masters," Tony said. "From the time I started playing, I would dream about playing with Tiger in the fourth round of a major, both of us in contention. And now I'm playing with Tiger, fourth round of the Masters." He often lapsed into the present tense like that.

"Everything was magnified by a hundred," he said. "I've played in the last group of a U.S. Open on a Sunday. I've played in a Ryder Cup. Incredible experiences. But a Sunday in the Masters with Tiger is like nothing else."

We were at the Liberty National Golf Club, in the dining room of its space-age clubhouse, a study in glass and chrome. George Jetson could have walked in at any moment.

Finau's profile had changed after the Masters, permanently. For as long as golf tournaments continue to be a conversation topic in civil societies and on Delta flights, Finau will be remembered as one third of the unlikely group that made up the final threesome in the final round of the 2019 Masters. None of the three—not Finau, not Molinari, not Tiger—had been raised in the American country-club system, the one that has produced golf stars from Bobby Jones to Jordan Spieth, with Jack Nicklaus and Tom Watson in between. The members of that last-off threesome looked different from many of their fellow pros. Their manner was different. They were different.

Finau, Tongan and Samoan by ancestry, talked about the summer of '97, his first as a golfer. It was all parks-and-rec. A decade later, right after graduating high school, he turned pro. He was seventeen, and the Tiger dream was taking shape. You don't think about the presence of a third guy when you're a kid imagining a Sunday showdown at a major with your hero. But you take what you can get, and in real life there Finau was, standing on the twelfth tee with Tiger and Molinari, Molinari with his two-shot lead and the honor. Finau was watching closely.

"You never want to hit a full shot on twelve," Finau said. "You don't want to hit something hard and high and have it get in the wind. You're trying to keep it below the trees. Frankie tried to chip an eight-iron. I knew his tee shot was in the water the second he hit it. He caught it a little heavy. He caught a lot of tee. You could hear it. You catch a lot of tee, you hit the ball high on the face, and you get a little chunk sound. That ball won't have much spin on it. It won't go its full distance."

Finau was not surprised to see Tiger, playing second, hit a full 9-iron into the heart of the green. Even though he was fifty feet from the hole, Finau was certain Tiger would make par. He imagined Molinari would make 5. He thought he was one swing and one putt from getting himself into the tournament. A birdie 2 would have done wonders for him right there. He made one bad swing instead. Like Molinari's, his ball started too far right and finished in Rae's Creek. He and Molinari walked mournfully to the creek while Tiger went to the bridge. "My coach told me that Tiger was giddy when he got to that green," Finau said.

The dining room around us was nearly empty. Finau was eating a series of sliders, each one looking like a brown M&M in his enormous hands. It was mid-August. Finau and his wife, Alayna, and their four young children had been traveling together for much of the summer, but that week his family was home in Salt Lake City, getting ready for the start of the school year. Tony was raised in the

Mormon Church. The vertices in the triangle of his life are home, church, and family. The prevailing attitude on the PGA Tour is get it while you can. Tony's different. But the 2019 Masters is now part of his life, too.

On the eighteenth green, as their shake became a hug, Finau said to Tiger, "I'm so proud of you." It's not the comment you would expect from a young golfer with one win to the game's most iconic figure. But Tony Finau has an old soul. Finau knew that Tiger had been on some journey. He didn't know or care about the details, he just knew the most important part: that Tiger Woods had come a long way, from where he had been to where he was. For a moment there, it was as if Tony were the father and Tiger the son.

· · ·

Earl predicted that Tiger would win fourteen majors before he had won his first. He shared the number with Tim Rosaforte, then of *Sports Illustrated*, in the form of a declaration at the 1995 U.S. Amateur, the one at the Newport Country Club in Rhode Island. Tiger had defeated Buddy Marucci, but he needed thirty-six holes to do it. Marucci was forty-three. Tiger was nineteen. He was wearing a Stanford hat. His father was wearing a TaylorMade hat, one hat from his extensive collection. In the interest of whetting the appetite of different manufacturers, he had hats from all of them. When Tiger turned pro in 1996, he played Titleist clubs. Later, he switched to Nike, and TaylorMade later yet. They all paid big money. Earl could see what was coming.

In his remarks at the trophy presentation at Newport, Tiger didn't mention the club or the USGA, but he did make nods to Buddy Marucci, to Butch Harmon, and to Jay Brunza, the navy psychologist who caddied for him. Tiger dedicated the win to Brunza and his family, a month after Brunza's father had died.

Brunza was part of the inner circle. He had caddied in all three of Tiger's USGA junior titles and his first and second U.S. Amateur titles. But the next year something happened. In 1996 the U.S. Amateur was played in Portland, and Brunza caddied for Tiger in the stroke-play qualifying rounds. But by the time Tiger was playing in the final, in a wild topsy-turvy match against Steve Scott, Tiger had a friend caddying for him, Bryon Bell, who much later became the president of Tiger's golf-course design company. Brunza was in, visibly so—and then he was not. He has never said what happened, not publicly.

Brunza's legacy is incalculable. Anytime you see Tiger close his eyes for a moment of silent meditation when considering a shot or a round, he's continuing, in some manner, his work with Jay Brunza. When Tiger got on Tour in 1996, there were players who were sure that Brunza had practiced hypnotism with Tiger, allowing him to play in a state of hyperfocus straight out of *Zen in the Art of Archery*. It was never true. Brunza's approach was much more on the ground. All these years later, he continues to emphasize breathing and mental preparation, and he uses the phrase "relax, review, and refocus" with his players. You wouldn't immediately identify Tiger Woods as a relaxed golfer, but he is by the time he gets over his ball. Relaxed and aggressive. It's some combination. It would be natural to focus on Brunza's departure, but the telling thing was Brunza's arrival. Sports psychology was a nascent field when Brunza started working with Tiger. It was Earl who brought Brunza in. Earl was a visionary.

He stood out at Newport in every way. He walked the course wearing a striped golf shirt, shorts, sneakers, and longish white socks. He smoked Merits and signed autographs with an elongated *z* underneath his name. In the break between the morning and afternoon rounds, Earl rolled a reclining desk chair out of the press tent and into a warm spot and napped for a while. He received visitors there, too.

At the end of the day, Earl stood in a small near-empty tent and hoisted the winner's trophy, which he had repurposed as a drinking vessel, with champagne in it. In a believable version of the quote as it came to me, Earl said, "Bobby Jones, you can kiss my black ass. I hope you're rolling over in your grave, knowing that this trophy is going to a black man's home for another year." I have heard other, similar versions. Whatever Earl's precise words were, his comments made the rounds at the game's highest levels. There were people at the USGA who knew Earl well, who were working closely with him to make sure Tiger didn't do anything to violate his amateur status. People found what they wanted in Earl's comments: racism, classism, anger, humor, vengeance. You'd have to be some kind of verbal genius to get that much done in two sentences.

Earl was. When Tiger was newly sixteen, he and Earl were in Miami for the Junior Orange Bowl, an important junior-golf event. A spectator mentioned to Earl another similar event, the Future Masters, played annually in remote Dothan, Alabama. "Tiger will play in the Masters before he ever plays in the Future Masters," Earl said. In fourteen words, he managed to be insulting, pointed, dismissive, and arrogant. Also funny.

Earl could go long, too. He was a soliloquy king. I had several late-night interviews with Earl over the years. He went on forever without being boring or repetitive, and he spoke at such length that it was impossible to parse his words. He was New Agey before that was a thing. I found him to be smart, insightful, and loaded with bullshit. He was fun. One of his intentional messages was that Tiger would make mistakes once but not again, because Earl was on the scene, riding herd. One of his unintentional messages was that the father had a god complex. The prediction for fourteen major titles had to be straight out of Earl's grand plan. This is over the top, but with Newport in the air, here goes: Earl was to Tiger as old Joe Kennedy was to JFK. (JFK and Jackie were married in Newport.) Each father shaped each son immeasurably. Both sons prospered and suffered more than we could know. But John Kennedy's "ask not" moment in 1961 inspired millions. You could say that Tiger's twelve-shot win at Augusta in 1997 did, too.

That win came right on the heels of Tiger's three straight U.S. Amateurs. If Earl was getting his wish, afterlife Bob had to be dizzy by then. (A tip for tourists in Atlanta: Consider a visit to the husband-and-wife Jones burial site, followed by a quick one across the street at Six Feet Under, a bar and restaurant where they serve a drink called Mr. Jones, an Arnold Palmer with vodka.) I once asked Dr. Bob about Earl's Newport remarks. "It demonstrates a profound lack of understanding about who Bub was," Jones said, using the family nickname. "My grandfather was all in for anybody who could shoot the scores."

But Earl understood the real problem—that without unfettered access to courses, equipment, and instruction, you would never have the chance to shoot the scores. Earl came up in "separate but equal" as a matter of law and separate and unequal in his daily life. He knew firsthand about closed doors and NO COLOREDS ALLOWED. Despite all that gorgeous Southern California light, Tiger spent a lot of his amateur years trying to settle the wrongs his father incurred. Tiger played a lot of his best golf on edge and with focused anger.

If you ever saw Earl and Tiger together, including that day at Newport, you could sense their powerful bond, their love, and their playful friendship. Shortly before Tiger was handed the winner's trophy at Newport, he leaned toward Earl's mouth as Earl cupped his cigarette. Some kind of intimate fatherly commentary was being delivered. Tiger grew up with the smell of Earl, his whiskey, his smokes, his steak sauce. His driving-range perspiration, trapped by his windbreaker until it wasn't. A father doesn't know his own smells, but a son does. Palatial, air-conditioned South Florida living is practically scent-free, but that's not how Tiger grew up, in that little house, on that little street, in a flat, sunbaked development well south of L.A.

There was no room for the Plymouth Duster in the garage, what with all of Earl's golf stuff in it. Tiger's came later.

Tiger was Earl's pride and joy. What could be wrong with that? But Project Tiger gave Earl's life meaning, and for Tiger, or any kid in a similar situation, that's some sack to carry. It could not have been easy being Earl's son. Which means it could not have been easy being Tiger Woods. This is from Dr. Bob: The mule asks the pack mule, "How's that load?" The pack mule says, "What load?"

Tiger's opponents were enemy combatants. They were expendable. That's why many of his Sunday marches to victory were borderline boring. There was seldom anything personal at stake except Tiger's desire to bury his nameless opponents. The winner was a winner, and it was often Tiger. What was traditionally called second place or runner-up was, in Tiger's accounting, "first loser." Another charmer of his in that vein: "Second sucks." Yet millions of people were drawn to all that. They were captivated by the many knockout punches Tiger threw en route to the trophy presentation. Other professional golfers won and organized a party. Tiger won and ate a sandwich.

One of the impressive things about Tony Bosch, Miami pharmacist without papers, was his commitment to being a more empathetic person. Tiger has never made it easy for other people to see him, as Rory McIlroy does, through the lens of empathy. When a person is so dominating, rich, cold, famous, and abrupt, what is there to hold on to? Tony Bosch's advice to anybody in that situation would be to dig deeper. Bosch's diesel therapy, the many bus trips from one prison to the next, paying off.

Imagine Tiger at twelve, at fourteen, at sixteen. The more you win, the prouder your father is going to be of you. That's natural. But it's difficult to have pride and love mixed up like that. Plus, what's going to happen when the winning stops? Because that's what happens sooner or later. Most of us grow up with try-your-best. It works fine.

But try-your-best alone won't produce a Tiger Woods. Tiger grew up on the Al Davis Raiders and the NFL owner's legendary motto: "Just win, baby." Al Davis was an expert showman, a brilliant strategist, an agitator for civil rights. There was a lot of Al Davis in Earl Woods. Tiger was watching and learning, from both of them.

Tiger was Earl's son. If there was one message I got from talking about Tiger with Arnold—at length, on several occasions, late in his life—it was that. Arnold was in his mid-eighties and much wiser as a reader of people than you might know or guess. He saw his own father, Deacon Palmer, in Tiger's father. Deacon, course superintendent at Latrobe Country Club and later its golf pro, had taught Arnold how to grip the club, just as Earl had taught Tiger how to putt. Arnold used his golf grip as a lifelong tribute to his father, and Tiger used his putting game as a tribute to his. Both fathers knew what it was like to be poor. Both knew what it was like to be shunned, Earl for being black in white America, Deacon for having a physical disability in an able-bodied world. (His left leg was deformed by a bout of childhood polio, and he wore a heavy metal brace.) Both were drinkers.

Arnold felt that his relationship with his father gave him insight into Tiger. The way he read it, Earl died and Tiger, lost, started wandering. Tiger was thirty and married but not really an adult. Arnold knew about that, too. At twenty-four, Arnold was selling paint Monday to Friday, drinking and chasing at night, playing weekend golf as the boss's show horse. In Arnold's telling, Tiger went along on autopilot for a while after Earl's death in 2006. Tiger was so good that even the fumes were enough to get him from one event to another, and to fourteen major titles. But Tiger never learned to fly the plane by himself.

For sheer craziness, the fourteenth—the 2008 U.S. Open at Torrey Pines, where Earl and Tiger had logged so much time—was the most dramatic of them all, Tiger winning on a "broken leg," limping down hills, holing improbable putts on bumpy greens. It was after that win that the serious wandering began. The knee operations, the

Canadian doctors, the girlfriends with stage names, the rule-book issues, the high scores, the chip yips, the weird claims about bad mattresses and a missing tooth, the long absences. Then, on Memorial Day 2017, he came out of the desert, under duress. Yes, he won plenty of tournaments in those nearly nine years, but you could also say they weren't the right tournaments and that they weren't won in the right spirit. Then came 2018 and his first win in five years. Then came the 2019 Masters. Then Japan. Then Melbourne. Another birthday, number forty-four. The start of another new year. Tiger saw Greg Norman and thanked him for his congratulatory note.

There are problems with this summation. For one thing, it's too tidy. It presumes too much about Tiger's overall health, mental and otherwise, in the aftermath of his infamous Memorial Day. He seems better, and he looks good and sounds good, but who really knows? People have wondered if Tiger joined a twelve-step program or another abstinence program. It would seem unlikely. For one thing, he's so private. Friends of Tiger's have said that after his year of plea-required alcohol abstinence concluded on September 12, 2018, he resumed drinking, but in a tempered way. After the Masters Tiger made at least one casual public reference to his own beer drinking. Someone in an abstinence program would not likely do that.

I asked Tiger once how his life had changed since that long Memorial Day night. "It's gotten better," he said. There was no second sentence.

. . .

After the Masters, fifteen was golf's new number. Jack still had the most important one, eighteen. But nobody was sitting shiva for fourteen. As Rob McNamara said, "Fifteen sounds a lot better than fourteen." When fourteen was new to him, in 2008, Tiger wore the number with joy. But in time it became a fifty-pound chain. It contributed to his bad back.

Nick Faldo had told me at the end of 2018 that he felt Tiger could win a Masters, if he had four days of warm weather. Four months after Tiger's win, I asked Faldo to analyze Tiger's chances of winning a sixteenth major. Few people have seen Tiger's career at closer range, or so dispassionately, and few people have a better understanding of Tiger as a golfer and a man.

Tiger could win another major, Faldo said, but everything would have to fall his way, as it did at Augusta. Warm weather again, good mental and physical health, swing in a good place, a course with no rough. In other words, as Faldo saw it, there continued to be only one major Tiger could win again—the Masters—and then only if the moon was in the seventh house.

And even if Tiger did win a sixth green jacket, Faldo said, it would never mean as much to Woods as his fifth did, fourteen years after his fourth, with his daughter and son waiting for him. During the frenzy of victory, and on the CBS broadcast, Faldo had said, "That will be the greatest scene in golf forever." It was some statement, given their icy relationship.

The wall between them has benefited Faldo as a commentator. It's been his liberator. On the Saturday of the 2013 Masters, Faldo was the most prominent golf person to say publicly that Woods should withdraw from the tournament. "Greg Norman said, 'That's the best call you've ever made on TV,'" Faldo said. "It's not complicated. If your scorecard is wrong, you're out of the tournament. You're at dinner, you get a call from a tournament official. 'What did you do on twelve?' 'Oh, my ball was in the ditch, and I dropped it to the left.' 'Yeah, that's not a lateral. You're DQed, sorry.' 'Oh, okay.' You take it on the chin. We've all been there."

Faldo sees Tiger only now and again. Faldo's own manner has changed markedly since his prime. He's approachable. When he was the number one player in the world, he was not. He sees a similar evolution in Tiger, to a degree.

"I think he's tried to open up, but he's led essentially a weird life, to be honest," Faldo said. "You're a golfer from age three, you follow your father's guidance, you're under the spotlight, you create your own world. I think of what Charles Barkley said: 'I was on his list, and then I wasn't.' Tiger's ever-changing. Two years ago he shows up and suddenly he's hugging everybody." Almost everybody. "I never got my hug," Faldo said.

We were standing on the back of the range at Liberty National. Brooks Koepka was the only person hitting balls. Faldo watched him smash another and said, "Tiger's not going to beat him, not if they're both playing out of the rough." Earlier in the year, Woods was asked to compare himself to Koepka when he was Koepka's age, twenty-nine. "Does Brooksie look like a young me?" Woods said. "No. I wish. I was never that big. I was a hundred and thirty pounds."

Faldo got big and strong in his prime, as Tiger did later. Faldo never dominated the game the way Tiger did, but he knows what it's like to be the best player in the world, and he knows the isolated life you lead in an attempt to stay there. Faldo was also once a single man in his mid-forties with young children. Faldo has been married and divorced three times. He has three daughters and a son.

"When you're on a mission, like Tiger was, like I was, you're at the front of the ship, and you're creating a wake, and sometimes that wake isn't pretty, but still you plow on," Faldo said. "Then your children grow up, and that changes you. You learn to forgive and to ask for forgiveness." You never hear Faldo get introspective like that on TV.

Faldo talked, just as Tony Bosch did, about his growing sense of gratitude. "I don't think you find gratitude," he said. "I think it hits you. Seeing Seve decline, I realized I was lucky." There were two major components to Seve's decline. First, he lost his golf game, then he lost his health. "I realized that I had had my time, that I had given it my best with the knowledge I had. I had a twenty-year opportunity. When it's over, you realize it goes by like *that*." He snapped his fingers.

"And now it's thirty years ago that I was really good. That's half my life ago." His broadcasting career is now as long as his playing career was.

"I didn't know myself then," Faldo said. "I was a driven golfer. That's it. If I met people for five seconds and they thought I was an ass, then I was an ass to them for the rest of their lives." Faldo was talking about himself, but Tiger was lurking.

When Nicklaus won his sixth Masters in 1986, at age forty-six, he said, "I'd quit now, but I'm not that smart." Faldo knows how hard it is to say goodbye to the thing you do best and, at least for a while, better than anyone else in the world. "There was a five-year period when I couldn't play like Nick Faldo could play, and it hurt like hell," he said. "You want so desperately to go out on a high note. You actually dream of doing that. You say to yourself, *If I could just win this one and leave and wave and say, 'Thank you very much.'*"

He tried to imagine Tiger doing that. Just walking away. But he knows that it's impossible. The drug is too powerful. If you win—if you place, if you show, if you top-ten—you want to keep going. Tiger, Faldo said, would someday find the same thing. There was no way to warn him, to tell Tiger that his own half decade of golf-career purgatory was coming. But it will. Faldo was certain of that.

And then what do you do? The question has been asked forever. There's the era you own, when you're in it, and then there are all the days after it, and you have to fill them, too. Michael Jordan found that out. So did Muhammad Ali, Ted Williams, Jesse Owens, the boys in the boat, Seabiscuit, Bobby Jones, and all the others. The days do get filled. But it won't be the same as playing and winning and all that invincibility.

Faldo spoke of the talent, determination, and nerve that tournament golf requires. It takes talent and determination to contend. It takes nerve to close. And nerve dies through lack of use.

"Tiger spent eleven years climbing Mount Everest without oxygen," Faldo said. From his U.S. Open win at Torrey Pines in 2008 through his fifth green jacket in 2019. "Basically, for eleven years, it all went wrong. And then there was a chance, and he grabbed it."

That's what impressed Faldo most—what Tiger did with his chance at that Masters. "To win a Tour event after a five-year hiatus is incredible," Faldo said. "But to win a major eleven years after you've won your last?" Nick Faldo is a good talker, but he had no words.

• • •

Tiger's fifteenth major was different from the fourteen before it. He didn't win it as Earl's son. He won it as Charlie and Sam's father. He didn't win it walled off from his fans. He won it bringing his fans in. In his prime, Tiger won majors by twelve, by eight, by five, by fifteen. Nobody else had done that. Not Faldo, not Norman. Not Arnold, not Jack. Not Hogan. Not Jones.

Tiger was above the game. "He sucks all the air out of the pairing," as Gary Koch, an NBC commentator, once put it. Nicklaus nearly always had to beat guys down the stretch, or try. That's why he had nineteen second-place finishes, just in the majors. How he handled winning, and not winning, is what makes Jack the greatest golfer ever. He wasn't warm, but he had good manners in the truest sense. He had an underlying decency. He was Jones's successor.

Nobody has ever dominated an era as Tiger did his. Tiger Woods is the best player in history. But Nicklaus owns some other category. You can call it what you wish, but it's bigger and more important. Ali used to say, "I am the greatest of *all time*." He didn't need to cite a category. Jack would never say anything like that. But he's the greatest of all time.

Have you ever seen those Andy Warhol portraits of Nicklaus? They're wild. Early in their session, Warhol was snapping some Polaroids and Jack said to an acquaintance, "Does this guy know what he's doing?" The works portray Jack's immense confidence and self-reliance. Nicklaus embodies mid-century, mid-country American prosperity in

Warhol's work. In Annie Leibovitz's portraits of Tiger, shirtless and wearing a watchman's cap, she also captures the essence of her subject. You can see Tiger's need to prove something to others without saying a thing. As artworks, they couldn't be more different, and they couldn't be more revealing.

The golfers Jack beat, and the golfers who beat him, were gritty men playing with mom-and-pop equipment on courses that were sometimes so dry you couldn't take a divot. Those men made Nicklaus's career far more interesting, for us and for him. Arnold Palmer. Gary Player. Billy Casper. Raymond Floyd. Lee Trevino. Johnny Miller. Tom Watson. Hubert Green, Tony Jacklin, Lanny Wadkins, Hale Irwin, Larry Nelson, John Mahaffey, Dave Stockton, David Graham, Andy North, Ben Crenshaw, Tom Weiskopf. Early Seve, early Langer, early Faldo. Jack had their numbers, except when he didn't. But Jack never developed a fanatical following because, as Warhol figured out, he won with his head as much as anything else.

Arnold's program was totally different, in terms of how he played, how he thought, how he walked, the chemistry he had with fans, in person and even through the magic of TV. He was one of the first TV superstars, along with JFK and Jerry Mathers (as the Beaver). Arnold treated his fans as if they were paying him directly, and he had tens of thousands of interactions over the years, right up to the end in a Pittsburgh hospital. It was easy for him, because he liked people. Also, Arnold always understood that the game was much bigger than he. By the 2019 Masters, Tiger had figured that out, too.

• • •

No golfer before Tiger had led a life remotely like his. Not Arnold, not Jack. Not Hogan. Not Bobby Jones. Jones had a ticker-tape parade down Broadway after completing the Grand Slam, but most days he didn't encounter a camera at all. Tiger couldn't possibly relate. He has tolerated the ubiquity of cameras most days and fought them on others. Cameras have made Tiger millions and cost him more than any forensic accountant could determine. The *National Enquirer* snaps of Tiger at Pine Grove in Hattiesburg would be a prime example, but only one. The video footage of him as he tried to move the stubby stick beside his ball at that tournament outside Chicago would be another.

Then came Memorial Day 2017, when Tiger unwittingly appeared as himself. A half year later, when Tiger reemerged as a professional athlete and as a public figure, he seemed different. He was more accepting, if you had to get it down to a single word.

The changes have been subtle, and there are insightful people who see Tiger at close range who wouldn't go even that far. They wisely remember what a good actor Tiger is. They presume there was a PR makeover behind a curtain. They cringed when, after the Masters, people began saying, "Tiger's changed." This might be nearer to the truth: Tiger's changing. But who can really know? Likely nobody, including Tiger.

• • •

Over the course of 2018 and 2019, Tiger used the word *gratitude*, in its various forms, far more than he ever had. He became part of the game, part of the community of golfers, in unprecedented ways. His decision, early in 2018, to accept the captaincy for the 2019 U.S. Presidents Cup team showed he was thinking about his place in the game in a new way. That commission required him to pay attention to a large group of players, foreign and domestic, in ways he had never done. It required him to think of his fellow golfers as something other than faceless bodies that exist for Tiger to defeat. The event was challenging. Tiger handled it. He led.

In Tiger's absence, a long list of players began to assume prominent roles in the game. In his return, they showed their admiration for Tiger repeatedly. Bryson DeChambeau, Justin Thomas, Jordan

Spieth, Rickie Fowler, Rory McIlroy, Tony Finau, Patrick Reed, Brooks Koepka, Jon Rahm: they weren't scared of Tiger. They weren't swimming with the old Tiger, always in motion, like a shark. They knew the new Tiger. They liked him. And vice versa. To Tiger, they represented a fresh start.

Tiger won the 2019 Masters by one thin dime, aided by Molinari's two back-nine disasters. The win was made more significant because he had to beat guys who knew what it was like to win a major title and had done so far more recently than he. Some commentators have said the other contenders backed away from Tiger, as golfers did in the past. Another view is that they just didn't get to 13 under. It's golf. Golf's hard, and harder yet with that green jacket beckoning. Tiger squeaked out a victory on the basis of skill, knowledge, guile, timing, and luck. Tiger won. It was like being at a concert. Your watch stops, your eyes close, your mind drifts. You're young.

· · ·

In that greenside pandemonium, everything was coming out: bliss, relief, *well done* in all its various forms. It was a salute to mixed-ancestry greatness and made-in-America excellence. It was we-gonna-celebrate-your-party-with-you.

Ev-ree-one a-round the world, c'mon!

Eventually, decorum was restored, and before long Tiger was in the basement of Butler Cabin, in a living room converted into a TV studio for one week a year, seated in a dining-room chair between the defending champion and the low amateur. He was facing Fred Ridley and Jim Nantz. Tiger knows what it's like to be the low amateur, with finals coming and your schoolwork mounting. He knows what it's like to be the defending champion, unable to get anything going. He knows what it's like to be interviewed by the club chairman and the voice of CBS. Tiger's experience in the game is vast.

He sat there, waiting for Patrick Reed to help him into his green jacket. It was resting on Reed's left knee. Nantz asked the low amateur, Viktor Hovland of Norway and Oklahoma State University, about his plans. *NCAAs are coming up, and we're gonna try to defend.* Tiger was at least half listening. There was a little microphone under his chin, tugging on the collar of his mock turtleneck. The camera would be coming to him soon enough, just as it had for forty years, in some bad times and many good ones.

"Well, Tiger," Jim said.

"Jim," Tiger said.

"Welcome back to Butler Cabin."

"Thank you."

Tiger's chin went down. He smiled.

He was modest, appropriate, natural. He was different than he was in his other Butler Cabin appearances over the years. This time, he had no talking points. Nothing seemed forced. He had won his fifteenth major and his fifth green coat, and he had done it without a swing coach. There was no Butch in his life, no Hank. Stevie was in New Zealand. Earl was long gone. Tiger was flying solo.

Nantz could see what we all could see: A proud, aging athlete with a bad back, not what he was but still able, with effort, to stand straight and make good swings while thinking clearly.

We could see Tiger as a father and as a son. We could see his appreciation for his team and his fans. We could see him embracing the traditions of this most hidebound of games and at this most hidebound of tournaments.

For almost eleven years, Tiger seemed to be desperately trying to find a precious thing he had lost. Maybe he actually believed the words Nike had put in quotes for him. Maybe he was a prisoner of his own marketing and his own success, a prisoner of all the roles he had been playing for all his life. Every day he carried the conflict of his just-the-numbers tournament life, which required no acting, and the rest of his life, which did. We all have that in our lives, but Tiger has it more.

Physically, Tiger looked, understandably, far different than he did on that Sunday when he won his fourth coat in 2005. Now you could see his father's hairline. Now there were pronounced vertical lines between his eyes. Now he spoke more slowly, and his demeanor was softer. He was more patient. (Parenthood.) He seemed aware that the euphoria of victory would disappear before long, as all highs do.

He was still *Tiger Woods*, with all the talent, fame, and wealth you associate with that name. But now and for the first time you felt like you could touch him, that you knew him. Who in middle age doesn't have job worries, health issues, family travails? You would hope for Tiger what you would hope for anybody, for the protection that comes from giving and getting love. That Sunday afternoon at Augusta was spectacular, and it was watched by millions of people who don't care about golf. A long day's journey into the rest of his life. It lifted many.

As Picasso had his Blue Period, Tiger had his Callow Years, marked by his pleated pants and his tunnel vision. He was twenty-three when he asked the guys to move that boulder in an Arizona desert. He was thirty-seven when he had all those rules issues. Just-win-baby was good for winning and not much else. During 2018 and 2019, he was doing the only thing that works over the long term: He was trying his best. He was actually doing it that night with Officer Fandrey. Tiger was a mess, but he was trying his best.

He had always done that in his physical life. That's how he became Tiger Woods. But by that Masters, and at that Masters, he seemed to be expanding try-your-best into every realm of his life. Fortune-tellers and leaders of group therapy sessions will sometimes speak of *psychic shifts*. It's not like tectonic plates are on the move. The tells are subtle. In victory, Tiger high-fived an ordinary fan, a random middle-aged lady, not any kind of insider, just another person leaning on a rope with her hand out. That was something. She was there for him, and he found his way to her.

. . .

Tiger made the rounds in his golf shoes. After his stop in Butler Cabin, where Patrick Reed helped him into his green jacket, Tiger made a short walk to the practice putting green, now encircled by fans. Tiger took his coat off so that Reed could help him into it again, this time outside, with cheering witnesses. With his coat on and unbuttoned, Tiger lifted the winner's trophy, a silver replica of the Augusta National clubhouse. You could see the red front of his shirt, its Amen Corner perspiration long since dried. As he raised the trophy, the coat's sleeves went up and you could read the time on Tiger's watch. The beaded bracelet from his daughter was right up against it. The air was filled with chants, with cheering, with the whir of high-speed shutters amid the threat of rain. Tiger made a circle with his index finger, sign language to a club staffer asking if he needed to do a 360 so all the photographers could get shots of him. He was smiling, and not just for the cameras.

From the practice putting green Tiger went by cart to the press building for the winner's press conference. Sam and Charlie sat in the back row, and their father ended his remarks with that charming nod to them, without even saying their names. After the press conference, he went to the champions locker room, where two tailors did some quick work on his coat, improving its fit. He then returned to Butler Cabin for the interview with Faldo and Nantz, and that was when Tiger remembered his mother's old Duster. From there he went to a clubhouse dining room to be toasted by the club's chairman, scores of members standing with him. *To Tiger.*

Eventually, Tiger arrived in a parking lot beside the clubhouse, the one reserved for past champions. He got behind the wheel of a big silver Mercedes SUV, a loaner from the club, now filled with his golf bag and his people, various suitcases, the yellow flagstick that a few hours earlier had marked the location of the hole on the eighteenth green. Joe's trophy, in a manner of speaking. Tiger was wearing his green jacket.

He headed down Magnolia Lane, drove over the descended bollards, turned onto Washington Road, and proceeded to the airport. It was the first leg of his trip home, to his hidden estate on Jupiter Island, the Indian River in his backyard, the Atlantic Ocean in his front, Greg Norman's estate a little north on Beach Road, the Blowing Rocks beach, desolate and beautiful, a little south. Tiger's restaurant was farther south still, over the bridge and off the island. His other life.

Tiger plays in only about fifteen tournaments a year, and he'll play fewer in the years to come. The main goal, Tiger said in Butler Cabin, was to have his "mind and body come together four times a year." *Mind and body*. One for the yoga buffs. As for the four times, once more, with feeling: the U.S. Open, the British Open, the PGA Championship—and the Masters.

The storm that had flirted with Augusta all day finally got serious in the late afternoon. It poured. The practice putting green: drenched. The clubhouse awnings, the magnolia trees along the driveway, the four lanes of Washington Road: drenched. The club had made a good call, moving curtain time up by five hours. The outdoor program was done by the time the rain came, at least those events meant for players and fans. Workers were collecting trash. Reporters were scurrying to their laptops. Fans were driving home. Monday would be a school day for Sam and Charlie. The real world was crashing in.

The deluge was powerful and intense but long over by the time Tiger boarded his plane. The dusk sky was pink and blue. The was no wind and the night was warm. For the first time in fourteen years, Tiger could take his coat home, free and clear. Maybe the kids would want him to bring it to school. He could. He could absolutely do that, bring it in for show-and-tell, if that's what they wanted.

About the Author

Michael Bamberger was born in Patchogue, New York, in 1960. After graduating from the University of Pennsylvania in 1982, he worked as a newspaper reporter, first for the (Martha's) *Vineyard Gazette*, later for *The Philadelphia Inquirer*. After twenty-two years at *Sports Illustrated*, he is now a senior writer for *GOLF* magazine and Golf.com. He and his wife, Christine, live in Philadelphia.